Families at Risk
Treating the Multiproblem Family

Families at Risk
Treating the Multiproblem Family

Katherine M. Wood, Ph.D.
and Ludwig L. Geismar, Ph.D.

Rutgers University School of Social Work
New Brunswick, New Jersey

Foreword by
Werner W. Boehm, D. L., M.S.W.

 Human Sciences Press, Inc.

Library of Congress Cataloging in Publication Data

Wood, Katherine.
  Families at risk: treating the multiproblem family / Katherine M. Wood, Ludwig
L. Geismar.
     p.   cm.
  Bibliography: p.
  Includes index.
  ISBN 0-89885-437-7
  1. Family social work — United States. 2. Family psychotherapy — United States. 3.
Problem families — United States. I. Geismar, Ludwig L. II. Title.
  [DNLM: 1. Family — United States. 2. Family Therapy — United States. 3. Social
Problems — United States. 4. Social Work — United States. HV 699 W876f]
HV699.W68   1989
362.8′2′0973 — dc19
DNLM/DLC   88-855
for Library of Congress   CIP

© 1989 Human Sciences Press, Inc.
A Subsidiary of Plenum Publishing Corporation
233 Spring Street, New York, N.Y. 10013

Printed in the United States of America

To Alice Overton (1907–1987), who gave hope
to the families whom society passed by.

Dedication

Serving as director of the St. Paul Family Centered Project between 1954 and 1959, Alice Overton translated the concept of family-centeredness and the mechanism of reaching-out into an exciting community endeavor that served as a model for countless projects and services throughout North America and other Western societies. Although she was not the only professional to use these concepts to pull back seriously problematic families from the outer fringes of social existence, she was unique in moving from the concept to the deed. It is to her teachings and example that this work is greatly indebted.

The authors came to an appreciation of her contributions from very different perspectives. The senior author learned about the work of Overton and her associates from a close reading of the literature on services to the dysfunctional family over the last 100 years. The junior author was privileged to serve on the Overton team as director of research. Thus, he knew her much more directly, not only as Alice the thinker and doer, but also as a charismatic social work leader and delightful human being. From both viewpoints Alice Overton's work can be seen as a great pioneering wellspring for those who seek to intervene in the plight of seriously malfunctioning families.

Writing this book in the late 1980s, we attempt to put the Overton model, especially as it is spelled out in the 1957 *Casework Notebook* by Overton, Tinker, and associates, into a broader theoretical and historical perspective. Despite a mushrooming literature with a growing theoretical sophistication, the Overton work can serve as a baseline against which to compare these later, related developments. The concepts are clear and the language of the prescriptive model is direct. The researcher takes delight in the potential for operationalization. The work of the Family Centered Project has given rise to a fair amount of practice research, and although it is not nearly enough to establish a firm empirical basis for practice theory, it is still much more than has been produced by most other programs of professional intervention.

Of late, there has been a resurgence of interest in and service to multiproblem families. Although the movement to launch the Great Society of the Johnson administration has run its course, we find the dysfunctional family is still with us, perhaps in greater numbers than ever before. Furthermore, the conservative ethos that gave rise to the Reagan administration stands in the way of structural reform that might conceivably improve the lot of many socially handicapped families.

Casting about for ideas and models to help deal with the problem, social work practitioners and educators are likely to come across a few published articles by Alice Overton— although historical scholarship has never been one of the strengths of social work—and perhaps the aforementioned Overton–Tinker *Casework Notebook*. Many thousands of copies of the book were sold, and it is still available at the noninflationary price of $4.50. The inexpensive, softcover, looseleaf format was deliberately chosen by Alice so that it could be placed into the hands of a maximum number of practitioners and thus be put into immediate use serving the multiproblem population.

The volume of sales indicates that the plan worked exceedingly well. The problem posed by the book design is of a different nature. Libraries are reluctant to place books of a nonstandard format on their shelves. There is yet another reason for the limited visibility of the Overton contribution. The writings of Overton were a model of simplicity, designed to speak to the beginning and often untrained practitioner. That style is not in tune with the language of the family therapy movement presently sweeping the country. (We comment on this in more detail in Chapter 6.) For these reasons and perhaps also because of social work's lack of historical perspective, Overton's work has remained relatively obscure.

Alice Overton's Family Centered Project anticipated some of the key developments that were seen in social work in subsequent years. Her keen perception—derived from her work with juvenile delinquents at the New York Youth House for Girls—of the interconnectedness of individual behavior and family functioning became a central organizing theme for the St. Paul Family Centered Project. Social work direct practice was only beginning to loosen its psychiatric bonds and explore the contextual aspects of human behavior. The Family Centered Project was a highly visible demonstration of this development. As is often the case, the more articulate theoretical formulations followed rather than accompanied this event. Alice Overton's work occupies a central place in these developments and should continue to influence the direction of professional practice.

Katherine M. Wood
Ludwig L. Geismar
New Brunswick, New Jersey

Foreword

In this work, Wood and Geismar seek what has often been wished but seldom accomplished, namely a marriage between theory and practice in social casework. The focus is on work with multiproblem families, the work imaginatively initiated by Alice Overton in the St. Paul Family Centered Project between 1954 and 1959. Much time has passed since that period and much development has occurred in social work, particularly in social casework. The concept of the multiproblem family has undergone change over time, but the essential concern with families who "have been bypassed by society" has endured.

The authors' endeavor is not primarily to bring the reader up to date on the current status of the multiproblem family in American society or, for that matter, in American social work, but rather to utilize the practice innovations of the St. Paul Project as a springboard for developing theory and practice concepts that are useful for working with today's disadvantaged families. Writing as they do some 30 years after the St. Paul Family Centered Project has ended, the authors review developments in social casework that are pertinent to working with the family (Chapter 4). The reader is treated to a history of the family therapy movement and a critical examination of casework's efforts and struggles to move from predominant consideration of the individual as the client, to a consideration of the interactions of the members of the family with each other and the family's interaction with its material and social environment (Chapters 5 and 6).

As we witness social casework's slow and at times painful rediscovery of the "social" in social work, we observe the inevitable reemergence of the family as a focus of concern. The stage for this discussion is set in Chapters 1 to 3, which provide an analysis of the sociological literature pertinent to understanding the problem family. Dr. Geismar, the junior author of the book, identifies two categories of family functioning—task functioning and role functioning—which are "essentially two sides of the same coin" (Chapter 2). Tasks and roles together constitute the interplay of the individual and the group, the exterior and interior of the family—the total array of the relationships of the family with society and of the family members with each other.

This analysis is the fruit of Geismar's work as Director of Research of the St. Paul Family Centered Project, but goes beyond it and incorporates his more recent work in the 1960s, 1970s, and early 1980s. The advantage of Geismar's perspective for the development of a theory-based practice is that he clarifies not only the "what" but also the "how" and the "when" of task performance and role functioning. The "how" can be measured through the use of the health-welfare criteria for the tasks, whereas criteria of competence, satisfaction, and nondeviance apply to the roles. The "when" calls for placing family functioning within a time span, namely the family's life cycle. Geismar also critically examines various ideologies that have been invoked over time to explain family malfunctioning—namely poverty, deviant behavior, and psychopathology. His examination of the literature dealing with these assumed causes of family dysfunctioning identifies the scholarly limitations inherent in these approaches (Chapter 3).

This analysis of the sociological literature is followed by Dr. Wood's historical survey of 100 years of concern by social work with the problem family (Chapter 4). The review reflects the ebb and flow of identification of societal deficiencies versus the attribution of family dysfunctioning to shortcomings of individual members of the family. It depicts the ongoing struggle to assimilate Freudian and other psychological explanations of family dysfunctioning, the shift away from the family to an emphasis on the individual, and the often limited attempts to bring the family back into focus without abandoning concern with internal individual processes. The reader who is interested in the development of social casework will be particularly pleased to find an assessment of the powerful role played by Mary Richmond and her bias in favor of the individual approach and, on the other side, the somewhat submerged but nevertheless substantive emphasis on the total "situation" of the family and its context in the work of Ada Eliot Sheffield.

Dr. Wood provides the student of recent social casework history with an opportunity to relive some of his or her own participation in the struggle between the "people-changing" approaches and the "situation-changing" approaches. She singles out the writings of Gomberg and other members of the staff of the Jewish Family Service in New York City during the late 1940s and the middle 1950s that reflected their pioneering family emphasis, deviating from the mainstream individualistic thinking of the time that was characteristic not only of social casework but also of psychiatry and other helping professions.

Two chapters dealing with descriptive theory (Chapter 5) and prescriptive theory (Chapter 6) for family social work set forth and clarify the requirements of theory development for the purpose of its use in practice. Alice Overton's formulations, because they were couched in operative terms, permitted ready utilization in practice. These formulations led to the creation by Wood and Geismar of a framework of practice principles (Chapter 7), consisting of a series of theoretical premises on the level of practice theory that were operable and capable of being tested through research. This framework is a tribute to the genius of Alice Overton, to whom this book is dedicated. The Overton–Tinker *Casework Notebook*, which is still available to the practitioner, serves as the jumping-off point for the authors' theoretical work.

Drs. Wood and Geismar do not neglect to develop the administrative and research contexts in which family practice and casework need to be placed (Chapter 8). They identify issues and problems, and provide suggestions for appropriate administrative structures to facilitate research in conjunction with practice.

This book should go a long distance to give comfort to the student of social casework, because it succeeds in establishing historic continuity in an area that has been much neglected. Further, because it was written by two teachers and researchers in social work, it underlines the convictions and provides the evidence that research need not and should not be separated from practice. Finally, and this gives particular joy to this writer, the book makes plausible the notion that the teacher of social work, concerned with the development of practice skills by students, needs to provide in his teaching and afford students in their learning the opportunity to engage in practice by doing research and engage in research by doing practice.

Werner W. Boehm, D.L., M.S.W.
Distinguished Professor Emeritus
Rutgers University

Contents

Contents

Chapter 1

Introduction

The volume before us examines the role of professional services in helping the problem-ridden family to endure as a viable institution. Throughout recorded history, the family has been a core element in human groupings ranging in complexity from tribal organizations to postindustrial societies. The family has ensured the survival of these segments of mankind by carrying out procreating, socializing, nurturing, material, maintenance, and various social-control functions.

By and large, the relationship between family and the larger societal institutions has been a symbiotic one. Each has been clear about the roles of the other and, by relying on the performance of these roles, has achieved continuity and stability. The recorded history and the archivers of anthropological investigations show an enormous variety of patterns marking the relationship between the family and larger human groupings. These patterns, though beset occasionally by friction and conflict, are nonetheless impressive in their capacity to endure.

Durability, most observers tend to agree, is inversely related to societal complexity. Although our methods for observing historic or primitive societies lack the sophistication of techniques of investigation we apply to modern societies—another way of saying that we may be unaware of some problems in other times

We are indebted to Professor Max Siporin for a critical reading of the manuscript and for helpful suggestions to strengthen it. Its shortcomings, however, are the responsibility of the authors alone.

and places—the evidence is still overwhelming that complex societal forms confront the family with special challenges to its existence.

The relationship between family and society is thus marked by ongoing reciprocity. Each relies on the other for legitimation and support, particularly in times of crises such as natural disasters, wars, social and economic upheavals, and other threats to stability. Society expects from the family loyalty, ideological conformity, reliable and stable functioning—particularly with regard to socializing the young—and provision of resources in the form of taxes and services for maintaining the societal structure. The family in turn is dependent on society for legitimation, physical and social security, order and continuity. When society is in trouble, it can call on the family to bail it out (though this may not be the most efficacious way of dealing with the trouble) by way of increased material and social support or more appropriate functioning, or both. When the family encounters problems, it may as one of its options look to society for help in coping. Such help can take a variety of forms, depending on the type of society and its particular orientation toward helping.

The more developed the society, the greater the number of options—partly because of the variety and complexity of its institutions and partly because of the diversity of views that come into play and that have a bearing on the choice of options, at least in a democratic society. Modern American society furnishes a good illustration of how the well-being of the family can become a societal agenda item, and of some of the ways in which options dealing with the problems of the family are played out on a nationwide scale.

Families can be rendered assistance and services from two vantage points: the macro and the micro. The macro perspective comprises all measures that are beyond the micro or direct person-to-person contacts with family members, such as legislation, the programmatic provision of resources and services, and all other measures under the general heading of policy. The macro aspects of activities on behalf of families have received considerable attention in this country in the professional literature, and even at the level of government during the 1960s and 1970s. A number of European nations, including Sweden,

France, and Norway, had been addressing the issue in a more sustained and productive manner at least two decades earlier.

The micro perspective, the subject of the present volume, deals, as already indicated, with the services extended directly to the family by individuals and organizations authorized to render such services. Although most services in any society, primitive as well as modern, are furnished informally through the family (nuclear and extended) itself, and through friendship and neighborhood groups and the like, specialized services tend to come into play to complement or supersede informal ones whenever the family experiences a serious crisis or encounters situations where one or more members find it difficult to cope.

In the United States and most other Western nations, such services tend to be of a professional nature. In most general terms, *professional* means (1) being rendered by persons who have received specialized training (more often than not) in institutions of higher learning; (2) being given official societal recognition, by way of licensing or related means, to be the only agents to render such services; and (3) receiving monetary compensation for the services.

The problems of the problematic family have in recent decades been the province of professional agents and agencies. This is particularly true in the United States. In this country, also, the social work profession has been assigned major responsibility for attending to the needs of the seriously troubled family. The beginnings of social work as a specialized, skilled service during the last third of the 19th century showed a concern of the emerging profession with the poor, the foreign-born, the mentally retarded, the delinquent, and children in need of care. Service to families was a legitimate and normal activity of the social work practitioner. By the third decade of the 20th century, these concerns had given way—at least in the minds and writings of the professional leadership—to a preoccupation with the intrapersonal and interpersonal problems of the individual. This movement was strongly influenced by Freudian and neo-Freudian psychiatry, which, although transferred from continental Europe, found in this country a most receptive climate.

By the 1950s, however, the pendulum had already begun to swing in the other direction. Social work was being accused of disengaging from the poor. Some professional voices were heard asking what happened to the "social" in social work. Social science subjects were introduced in the curricula of many schools of social work. But the new impetus to give services to families rather than to individuals came from within the social work profession. The writings of such authors as Scherz (1953), Overton (1953), Regensburg (1954), and Fantl (1958) indicated a new direction (new from the vantage point of where social work stood in the 1940s) in the treatment of troubled people who are members of a family. Overton's work in particular was rooted in her professional experiences as director of family treatment programs at the New York Youth House for Girls and the St. Paul Family Centered Project. Psychiatry followed the social work lead, having Nathan Ackerman (1958) as one of its earliest and most visible spokesmen during the 1950s and 1960s. Most of the initiative for serving the seriously malfunctioning and resistive family, however, came from social work.

During the 1960s, the concern with service to the family became temporarily subordinated to the War on Poverty and other efforts to bring about social change. The prevailing ethos of this period tended to shift the blame for human malfunctioning away from the individual and the family to society as a whole.

In the 1970s, partly as a result of disillusionment with efforts at social reform and as a reaction to a meaningless war in Vietnam, there was a turning inward toward microstructures, including the family. Work with families gained momentum under the label "family therapy." The Carter government put the stamp of the White House on efforts to strengthen the family. At the start of the last tercile of the 1980s, the family therapy movement was still going strong, but work with seriously problematic families was given only minor attention. There was a proliferation of treatment schools, most of them claiming to incorporate a systems orientation and competing for adherents to methods with as-yet minimal empirical validation. Psychiatry is strongly represented among the family therapist leadership, but clinical psychology, social work, marriage counseling, child guidance, and related disciplines contribute at all levels of the family therapy enterprise.

The alternating periods of concern and unconcern in social work for the collective welfare of the family are more easily delineated than explained. They reflect in part, of course, the ethos of the larger society in which liberalism and conservatism in government alternate with some regularity. But the development of a profession, particularly one that is still evolving, follows its own dynamic in which theory and practice are greatly influenced by concerns with identity, image, and social rewards.

The succeeding chapters examine some of these issues, beginning with a review of theoretical perspectives (Chapter 2) and problem foci (Chapter 3) in meeting the needs of the severely dysfunctional family. Subsequently, social work's treatment role is scrutinized in a historical perspective (Chapter 4). This is followed by a critique of some of the major descriptive and prescriptive intervention theories (Chapters 5 and 6), juxtaposing the claims of their authors with principles of scientific theorizing, including the use of empirical data to support such theories. In addition, the authors have attempted to identify a set of professional practice principles (Chapter 7) designed to guide future efforts to serve families in peril. Finally (Chapter 8), they examine the implications for research and administration in strengthening services to the multiproblem family.

Chapter 2

Theoretical Perspectives

Given the aforementioned interdependence between family and society, at what point does society consider a family at risk or in peril? In the broadest sense, a family is seen as being of societal concern when it fails to carry out its socially expected functions. Such a family tends to be labeled as dysfunctional or malfunctioning, meaning that some of these functions are not performed at all or are performed so badly as to bring about negative consequences both for the family itself and for those who are associated with it.

Sociologists have attempted to differentiate between functions performed for the family itself and on behalf of other institutions (Bell & Vogel, 1960, pp. 6–8). Managing of tension and conflict would belong to the first group of functions; maintaining motivation for and promoting participation in society would belong to the second group. In actuality, the differences are far from clear-cut. What may be of major immediate concern to the family, such as poor impulse control in family relations, may affect the society greatly in the long run. And conversely, acting out against the community, such as stealing from neighbors, may have dire consequences for the whole family. There is no question, however, that society is least tolerant of malfunctioning that has a direct impact on the social order, as for instance, does dealing in controlled substances.

The question then arises whether any measure of functioning or dysfunctioning has to give weight to whether its impact is greatest on individual family members, the family as a whole, the neighborhood, the community, or society at large. An unequivocal "no" would, of course, deny the essentially sociological nature of most criteria of behavior, including family functioning. Judgments about the desirability and acceptability of behavior are rooted in the values of those who do the judging. Given the differences in value systems across societies and cultures, a search for true universals would probably net few if any criteria that are accepted everywhere.

To avoid the impossible task of generating universal standards for judging family functioning, we must realistically confine our efforts to settings that share a common culture and value system. This does not necessarily mean populations that show conformity in language, beliefs, and values, but rather those that manifest similar concepts regarding the sanctity of life, the rights of individuals, civil liberties, the role of the individual in decision making, freedom of expression, tolerance of differences in conduct and beliefs, and the like. The common denominators on these dimensions often stretch across national frontiers.

It is then possible within the framework of such broader cultural similarity to posit criteria for the social functioning of families? The behavioral science literature on the family is more explicit in delineating categories or areas for organizing information (descriptive approach) than in specifying criteria for evaluating (evaluative approach) the social functioning of families. The former efforts follow the tradition of Ogburn (1938), Parsons and Bales (1958, pp. 16–22), and Bell and Vogel (1960) by identifying categories designating major activities that the family performs on behalf of its members, or the family as a group, or society. Scholars and writers have been reluctant to specify evaluative criteria that are held to run counter to the modern social science tradition of maintaining objectivity and keeping values separate from scholarly analysis.

Assorted efforts at evaluation, generated for the most part in various applied fields, have focused predominantly on specified tasks, such as meeting health needs, decision making, maintaining cohesion, interpersonal communication, furthering growth and change, or generating marital satisfaction

(Roghmann, Hecht, & Haggerty, 1973; Pless & Satterwhite, 1973; Lewis, Beavers, Gosset, & Phillips, 1976; Smilkstein, 1978; Olsen, Sprenkle, & Russell, 1979; Linder-Pelz, Levy, Tamir, Spenser, & Epstein, 1984).

A more comprehensive effort at evaluating family functioning was carried out by Nye and associates (Nye, 1976) who assessed six family roles (socialization and child care, kinship, provider and housekeeper, sexual, therapeutic, and recreational). The performance or enactment of these roles was rated in terms of competence (as perceived by the spouses), identification with role, value placed on role, role strain, role conflict, and resolution of conflict. Parallel questionnaires for husbands and wives ($N = 210$ couples), drawn in a county-wide sample in the state of Washington, were the source of data. Despite the evaluative aspects of this remarkable study, its primary emphasis was description rather than evaluation of the family's ability to function as a viable institution.

TASK FUNCTIONS AND ROLE FUNCTIONS

The goal of evaluating the family's functioning was sought by Geismar & Ayres (1959a) and subsequent related efforts (Geismar, LaSorte, & Ayres, 1962; Geismar, 1980), and is cited here in an attempt to furnish some guidelines for judging families to be at risk. The scheme presented here, which is an extension of the above-cited works, draws ideas and formulations from the structural-functional framework and the role structure analysis of Nye (1976).

Evaluation of any kind must proceed within a structure of descriptive categories that designate the "what" of evaluation. The "how" of evaluation requires criteria to be applied to specified behaviors or functioning in the various descriptive categories.

The present scheme differentiates between (1) task functioning, which represents socially assigned activities family members engage in, individually or jointly, in order to accomplish given goals; and (2) role functioning, which represents the behavior of individual family members. The former are made up of role clusters that bring together individuals' roles, which are joined to accomplish the designated tasks. The latter constitute role sets that are associated with each family member and that represent the sum of roles he or she is performing. Knowing an individual's role set is unlocking the key to his or her personality. Knowledge of the tasks provides us with a comprehensive view of family role allocations, decision making, cooperation, and conflict.

The tasks are broken down into seven areas (each of these is further subdivided), which are: intrafamilial relationships, extrafamilial relationships, socialization of dependents, economic functioning, health functioning, home conditions and practices, and use of community resources. The first three are predominantly expressive functions, which is to say their goal is providing psychosocial satisfaction for family members and group identity and solidarity. The other four areas can be designated as being predominantly instrumental in nature, meaning their aims are to maintain the family as a physical system and to guarantee conditions of biophysical well-being.

Task functioning and role functioning are essentially two sides of the same coin, different perspectives of viewing the family. Task analysis focuses on the functions, whereas role analysis puts the spotlight on the functionary. The two are interrelated (this has some empirical support: Geismar, LaSorte, & Ayres, 1962; Wallace, 1967) but are not identical. In a systems perspective such as we are using, the family functions are not merely the sum of its parts, namely the actions of its membership, although there is no denying that members greatly influence the manner in which the family system functions. However, many functions are decisively affected by factors outside the family, whereas other functions emerge only as a result of the interaction of family members.

It is not easy to abstract task functioning from the people performing the tasks, but proper evaluation requires that this be done. A particular task, such as homemaking, for instance, can be carried out effectively and agreeably even though the persons involved in it do not get along well in other areas or function poorly in some other respects. A judgment on good homemaking has more to do with the conditions in which the house is kept, the quality of meals, the maintenance of routines for eating, resting, and relaxing than with the quality of behavior of family members involved in the task.

Role functioning, by contrast, takes into account the variety (set) of roles each family member plays. These roles may be uniformly successful or, more typically, may differ, such as the case of the woman who is a loving mother and competent housekeeper but an ineffectual and frustrated worker outside the home. Her overall role performance is thus of unequal quality, but the intrafamilial tasks in which she is involved benefit from her competence in the home areas.

HEALTH-WELFARE DIMENSION

After having delineated areas of social functioning composed of tasks and roles, the next logical step in evaluation is designating the "how" of the evaluation process. The approach selected here (somewhat different from an earlier one: Geismar, 1980) uses one-dimensional ratings for task functioning and three-dimensional ones for role functioning. The quality of task performance needs to be judged in terms of how it affects the well-being of family members, as well as individuals and groups in the family orbit. We shall refer to this as the health-welfare dimension. Well-being is to be interpreted broadly to cover social, psychological, medical, and material conditions, and task functioning will be rated by degrees of adequacy or inadequacy in task performance.

A simple but reasonable coherent way of differentiating among degrees of adequacy is to define positions of adequacy and inadequacy on each of the four dimensions as well as a middle position, which will be termed marginal functioning. For purposes of measurement (dealt with below) the three anchor points can be assigned values of 1 (inadequate), 3 (marginal), and 5 (adequate), with the in-between values of 2 and 4 representing functioning falling between the anchor positions. In rating conformity–deviance, however, lower weights of 1, 2, and 3, respectively were assigned because of the lesser saliency of this dimension in family life. The definitions as applied to the health-welfare dimension are given below:

Health-Welfare Dimension

1. Functioning is harmful to the point where the community has a right to intervene. Family life is characterized by extreme conflict, neglect, severe deprivation, unhappiness, or very poor relationships, resulting in physical and/or emotional suffering of family members. Children are in clear and present danger because of the above conditions or other behavior inimical to their welfare.

3. Functioning is not sufficiently harmful to justify intervention. Family life is marked by conflict, unhappiness, apathy, or instability that represent a potential threat to the well-being of family members and others. Although children are not being properly socialized, they are not in imminent danger.

5. Functioning is at a level where the basic needs of family members are being met and where family members are satisfied with their lot. When problems arise the family is able to cope with them. Family life is stable, and members have a sense of belonging. Children are being raised in an atmosphere conducive to healthy growth and development.

COMPETENCE, SATISFACTION, AND CONFORMITY–DEVIANCE DIMENSIONS

In keeping with these definitions for adequacy, intrafamilial relationships (representing one of the task areas) marked by apathy or conflict would be characterized as inadequate, or nearly so, depending on the seriousness of the problems. But so would high family solidarity that is fed by community hostility that is the result of antisocial behavior, such as stealing from merchants.

Evaluating role functioning is essentially multidimensional in nature because it needs to take into account not only how a family member's behavior is viewed by others but also his or her subjective perspective, better known as satisfaction, on that behavior. The salient criterion for judging the roles of an individual is the degree of competence—according to standards set by the community—with which roles are performed. Competence is ability to cope according to widely accepted standards. Serving the well-being of self and others enters here, but it is only one of several competence criteria that include efficiency, timeliness, and appropriateness.

Competence, however, needs to be balanced against satisfaction, because the quality of the social roles is at least partly determined by whether or not the role incumbent enjoys them. Even though a broad correlation between competence and satisfaction may be safely assumed, everyone knows of situations where persons do something well without enjoyment or, conversely, greatly enjoy an activity without doing well at it.

Competence and satisfaction as criteria for evaluating role functioning need to be judged within the parameters of conformity and deviance, because the societal perspective inevitably takes into account whether behavior is in keeping or at odds with social expectations. This third dimension of role functioning, however, comes into play mainly at the deviance end, because degree of conformity (from moderate to high) is a questionable standard for judging role behavior.

To summarize, the proposed framework for evaluating a family's social functioning applies a health-welfare dimension to task functioning and the competence, satisfaction, and conformity–deviance dimensions to role functioning. Evaluation along the last three dimensions relies on the definitions for anchoring the actual social functioning of family members according to degrees of adequacy listed below.

Competence Dimension

1. Family member performs poorly in all or most of his or her social roles, is unable to live up to even minimal expectations of others in the family, at the work place, or in the community. He or she is totally unable to cope with changing situations. Serious mental illness, defectiveness, other psychosocial or physical handicaps require institutionalization or extensive intervention.

3. Family member's role performance is problematic with regard to his or her ability to meet about half the role

requirements, or family member is failing badly in one or two crucial roles. He or she has a problem coping with changing situations. There are illnesses and/or handicaps adversely affecting some roles, but the person's functioning does not require continuous or extensive intervention.

5. Family member's role performance reveals ability to perform well in all or nearly all social roles. He or she is able to satisfy the expectations of others in the family, at work, in social groups, in the community, and so forth, and is able to cope well with changing situations. If psychosocial or medical problems arise, the person shows flexibility and resourcefulness in coping with them.

Satisfaction Dimension

1. Family member is chronically and seriously dissatisfied with his or her roles, expresses great anger or total apathy about the situation, takes no joy in any of these roles.
3. Family member expresses frequent dissatisfaction with one or more roles, believes he or she is barred from living up to his or her potential. There are, nonetheless, occasions where some joy and satisfaction is experienced, or else the degree of overall dissatisfaction is moderate and fluctuates over time.
5. Family member is generally satisfied with his or her roles in life, experiences much joy in some or most of the roles he or she is performing, believes that he or she is or is about to achieve his or her potential, and generally has a sense of fulfillment.

Conformity–Deviance Dimension

1. Family member is deviant to the point where he or she has come into conflict with the law, has violated laws and mores that are clearly enforced by the community or society. For example, he or she drinks or takes drugs to excess, to the point where such behavior seriously interferes with the performance of key social roles.
2. Family member's deviant behavior does not violate laws that are being enforced. There are instances of deviant

sexual conduct, excessive drinking and consumption of drugs, offensive behavior in interpersonal areas—but these behaviors do not seriously affect family welfare or the well-being of the individual and others in the community.

3. Deviance is limited to minor infractions and idiosyncratic behavior. Family member basically conforms to social expectations of community and society. Nonconformity is allied with an emphasis on the esthetic and creative side of human differences, and with social skills to counter opposition to nonconformity.

Does the conceptual framework laid out here provide the key for operational definitions of *problem family* or *family at risk*? This framework, derived from an earlier one (Geismar, 1980), has not yet generated enough empirical data to generate norms of family functioning and malfunctioning. However, from prior research (Geismar, LaSorte, & Ayres, 1962; Geismar, 1964; Geismar & LaSorte, 1964, pp. 88–89; Geismar, 1973, pp. 41–44; Geismar & Wood, 1986, pp. 37–41) it is possible to extrapolate some rough indicants of family malfunctioning within the scheme laid out above.

Task functioning for which mean values are at or below 3 (marginal) indicates functioning levels where the well-being of family members is given a low priority. Seriously malfunctioning people characteristically perform submarginally in the expressive areas, that is, intrafamilial and extrafamilial relationships and the socialization of dependents (Geismar, LaSorte, & Ayres, 1962). The highest degree of malfunctioning, of course, takes the form of problematic task performance in the expressive and instrumental areas, denoting a situation where the physical structure of family life is shaky, and where basic routines such as feeding family members and attending to their health needs are being neglected. Problematic task functioning is generally correlated with poor role functioning of one or more family members, but even in the most disorganized family there is likely to be a range of role performance levels among the various family members.

The present conceptual framework postulates a broad correlation between competence and satisfaction, based on the notion that people who are competent tend to be more satisfied with what they are doing than those with lesser competence. Conversely, one might argue that persons with a generally positive outlook on life are more likely to do well at any task than those whose view of life is more gloomy. The relationship between competence and satisfaction may also be circular in the sense that one reinforces the other.

Although this project has not yet generated sufficient data for this proposition, some empirical support for its rationale comes from Nye & McLaughlin (1976) and Hicks & Platt (1970). Yet competence and satisfaction are likely to diverge in situations where individuals are lacking in sensitivity or empathy, or where family members are guided by different sets of values.

Conformity–deviance as the third dimension of role functioning is theoretically relevant in any assessment of human behavior because that dimension is a basic measure of how an individual fits into the larger social systems comprising family, neighborhood, community, and other groups with which he or she maintains contact. The conformity end of this dimension, however, is not a sharply delineated criterion of performance, simply because so-called normal functioning within or outside the family ordinarily covers a range of behavior from overconformity to conduct that deviates in numerous ways from generally accepted standards. Deviance becomes critical with the transgression of laws (those that are generally enforced) or the violations of norms considered important by the community. Such behavior, though relatively uncommon among American families as a whole (Geismar, 1973, pp. 180–190), is more widespread among the most disorganized families (Geismar & Ayres, 1958, pp. 29–33) and is clearly correlated with the other two dimensions of role functioning.

To summarize: The family at risk, seen as seriously malfunctioning within the conceptual framework laid out here, is characterized by overall functioning at a marginal or submarginal level. Malfunctioning is punctuated by special deficits in the intrapersonal and interpersonal relationship areas. The role performance of at least one of the core members of the family is below the socially expected level and reflects limited competence as well as general dissatisfaction with the situation in which the person is cast.

Few people would question that this type of social functioning is the concern not only of the family members affected but also of the larger community. Such malfunctioning most directly affects the children with likely long-term consequences; but it also affects relatives, neighbors, schools, the workplace, and agents of social control. Families with severe malfunctioning lack the resources to cope with the problems on their own and are dependent on the community for corrective intervention.

Before taking a close look at treatment alternatives to cope with family malfunctioning, we shall examine the subject before us relative to several societal phenomena (problems and processes) that are presumably associated—as cause or effect or both—with family dysfunctioning.

Disorganization, rather than malfunctioning, is the construct used most often in the sociological literature to describe the severely problematic family. We shall for the purposes of this discussion use the terms interchangeably even though disorganization, in our view, is more narrow conceptually, denoting malfunctioning that revolves in the main around deficiencies in the assignment and/or performance of social roles, but that neglects to take adequate account of the quality of tasks. We assume, nonetheless, that the two concepts, when correlated empirically, are sufficiently closely associated to justify interchangeable use. The correlates we chose to deal with are: the family life cycle, poverty, social deviance, and psychopathology including substance abuse. This is neither a finite list, nor is it the only plausible way of conceptualizing factors associated with problematic family functioning.

An investigator working in the more exact sciences would naturally begin his or her research by identifying assumed causal or quasi-causal factors that have a bearing on the phenomenon under study. The social science student who wishes to follow such a model encounters a reality that mitigates against such an approach. At issue is not only the multicausal nature of most social problems but also the difficulty of pinpointing the direction of causal flow among variables. An alternative approach, more geared to the state of knowledge in social science fields, consists of identifying from the literature variables associated, in determined and undetermined ways, with the problem to be studied. Given a fair measure of conceptual clarity, it is then possible to explore the nature of association in successive endeavors, ranging from existing cross-sectional research to studies with a longitudinal design.

Our goal here is confined to the first stage. We have selected from the literature those concepts that investigators see as being connected with the malfunctioning family. Out of the four chosen, three of them can be termed normative behavior, confined to a clearly circumscribed area of functioning. Poverty, for instance, denotes insufficient material resources to accomplish normal family goals. Social deviance means one or more family members have engaged in behavior that is either illegal or in violation of social norms to a degree at which it offends members of the community. Psychopathology represents behavior at variance with widely accepted criteria of psychosocial normalcy. The family life cycle as a correlate of family disorganization, by contrast, does not represent a form of normative behavior. On the contrary, all families experience the life cycle, which in the most basic terms is a way of descriptively conceptualizing stages in family development. The concept is relevant because family malfunctioning is more closely associated with some life cycle stages than with others. The categories of normative behavior, by contrast, constitute factors that may (1) contribute to family disorganization, or (2) be one of its results, or (3) interact with it to the point where the normative behavior and family malfunctioning mutually reinforce each other.

FAMILY MALFUNCTIONING AND THE FAMILY LIFE CYCLE*

Family malfunctioning or disorganization is by definition a phenomenon that affects individuals while they are members of a family. Their membership can comprise the role of parent(s) or child(ren) at a time when they maintain ties with the

*We gratefully acknowledge the assistance of Joan Axelrod in reviewing the literature under this heading.

family unit. In the traditional family, family membership extends over most of an individual's life cycle and takes the form of belonging first to a family of origin and later to a family of procreation. Periods of nonmembership or attenuated membership occur between the two stages when (1) a son or daughter has become independent of the family of origin but has not formed his or her own family and (2) at the end of a person's life when he or she is the surviving spouse whose children have left home. Nonmembership also applies to the ever-growing group of individuals who live alone or in a group setting that does not meet the definition of family. The family life cycle in its present usage is a family's life span divided into developmentally meaningful stages.

The contemporary family structure no longer fits the traditional model very closely. There has been a rise in single-person households and nonfamily households (one person households as percent of total households were 13.1% in 1960; 17.1% in 1970; 22.7% in 1980; and 23.4% in 1985. Family households increased 15.7% between 1970 and 1980 and 5.3% between 1980 and 1985. By contrast, nonfamily households during the same periods experienced an expansion of 77.1% and 13.5% respectively. The Bureau of the Census (*Statistical Abstract of the United States*, 1986, pp. 39–40) provides a clear indication of a tendency for more individuals to live a substantial part of their lives outside a family framework and thus not be part of the family life cycle. However, birth and early socialization are still almost exclusively confined to a family environment, albeit often a changing one, and the overwhelming majority of adults spend at least a portion of their lives in a marital relationship. Therefore, the life cycle concept is still relevant to the study of life events emanating from within or outside the family.

The concept of a family life cycle has a long history in the social sciences. In 1901 Rowntree discussed the economics of the working class family in terms of its rise above and fall below the poverty line during the life cycle of a laborer (Rowntree, 1901, p. 171). In 1931, Sorokin, Zimmerman, and Galpin analyzed the rural family using the life cycle concept. Their study and others spawned by it firmly established the notion of stages in the family life cycle based on "expanding and contracting family size or based on the ages of children" (Hill & Rodgers, 1964, p. 173).

Loomis and Hamilton (1936) and Glick (1947) established life cycle analysis as sociological study through the use of census data, using household-composition, housing characteristics, income, and other demographic variables to bring about an understanding of family experiences in the various periods of the life span. It was Duvall (1957) who made family life cycle a household word in family study through publication of her book *Family Development*, in which she related eight stages of the life cycle to sets of developmental tasks. Rodgers combined a modified categorization of stages with interactional analysis (Rodgers, 1973).

By the 1970s, writing on the family life cycle had peaked with a large body of literature that, although creative, fell short in empirical support. The clinical use of the life cycle concept, however, is a continuing one, as a perusal of writings in psychotherapy and social work indicates (Gurman & Kniskern, 1981, p. 782; and Walsh, 1982, pp. 167–193, for instance).

The life cycle concept is serving a useful function in demographic analysis revolving around marriage, fertility, and family breakup (Spanier & Glick, 1980; Norton, 1983), with the life cycle concept used in a more general way to refer to clearly identified events such as marriage, birth of first child, and birth of last child. Interest has waned in pursuing the process of refining the conceptualization of life cycle stages. Analysis of survey data has tended to cast doubt on the superior value of multistage life cycle analysis as compared with the use of other stratification schemes such as age of marriage cohorts (Spanier, Sauer, & Larzelere, 1979) or length of marriage and presence of children (Nock, 1979). The life cycle approach, despite empirical limitations, will no doubt continue to serve as an important conceptual tool (Nock, 1979, p. 25), while its empirical significance is likely to be subjected to further testing.

One of the shortcomings in the empirical analysis of life cycle data is the choice of independent variables that center on simple demographic facts such as education, income, employment, separation, or divorce, or single relationship and attitudinal items such as understanding spouse, enjoying children, satisfaction with family and friends, satisfaction with living standard, degree of religiosity, or importance of money. Such analysis falls short of the promise of the pioneers of the life cycle movement, who sought to use the concept as an instrument for charting and predicting significant developments over the life span of a family. The early Rowntree approach (1901) of using the life cycle for studying such significant developments as the slide into poverty was not pursued on any major scale. It should, after all, be remembered that during most of this century family study has not concentrated its research efforts on the seriously dysfunctioning and socially handicapped family.

There are, it should be noted, a number of efforts to relate family development to variables that might be correlated with social dysfunctioning, and a few observations emerge that underscore the significance of the life cycle concept. Geismar in 1973 carried out a study that had as one of its goals to discover the relationship between family disorganization and life cycle stages. In surveying the existing literature at that time (Geismar, 1973, pp. 13–15), covering some two dozen studies, he found that they were heavily weighted on the side of concepts such as happiness, love, marital adjustment, companionship, and general satisfaction. Findings could be summarized as showing a curvilinear trend, with satisfaction and/or adjustment lowest during the child-rearing years, although Spanier, Lewis, and Cole (1975) found the evidence on curvilinearity not entirely convincing. It should be noted that studies that recorded separately the attitudes of husbands and wives tended to find differences between the spouses; however, taking the life cycle as a whole, similarities appeared to overshadow the differences.

Schram (1979) has criticized the "marital satisfaction over the life cycle" studies as lacking in methodological rigor and failing to take account of changing values and cultural changes. Rather than rejecting the life cycle approach, she proposed alternative research methodologies such as repeated and intensive interviewing of husbands and wives, and incorporation of such variables as changed commitments to marriage, dual career functioning, and alternatives to the nuclear family.

Research speaking more directly to the relationship between the life cycle and family dysfunctioning revealed that families function significantly better after the birth of the first child than they do 12 to 14 years later when the first child had entered the middle school (Geismar, 1969, pp. 58–68). In one of the few large-scale ($N = 1,000$) and long-term (20 years) follow-up studies on record, Dizard (1968) found that the middle years of marriage, in contrast to the beginning ones, are characterized by greater husband–wife disagreement over the performance of familial tasks and increasing dominance by one of the partners (pp. 15–21).

Seriously malfunctioning families have not been the subject of longitudinal studies. However, information on dysfunctioning relative to life cycle stage comes from two treatment studies in St. Paul, Minnesota, and Vancouver, British Columbia, which selected families from a community-wide pool of cases (Ns were about 5,000 and 8,000 respectively) known to social agencies. Cases were identified as being multiproblem on the basis of their having been known to several social agencies and manifesting serious problems in two or more areas of social functioning. The proportions of families identified as multiproblem were 19% in St. Paul and 21% in Vancouver. Generalizations regarding any characteristics of the dysfunctioning families obviously can be made only with regard to a universe of "known" cases, by which is meant families that have come to the attention of one or more social agencies in the community. The proportion of seriously malfunctioning families as a percentage of all families in the community is obviously much smaller, and was estimated by the researchers to be between 3% and 5%.

From a life cycle perspective, the age of the woman heading the household is worth noting. The median age of the St. Paul women was 38 years (Geismar & Ayres, 1958, p. 16), and of the Vancouver women 36.5 years (Ayres & Lagey, 1961, p. 16). The majority of the women were in the 26-to-50 age range, or the middle and upper childbearing period.

Noting also the nature of the identification process, which was similar in both cities, and assuming furthermore that families were identified at the point of greatest need (in both cities, research workers not only utilized central registration bureaus' data dealing with type and length of service but also read case records that contained social diagnostic information on the family), we are led to conclude that family life was characterized by serious malfunctioning at the point when most of the children were already born. The mean number of children in the home was 4.4 for the St. Paul group, and 3.5 for the Vancouver families (the latter may be an underestimate because some of the registration cards were not up-to-date; Ayres & Lagey, 1961, p. 54). The mean age of the children at home (data were available only for the St. Paul study) was nine years.

What emerges here from two separate surveys is a profile of a crisis-ridden family at roughly the midpoint of the family life cycle (stage V on a nine-stage scheme of Duvall; Rowe, 1981, pp. 208–209), with several children, some of whom are teenagers. Nearly half the men are out of the home. The families have serious problems in two or more areas of functioning, and the children tend to be at risk of facing neglect, abuse, delinquency, and other forms of deviant behavior. The family is unable to cope on their own, and they have been turning to several social agencies, but for a variety of reasons (which include client non-cooperation as well as poor quality of agency service) they have not been helped.

There is, nonetheless, one marked limitation to the generalizability from the group of families identified as malfunctioning in the two communities. The universe from which the identification was made excluded families that managed to stay out of the social agency orbit because they were economically independent and used private medical and adjustment services (that selection process was, of course, in line with the goals of the treatment projects to discover more effective intervention by publicly financed agencies).

There is, however, some good evidence of a strong correlation—in this country at least—between social class and family malfunctioning (Geismar, 1969, pp. 36–41), making the truly multiproblem family—as defined here—a relatively rare phenomenon among middle-class and upper-class populations.

The seriously dysfunctional family, it follows, is defined, in keeping with our framework outlined above, by degrees of malfunctioning in several behavior and task areas, and as being likely to manifest special problems in the economic area. Such a family usually lacks financial resources to meet basic family needs and to provide minimal security for family members.

Why is extreme family malfunctioning correlated with the middle stages of the life cycle? Longitudinal studies are lacking to furnish a conclusive explanation. Yet a few developments, coinciding with that phase of family life, offer a plausible interpretation. One or more children have entered the adolescent stage making greater demands on parental supervision. This is also the time period when children are most likely to manifest deviant behavior. Perhaps more important is the fact that at that point in time families are under a greater financial strain because of enlarged family size and the greater material requirements (food, clothing, etc.) of growing children. That strain becomes particularly pronounced when the family has but one wage earner or is on welfare, situations that are characteristic of malfunctioning families.

Only a small segment, of course, of all families at the middle of the life cycle and facing all these situations becomes severely dysfunctional. That means that more than a combination of these conditions is needed to bring about family breakdown. Such is indeed the case, and we shall consider other likely causal factors in subsequent chapters. What is important for this discussion is the more likely occurrence of dysfunctioning at that phase of the family life span than at other stages.

The present discussion brings into renewed focus the work of Rowntree (1901) early in this century. In his classic study on poverty, he showed how the typical English laborer drops below the poverty line three times in his life. The first time this happens is when he reaches adolescence and his family of origin has a difficult time making ends meet. His second slide below the poverty line occurs in his late 30s, when he is heading a family and his children are still in school and have not begun to earn and contribute to the family budget. His third encounter with poverty takes place when he retires.

The parallel between the Rowntree discovery and the findings from the two North American community studies is striking. Family economic vulnerability, it appears, is a long-standing phenomenon in Western societies, and there are two likely causal factors involved: (1) the internal forces, which prompt families to conceive and rear several children whose needs in time put a strain on the economic resources; and (2) the external forces, that is, the society, which make only inadequate provisions (and this is largely true for the United States nearly a century after Rowntree's observations) for helping families cope during the middle stages of the life cycle.

The relative salience of these factors in our society at this point in time is a matter of conjecture. The significance of external forces, in this case social legislation, is illustrated by the fact that in the 1980s the aged in the United States are no longer overrepresented in the poverty category as they were during earlier periods (*Information Please Almanac*, 1986, p. 742). But even prior to the step-by-step improvement in the social security provisions for the elderly, this age group was never known to have generated much family dysfunctioning, because the family functions of the aged have been scaled down due to the general absence of children and the frequent absence of one of the spouses. In other words, the internal, developmental forces are setting the parameters within which malfunctioning can occur. The smaller likelihood of family malfunctioning during the early life cycle stages in this country is probably due to such internal factors as couples' romanticism, which marks the beginning of family life, and the relatively limited economic burdens, because few children are present and they are still young. We have no up-to-date research on whether the increase in one-parent families has brought about a downward shift in life cycle time of family malfunctioning.

The descriptive family life cycle literature, from Sorokin, Zimmerman, and Galpin through Spanier and associates, has given a measure of recognition to the effect of economic variables on family functioning, but the dysfunctional family has not become an important focus. The subject cannot be studied effectively in a life cycle context without longitudinal research, which is, of course, both expensive and time consuming. This may well account for the dearth of research and writing on the subject. The converging evidence we have presented for the significance of the life cycle concept in the analysis of family dysfunctioning should, nonetheless, encourage research to fill an important gap in knowledge of the etiology of family disorganization.

The relationship of family malfunctioning to poverty, deviant behavior, and psychopathology is dealt with in terms of problem foci, which are the subject of Chapter 3.

Chapter 3

Problem Foci for Understanding Family Malfunctioning

FAMILY MALFUNCTIONING AND POVERTY

In the absence of empirically based theory, the issue of family disorganization is dominated by ideological positions, at least two of which have some influence on the ways in which society deals with the problem. The two positions could be termed *internal-cultural* and *environmental* perspectives. These notions parallel in part the concept of culture of poverty as used by Oscar Lewis (1959, p. 16), and the situational approach as represented by such writers as Rainwater and Duncan (James, 1972, p. 132), to name but two.

The internal-cultural approach places the locus of control inside the family and ascribes its problems in social functioning to psychological and social deficits in family members. Such deficits can be viewed as functions of the family's values, which are at odds with societal expectations for child rearing, economic behavior, maintaining a home, work habits, and so forth. The deficits can also be seen as rooted in family members' bio-

We are indebted to Leonard Feldman, Rosemary Kopacsi, Trudi B. Leech, and Norma Rodriguez-Roldan for reviewing the literature relevant to this chapter.

psychological development, which was burdened by problems in heredity and interpersonal relations rather than by inappropriate values.

The environmental perspective puts the onus for the family's problematic functioning on society, particularly its dominant ideology, legislative system, economic order, and social and political institutions. These, individually and collectively, are seen as having failed to furnish the conditions for socially and economically deprived families to live normal lives and to socialize their offspring according to accepted standards of child rearing. Extreme dysfunctioning is seen as being the direct result of societal neglect rather than of family failure.

The two positions, which we have labeled ideologies, meaning belief systems to which some people have committed themselves without examining the factual base of the beliefs, obviously represent a gross oversimplification of a complex problem. These perspectives have, nonetheless, had a major impact not only on research and writing but also upon the fields of practice concerned with helping dysfunctional families.

In this and the two subsequent sections, we address the subject of family dysfunctioning relative to the problems of poverty, social deviance, and psychopathology including addictive behavior. The first two obviously fall under the heading environmental perspectives, whereas the last subject belongs under internal-cultural variables.

The discussion in Chapter 2 regarding the relationship of the life cycle to family functioning set the parameters for examining the influence of poverty. The evidence uncovered thus far points to poverty as a major mediating factor between the life cycle of the family and seriously dysfunctional behavior. Economic deprivation places a strain on a family's ability to carry out socially expected functions because several of these functions require for optimal performance a modicum of material resources. The instrumental task functions that are devoted to housing and feeding the family in particular depend on an income source to pay for rent and food; and child rearing, which has both expressive and instrumental components, makes material demands that escalate with the children's growing material and educational needs. The interrelationship between expressive and instrumental functions (Geismar, LaSorte, & Ayres, 1962) suggests a reciprocal influence where material inadequacies contribute substantially to overall family dysfunctioning, and vice versa.

Given the definition of the concept of the multiproblem family used in surveys cited above, it should be kept in mind that economic deficit is one component in the cumulative character of that definition. That is to say, with the existence of the economic problem, a family's chances of being classified as multiproblem are enhanced. The coexistence of problems, nonetheless, does not reveal the causative flow of problem functions leading to comprehensive malfunctioning. The surveys we spoke of are at best suggestive of such a flow.

Community surveys of dysfunctioning families have, of course, a built-in bias. As a type of welfare survey—comparable to a survey of child neglect and abuse—the population studied is confined to individuals or families known to welfare agencies or social service organizations: These are, in short, cases that are receiving—or have received in the past—a service provided by the community. That population covers the lower segment of the economic spectrum. We do not know what proportion of families in the population totally outside the orbit of public health and welfare agencies is seriously malfunctioning. But based on the above premises, it can be safely assumed that, in the absence of poverty, multiproblem functioning is limited in scope.

Solid empirical evidence on the joint occurrence of family malfunctioning and economic deprivation is scarce, partly because the concept under consideration has been used mainly in a clinical rather than a research context. Although an inordinate amount of work has been done on the prevalence of poverty in the population, definitions of family dysfunctioning are by and large applied only to research encompassing treatment samples that are not representative of the population as a whole. Students of the family who have used survey and census data have generally settled for such indices of problem functioning as separation, divorce, institutionalization, juvenile and adult delinquency, and so forth, none of which are satisfactory indices of family dysfunctioning.

The community surveys alluded to above did yield some empirical data on the poverty-malfunctioning nexus, at least for populations that had been using community social services— but not necessarily public assistance. The 1958 St. Paul study showed that of the first 100 families accepted into the Family Centered Project's treatment program, 91% had economic problems (Geismar & Ayres, 1958, pp. 36–39). The Vancouver community survey found 88% of 1,407 families with *multiple* behavior problems also had economic problems (Ayres & Lagey, 1961, p. 30). By contrast, both surveys reported health problems in these families to occur in conjunction with behavior problems on a much smaller scale than did economic problems.

A number of students of the family cite more indirect em/pirical evidence about the connection between poverty and family disorganization. By indirect, we mean that these investigators did not study family dysfunctioning as such, but rather concerned themselves with indices that are generally considered highly correlated with family disorganization, such as abuse, neglect, and physical violence.

Gil's (1970) classic child abuse study revealed a significant association between poverty and violence against children. Gelles (1980, pp. 95–98), using data from a national sample survey, found income, occupation, employment, and education (except for families where the husband had an 8th-grade education or less) negatively related to child abuse. Wolock & Horowitz (1979) discovered that, even among families living under poor material circumstances, child maltreatment is related to greater economic deprivation. Smith (1984), summarizing empirical studies on the etiology of child abuse and neglect, identified social class, situational stress, social isolation and lack of environmental support—all correlates of poverty—as combining and interacting to produce these forms of maltreatment of children. Pelton (1987a, p. 26), surveying available statistics including his own investigation of confirmed neglect and abuse cases, reached the conclusion that "the lower socioeconomic classes are disproportionately represented among the child abuse and neglect cases known to public agencies." Steinmetz and Straus, while pointing to some contradictory findings, state "that research will eventually show that in the recent past intrafamily violence has been more common as one goes down the socioeconomic status continuum" (1974, p. 8).

Further indirect evidence about the relationship between serious family dysfunctioning and poverty comes from studies that correlated social functioning per se with social class indices. Two New Jersey studies furnished proof of a strong and significant association between social status (based on measures of education and occupation) and adequacy of social functioning among young families (Geismar, 1969, pp. 36–40; 1973, p. 57). Gecas, in drawing together an extensive literature under the heading of "deficit theory of poverty and socialization," reached the conclusion that "poverty is perceived to have a detrimental effect on family relations" (Gecas, 1979, p. 392; see also Garbarino, 1983).

The causal linkages between poverty and family malfunctioning are complex and, at this stage of the research, not fully understood. Given the apparent greater frequency of family disorganization among the poor, one naturally looks for a one-way flow from socioeconomic deprivation to familial dysfunctioning. That is a reasonable assumption, because poverty brings in its wake unhappiness, frustration, a lack of skill to deal with the complexities of life, and a deficiency in education needed for upward mobility. On the other hand, the vast majority of poor families are not dysfunctional if the above-cited community surveys and studies of families receiving AFDC (Aid to Families with Dependent Children) are a guide (Geismar, 1963, 1964).

Which families among those living in poverty became truly dysfunctional? If poverty makes families vulnerable to malfunctioning, there must be other conditions that increase the likelihood of dysfunctionality. There is little solid research to answer this question. Some evidence of a high rate of continuity in malfunctioning from family of origin to family of procreation (Ayres & Lagey, 1961, p. 51; Geismar & LaSorte, 1964, pp. 62–64) has turned up, but in the absence of control groups the findings are not incontrovertible. Individual pathology and deviant behavior of family members play a role, as is shown below. Poor health, frequently correlated with poverty, is a contributing factor. Illness and disabling conditions are inherently frustrating circumstances and limit people's options for attaining life goals. What combinations of conditions are most likely to lead to family disorganization we do not know, although clinical data point to crisis situations such as illness, accidents, institutionalizations, or death as triggering mechanisms. Moreover, the extensive research literature showing a strong inverse relationship between psychological impairment and socioeconomic status (Camasso & Camasso, 1986) has clear implications for the problem under consideration.

Research and writing, whether ideological or empirical, on the relationship between poverty and family malfunctioning has had considerable influence on the nature of professional practice. And because such influence is hard to measure, we might phrase such an assumed relationship more cautiously by speaking of writing and practice being carried out against the background of sociopolitical thinking—characteristic of the times— which influences both writing and practice and furthers a reciprocal influence between the two.

The development of services to seriously malfunctioning families in the 1950s represented a departure from an earlier social work practice orientation that was dominated by psychodynamic theories. The change in the 1950s coincided with a rapid growth of the social sciences, whose theory and mode of data analysis stressed the social context of behavior. The very choice of family rather than individual as the target of intervention was characteristic of this then-new approach. By the middle 1960s this perspective of individual as member of a family and family in the context of community paralleling the much earlier social work perception of "person-in-situation" (Hollis, 1971), was giving way to a belief system—in line with President Johnson's War on Poverty—that family problems are caused only by society, not by people.

The notion that social reform would cure all human problems, oddly enough, weakened social work's concern for the seriously malfunctioning family. The concept of the multiproblem family tended to be viewed as an expression of a reactionary point of view that puts all the blame on the family. A decade or so later, as the social-change movement had run its course, practice interest was once more swinging back toward a more intrapsychic orientation. Nevertheless, the writings of this period, in contrast to those of five decades earlier, still show considerable influence of sociological thought—including the role of social class and economic status—regarding the behavior of the client population.

FAMILY MALFUNCTIONING AND DEVIANT BEHAVIOR

Deviant behavior as an explanation of family malfunctioning belongs under the heading of the environmental perspective. The assumption underlying such an attempted causal interpretation is as follows: The incorporation of deviant attitudes and behaviors on the part of one or more family members impinges critically upon the performance of familial tasks and roles to the point where minimum functioning standards are not being met. Deviance is defined as norm-violating behavior that tends to be induced by association with delinquent groups, social and/or economic deprivation, discrimination, and other pressures emanating from outside as well as within the family. Deviant behavior may be of a law-violating nature, or it may simply violate significant community mores.

An inquiry into a causal connection between deviance and family dysfunctioning must start with some knowledge about the frequency of deviant behavior in seriously malfunctioning families. On this subject, as on the issue dealt with in the previous section, little empirical information is available because family dysfunctioning has not been used as a concept for survey research.

The St. Paul and Vancouver studies of multiproblem families known to local agencies once again furnish a rough indicant of the prevalence of deviant behavior. A first treatment sample of 100 multiproblem families identified in the former community and a random sample of 100 such cases in the latter yielded the following information: In St. Paul, 47% of the families contained youngsters with a record of juvenile delinquency, 37% had a member who had been involved in adult crime, 17% had had one or more members incarcerated, and 28% had petitions of neglect and dependency (covering 97 children) filed against the parents. The number of incidents of nonadjudicated devi-ant behavior of family members showed a range from 1 to 13 with a median of 4 (Geismar & Ayres, 1958, pp. 30–33). The Vancouver data, which provide less detail, reveal that 51% of families had received services from correctional agencies, and 15% of the families had a member in a correctional institution at the time of the survey or at an earlier time period.

These data, derived as they are from the register of families known to community agencies, point to the close interconnec-tion between serious behavior problems of one or more family members and general family malfunctioning. The present dis-cussion focuses on socially rather than psychologically deviant behavior, although the line between the two is often blurred or nearly obscure. In terms of the theoretical framework guiding this analysis, the meaning of the nexus between the deviance of individual family members and family dysfunctioning is that roles and tasks are intertwined. Deficient role performance does not invariably mean the breakdown in the functioning of the family, but the trend is in that direction when key members fail in roles affecting others in the family.

The causal connection between socially deviant behavior and serious family dysfunctioning is complex. Sociologists as far back as Park, Burgess, and McKenzie (1925) have demonstrated the effects of the environment on family behavior, particularly the behavior of children. On the other hand, the subject of intrafamilial social deviance as a factor influencing family life has been of concern mainly to clinicians. Bahr (1979), who was interested in deviance as the dependent variable, has drawn together the family literature on the effects of family factors on the delinquent behaviors of family members, and organized it under six theoretical headings. He finds that "existing studies have usually been limited to a few structural characteristics of the family (divorce, social class, employment of mother) and have focused primarily on delinquency" (p. 640). The theoreti-cal frameworks revolve around such external factors as differen-tial associations and economic opportunities, and internal factors such as family, values, parental control, self-esteem, and so forth. There is considerable overlap among these formula-tions, as might be expected, and empirical studies under the various headings tend to explain only a small portion of the variance in behavioral deviance. The literature cited reveals a predominant concern with deviance as the dependent rather than independent variable in the study of family life.

Causal analysis is handicapped by the conceptual intertwining of deviant behavior and overall family malfunctioning. Studies of dysfunctional families generally have as their starting point serious behavior problems of family members, particularly parental abuse and neglect or related forms of parental role failure. Malfunctioning in individual roles, when combined with serious deficiencies in task performance, produces a pattern of family life known as multiproblem functioning. For lower-class families that had been "flagged" because of deficiencies in the socialization of children, problemicity seems to be cumulative (in the Guttman sense) from the expressive to the instrumental area (Geismar, LaSorte, & Ayres, 1962), meaning malfunctioning in economic, health, and household tasks follows interpersonal malfunctioning. That pattern does not hold up for other types of families (no unidimensional scaling models were found) that have been studied by this method of measurement (Geismar, 1973, pp. 46–47; Geismar, 1964; and Geismar & Wood, 1986, p. 39), and differential shapes of family profiles appear to be a function of such factors as life cycle stage and social class.

None of these social functioning profiles, not even the ones showing Guttman scalability, reveal much about early causation. A cumulative pattern, such as found in seriously malfunctioning families, might be operative during the midlife stages, but the root of the families' slide into problematic functioning may be inadequacies in income, health, or housing. Without longitudinal research on family functioning, we are left with inferences from a few cross-sectional studies and deductions from the literature, which views social functioning primarily as an independent rather than dependent variable.

Jaffe (1969) also struggled with the complex interaction between family life and deviant behavior. From a study comparing delinquent and nondelinquent boys, he deduced that there is a relationship between value confusion in the family and juvenile delinquency. He also found more elements of family disorgani-

zation in homes of delinquents than in the homes of nondelin-
quents. This researcher stated, however, that the data permit no
conclusion about a cause-effect relationship. Johnstone (1978),
who explored the relationship between delinquent behavior of
youth and family disorganization, also concluded that no causal
relationship can be firmly established.

Despite an enormous amount of research and writing on
the subjects of the family and deviant behavior, work on the
relationship between the two areas is in short supply and restricted almost entirely to a one-way exploration of the effects of
family variables on deviant behavior. Several reasons have been
advanced for this situation. Gove and Crutchfield (1982) believe
that evidence regarding the critical role of the family has been
downplayed by sociologists because they consider the study of
family variables as too psychological. Wilkinson (1974) sees a
tendency on the part of sociologists to view the family as a not
very effective or viable institution. Geismar and Wood (1986, p.
9) point to a discipline separation that has retarded work in
areas of concern that are theoretically related but belong to
different academic disciplines. Finally, we would point to a tendency on the part of family researchers to avoid studies where
the dependent variable, family malfunctioning or disorganization, has not been readily subject to operational definitions, and
has been perceived as normative in nature (something the pure
sociologist tends to shun).

The lack of significant research does not, of course, denote
the absence of need for such. Because of its pervasiveness, social
deviance is a key issue in family malfunctioning. The deviance,
however, generally characterizes individual roles, not the system
as such. *System deviance*, according to Cohen (1966, pp. 21–22),
deserves the same claim to our consideration as individual deviance, but events defined as the deviant acts of collectivities require an analysis of the interaction process and are hard to
document.

System deviance as used here denotes a situation where
most family members share antisocial values and engage in antisocial behavior that results in harm to individuals, groups, or
institutions. This type of deviance is not the same as Lewis'
(1959, p. 16) *culture of poverty*, which also denotes a deviant and

shared lifestyle, but not necessarily one that has a seriously adverse effect on others. And although the culture of poverty concept has been variously challenged (James 1972, p. 132), there is little evidence, given the present state of research, of a significant prevalence of families whose functioning could be characterized as true system deviance. Role deviance, which is widespread, is more likely to be nourished by the subcultures of the neighborhood or special associations than by the values of the family. Family case studies from the many intervention projects on behalf of multiproblem families in the 1960s reveal very few cases of truly collective family antisocial behavior.

One could indeed argue with some conviction that the dysfunctional family characterized by role failure requires a core of traditional values from which it can draw goals and derive standards for resocialization. Unlike the criminal underworld family, which tends to function well internally and malfunctions mainly relative to the conventional world, the seriously malfunctioning family lacks internal cohesion and is therefore at risk as a system. A modicum of conventional beliefs is, therefore, not only a condition for survival but also a necessary avenue for intervention aimed at raising the family to a higher level of social functioning.

FAMILY MALFUNCTIONING AND PSYCHOPATHOLOGY

The term *psychopathology* represents a somewhat imprecise concept that covers various forms of mental disorders and deficiency as well as substance abuse that is severe enough to cause impairment in functioning. Psychopathology represents also, of course, forms of deviant behavior; but in contrast to social deviance, the subject dealt with in the previous section, the psychopathology concept comprises deviance that is rooted in biopsychological factors, although the line between the two types of disorders is sometimes hard to draw and occasionally confounds the diagnostic capabilities of professional practitioners.

Data on the prevalence of psychopathology among severely dysfunctional families, like data about other types of disorders,

Table 1. Incidence of Psychopathology[a]

Type of disorder	Number of families involved (N = 100)	Number of individuals involved		
		Men	Women	Children
Diagnosed mental deficiency and retardation	22	2	2	26
Diagnosed neurosis	3	2	1	1
Diagnosed psychosis	11	4	4	4
Diagnosed character disorder	2	1		1
Suspected mental deficiency	21	1	3	22
Suspected psychosis	5	1	5	
Suspected emotional disturbances or character disorders	45	12	21	34
Problem drinking	50	41	19	3

[a]From Geismar & Ayres (1958, pp. 31–32).

are in short supply (for examples of studies furnishing information on psychopathology, see Philp, 1963; Spencer, 1963). The study of the first 100 families served by the St. Paul Family Centered Project (Geismar & Ayres, 1958; see Table 1) does provide a listing of types of behavior disorders according to the number of families and individuals involved. The statistics represent Midwest families in the late 1950s, predominantly white, with an average number (mean) of 4.4 children in the home. *Diagnosed disorder* refers to an assessment by a project-affiliated psychiatrist, and nothing is known about the reliability and validity of the diagnoses. The term *suspected* represents a judgment by any professional helping person.

Granting all the caveats of uncertain reliability and validity, it is still obvious that by comparison with more normal populations studied (Stirling County Study, Leighton, Harding, Macklin, Macmillan, & Leighton et al., 1963; Midtown Manhattan Study, Srole et al., 1978; also Manis, Brawer, Hunt, & Kercher, 1964; and Dohrenwend, 1966) the prevalence of serious mental disorders, mental deficiency, and problem drinking appears high (substance abuse other than alcoholism went unrecorded in this 1958 study because it was apparently not found among the study population or not recognized as a behavior disorder). The low frequency of diagnosed neurosis can be explained because psychiatrists, overwhelmed by the many instances of serious pathology in project families, tended to downplay neurosis as a treatment concern. The much higher number of women than men suspected of suffering from a mental disorder reflected mainly the absence of men (in the 100 families, 45 men and 8 women were absent because of separation, divorce, or institutionalization) from the home. When account is taken of absences, the rates are more similar, 20% and 28% for men and women, respectively.

In proceeding from the relatively simple issue of frequency of psychopathology in seriously dysfunctioning families to the complex problem of causation, a number of questions can be raised but not necessarily answered. Are mental disorders and substance abuse, particularly in the parents, a condition that contributed to family dysfunctioning, or were they brought on by a disorganized mode of life? The few studies of disorganized families do not throw much light on the subject, because they lack research designs aimed at pinpointing causative factors. Nonetheless, some inferences might be drawn from the general literature on the sociology of mental disorder.

Frank (1965) and Mosher and Gunderson (1973), after reviewing the empirical literature of previous decades, found little evidence of a causal connection between family types and the presence of psychopathological members.

Fontana (1966) cast doubt on the methodological adequacy of family studies identifying etiological factors in schizophrenia and dismissed notions of parental dominance and mental illness. However, he found some evidence of conflict and of less clear communication among parents as correlates of schizophrenia.

Since the late 1970s, the tendency of writers has been to see the family as a reactor rather than a causal agent (Kreisman & Joy, 1981). This has been therapeutically useful in that it tended to shift the onus for the problem from the parents to a variety of correlates. Since 1975, family studies of schizophrenia have focused on two aspects of family life: deviant role relationships and disordered communication processes, and they have made use of psychodynamic perspectives and systems theories, respectively (Liem, 1980).

Dramatic advances in the fields of biochemistry and human genetics have in recent years given new impetus to research in these fields that is aimed at uncovering causal factors in mental illness, particularly schizophrenia. Findings in the biochemical area continue to be suggestive rather than definitive, whereas theories of inheritance of various behavior disorders have received considerable support (Nathan & Harris, 1980, pp. 165–171).

The divergence of theories contributing in some measure to understanding etiologies of mental illness points up the complexity of causal knowledge and helps us guard against commitment to any facile formulations no matter how popular they may be.

Substance abuse or "psychoactive substance-induced organic mental disorders" as they are termed in the *Diagnostic and Statistical Manual* [DSM III-R] (American Psychiatric Association, 1987) are "the various organic mental syndromes caused by the direct effects of various psychoactive substances on the nervous system" (p. 123). These substances include alcohol, drugs, and tobacco. Their causes are not more readily pinpointed than those of mental illness. Intensive explorations of biological determinants carried out during the 1970s suggest that there may be a genetic component of alcoholism, although its precise extent remains to be determined (Nathan & Harris, 1980, pp. 291–292). Sociocultural and psychological factors, however, have long been recognized as significant factors in the etiology of alcoholism and other forms of substance abuse.

Since the well-known Midtown Manhattan Study of the 1950s (Srole et al., 1978), an inverse relationship between psychopathology and social class has been uncovered repeatedly (Kohn, 1973; Brown, Bhrolchain, & Harris, 1975; Ilfeld, 1978). In other words, mental illness, particularly in its more serious manifestations, becomes more frequent as we go down the class ladder. Various forms of substance use disorders likewise show a negative relationship to social class (Fried, 1976; Martindale & Martindale, 1971, pp. 218–291; Nathan & Harris, 1980, p. 311; Cahalan, Cisin, & Crossley, 1969, p. 29 ff.; Chafetz, M.E., & Task Force Staff, *Alcohol and Health*, 1971, pp. 33–34; Schmidt, Smart, & Moss, 1970, pp. 35–52), notwithstanding that the upper status groups are doing most of the consuming of the dominant substance, alcohol. Their overconsumption is protected by lifestyle and socioeconomic resources, and does not entail the same dire consequences that excessive drinking has for the lower classes.

The greater prevalence of most forms of psychopathology in the lower status groups suggests that psychopathology has a greater presence among severely dysfunctional families, simply because the latter tend to be concentrated in the lower social strata. Whether psychopathology is cause or effect of disorganized family functioning cannot be answered without methodologically sophisticated research. Such research is lacking at this point, and a sound working hypothesis would place most forms of mental disorder in both the cause category and in the effect category. If considered in the cause category, their origin places them under psychological, sociocultural, as well as biological headings. If considered in the effect category, much remains to be learned about what specific conditions of family life and family-community interaction generate the type of disorders dealt with in this section.

IDENTIFYING MULTIPROBLEM FAMILIES AND FAMILIES AT RISK

Efforts to identify multiproblem families on a community-wide basis have slackened since the late 1960s. One of the reasons was social work's growing macro focus, which helped generate a widespread belief that family problems can be dealt with effectively by well-targeted social policies. Another reason was the mounting concern of the health, welfare, and corrections fields with the drug problem, which appeared to overshadow most other issues with the exception of AIDS.

Little is known at this point about the degree to which epidemics of addictive behavior, which reached peaks during the late 1960s and middle 1970s (Roffman, 1987) exerted a major effect on the social functioning of families. The study of drug abuse as well as alcohol abuse has focused mainly on the effects upon individuals, not families; and earlier surveys of family malfunctioning, as already indicated, did not address the drug problem. One must assume, however, that the seemingly newer phenomenon of drug abuse as a "cultural phenomenon" of the neighborhood has had a major impact upon families.

The foregoing discussion of correlates of family dysfunctioning puts the spotlight most clearly on poverty. Following a gradual drop in the percentage of Americans below the poverty line between 1965 (17.3%) and 1975 (12.3%), that rate has risen about two percentage points during the subsequent decade (to 14.4% in 1984). The poverty rate for persons in families rose from 10.9% to 13.1%, and for related children under 18 from 16.8% to 21.0% during the 1975 to 1984 period (sources Rosen, Fanshel, & Lutz, 1987, pp. 9 and 21).

A further index of trouble in families is the rate increase (per thousand population) in reports of child abuse and neglect from 2.7 in 1978 to 3.7 in 1981 and to 4.8 in 1984 (Bureau of the Census, *Statistical Abstract of the United States*, 1987, p. 161). Other social indicators of population problems such as youth and adult crime (Bureau of the Census, 1987, pp. 155–173, 171) and drug use (p. 106) show a generally rising, though in some cases fluctuating, trend. The percentage of children not living with their own parents rose from 1.8 in 1960 to 2.4 in 1970 and to 3.1 in 1978 (Bureau of the Census, 1980, p. 50). Children in foster care, however, show a 9% decline between 1980 and 1984, probably as a result of the growing emphasis on providing children with services in their own homes. Among so-called new factors that must be considered to contribute to family disorganization is homelessness. "Homelessness," it has been stated by the editors of *Face of the Nation 1987* (Rosen, Fanshel, & Lutz, 1987, p. 69) "became an increasingly important problem in all major metropolitan areas of the United States in the 1980s, on a scale not seen since the depression of the 1930s."

Beyond the various trouble indices and representing the substratum of data for assessing the scope of malfunctioning of the American family is the changing picture of the American family. In Chapter 2 we list some statistics on the shrinking family household. Its correlate, the percentage of married females and males, showed a steady decline between 1960 and 1984, from 71.6% to 60.8% for males, and from 76.4% to 65.8%

for females. The percentage of divorced showed a corresponding rise from 2.9% to 8.3% for women, and from 2.0% to 6.1%
for men over the same period (Rosen, Fanshel, & Lutz, p. 10).
One-parent families, which accounted for 13% of all families in
1970 and 22% in 1980, exceeded one quarter (26.5%) of the
family population in 1984. The vast majority of these are
headed by women. The U.S. Commission on Civil Rights predicted that by 1990 half of all American children would spend
part of their childhood living with one parent only (Wattenberg,
1987, p. 548).

Although the effect of single parenthood on the parent and
children has not been pinpointed at this stage—a number of
intervening factors appear to overshadow the structural aspect
of family life (Wattenberg, 1987, p. 554)—there is little doubt
that the female-headed household is greatly disadvantaged economically. Female-headed households with children under 18
have only a little over one third of the level of monthly cash
income going to households that are headed by married couples
(p. 552). With poverty being one of the most clearly identified
correlates of family malfunctioning, the researcher intent on
discovering the prevalence of this phenomenon might well focus
the survey tools on communities with poor single-parent
families.

In recent years a new term designating deprived and
problem-ridden living has joined the social science vocabulary:
the *underclass* (Wilson, 1985; Auletta, 1982). Even though it is
not operationally defined, the underclass refers to people who
are not only poor but who are also characterized by extensive
social pathology such as drug abuse, homicide, delinquency,
teenage pregnancy, and so forth. Unlike the concept of the multiproblem family, the term underclass refers to individuals living alone or in nonfamily households as well as to families. The
two concepts have in common the characteristics of poverty and
psychosocial deviance. Given the definitions most commonly
used, underclass status is generated from census data whenever
a census tract has an unusually high percentage of unemployed
or underemployed, families headed by a woman, welfare recipients, and children of high school age not attending school
(Wilkerson, 1987, p. 26).

One would expect underclass neighborhoods to contain a disproportionate ratio of multiproblem families. But because the latter is not part of official census terminology, that supposition cannot be verified. Therefore, we continue to operate with inferences derived from earlier studies and suppositions that seek to make a logical connection between the multiproblem family and comparable, officially recognized census definitions.

The above-cited rise of families living in poverty and the increase noted in underclass populations (Wilkerson, p. 26) point to a spread of multiproblem functioning in the country. But if relatively little is known about prevalence, there is even less information regarding the intensity and nature of malfunctioning. The only comparison over time, using the same instrument, namely the St. Paul Scale of Family functioning, showed malfunctioning families receiving public assistance in Elmira, New York in the early 1960s to be functioning at a somewhat higher level than dysfunctional female-headed families on public assistance at the Urban Family Center in Manhattan around 1980 (Phillips et al., 1980, p. 30 and Appendix C). Striking differences (over one scale step) were revealed in the social activities and use of community resources of the Manhattan families, indicating a lower degree of integration in the community. This difference may, of course, reflect primarily the more anomic conditions of life in the giant metropolis.

In the present chapter we review some of the problem correlates of family malfunctioning and raise questions about its prevalence over time. Although hard data are lacking about the multiproblem family, a concept that despite operational definitions, has not become part of the terminology of census takers or survey researchers, there is much evidence that this family continues to be a major concern to health and welfare systems in general, and the social work profession in particular.

In Chapters 4, 5, and 6 we take a critical look at past and present efforts to translate theoretical perspectives into programs of intervention aimed at helping multiproblem families cope and relieving the burden on the communities serving them. This analysis, it is hoped, will bring us one step closer to the point of sorting out promising approaches from those that merely follow tradition or the latest fad.

Chapter 4

One Hundred Years of Social Work with the Multiproblem Family

Social work owes its beginning as a profession to the multi-problem family. The existence of many such families in the slums of the great cities of England and the United States in the 19th century led to the development of organizations to deal with the problems these "dependent, defective and delinquent" (Brace, 1872) people posed for those members of society who were benefitting from, rather than being destroyed, by the Industrial Revolution.

The aims of the early relief organizations in this country were as much, or more, to protect society as they were to help the people who were the human fallout of industrialization: "to end the abuse of charity, especially by professional beggars; to make charity more effective for those who really deserved it; and to mobilize the forces of helpfulness" (Leiby, 1978, p. 111). Their basic "diagnostic" assumption was that "people are naturally lazy, listless, and self-indulgent, naturally dependent, that they find labor irksome, and that they will work or take responsibility only under pressure" (Leiby, 1978, p. 112).

Institutionalization—in almshouses, orphanages, and mental asylums—was the prevalent response in the 1800s to the needs of people with problems. Franklin B. Sanborn, Chairman of the National Conference on Charities and Corrections, argued in 1890 for a family-oriented approach: "The family must be taken as a whole, otherwise the strongest social bond will be weakened....Let us adopt as the starting point of our system of public charities what the French called Secours à Domicile, and what we have termed 'Family' or 'Household Aid' " (Pumphrey & Pumphrey, 1961, p. 220). Just such an approach had started even earlier, but at that time was not yet widespread; volunteer "visitors" to the homes of the poor were being used as early as 1818 by the New York Society for Prevention of Pauperism (Siporin, 1980, pp. 11–12).

CHARITY ORGANIZATION SOCIETIES AND SETTLEMENT HOUSES

Attempts to improve the conditions of the poor took the form of both macro efforts, or social reform via legislative and public policy change, and, increasingly, work with the poor directly at the micro level. Direct services began to organize into two parallel but different and sometimes competitive movements: the Charity Organization Societies, and the settlement houses.

Buffalo, New York was the site of the first Charity Organization Society in the United States, rapidly followed by others established in the 1870s and 1880s in several large cities. The new Societies came into being primarily to coordinate the efforts of a plethora of narrowly focused and overlapping charities, but they also differed from previous relief organizations in their aim for a "scientific charity" or "scientific philanthropy." A poet of the Irish poor in Boston commented scathingly on the "scientific" ministrations of the Charity Organization Society in that city:

> The organized charity, scrimped and iced,
> In the name of a cautious, statistical Christ.
>   (O'Reilly, 1886; quoted in Leiby, 1978, p. 116)

The Charity Organization Societies did emphasize, however, the individualization of the families they served, and the necessity that relief given had to be adequate to the need. Further, they set up as an ideal (although the poet's complaint indicates that it was not always realized in practice) that the volunteer "friendly visitor" of the Society should establish a personalized, nonpaternalistic, friendship relationship with the families she served. That is, beginning to take shape were both the idea that the personal qualities of the helper might be a variable in the effectiveness of the help, and the concept that was later to become perhaps too dominant in social casework, that of "relationship as the medium of treatment."

Like the Charity Organization Societies, the idea of the settlement house had been borrowed from England, where the first, Toynbee Hall, was opened in 1884; and again like the Societies, the settlement houses spread rapidly in the United States. In the beginning they were literally "settlements" in poor communities of socially concerned middle-class and upper-class university students and others, who resided together in the settlement house and shared their lives with the poor—a kind of Peace Corps of the time. The settlements sought to "bring together the privileged and the underprivileged for sharing...rather than giving" (Reynolds, 1963, p. 29). They had started partly as a protest against organized charity, which they saw as paternalistic and condescending; the residents of the settlements preferred their ideal of social democracy, "acting together in a common life, not divided by snobbish distinctions of class, race, and religion" (Leiby, 1978, p. 129). Fundamental differences existed between the approaches to the problems of the poor by the settlement houses and by the Charity Organization Societies. "The settlers defined problems environmentally and engaged in social melioration. The charity workers, for the most part, defined problems as personal deficiencies and emphasized the need for moral uplift to achieve social betterment" (Germain & Hartman, 1980, p. 329). There were sharp attacks on each other's perspectives by Mary Richmond of the Baltimore Charity Organization Society and Jane Addams of Hull House in Chicago, in which each tore the other "to shreds while maintaining an air of sweet gentility" (Germain & Hartman, 1980, p. 326). In addition to a wide variety of practical services—adult education, child care, health facilities, recreation, and clubs for children, adolescents, and adults—the settlement houses also became involved in research concerning the social conditions of the poor and the working classes, and social action and reform. As social work inevitably became increasingly professionalized, the unpaid agent of the Charity Organization Society was replaced by the professional social worker, and the volunteer resident staff of the settlement house by paid professionally trained personnel who had less interest in living in community with the poor for no remuneration.

From the beginnings of the Charity Organization Societies, the family rather than the individual was the unit of attention. Josephine Shaw Lowell in 1880 advised volunteer visitors "to find out all about the man in the family rather than dealing exclusively with the woman," and recommended conjoint interviews with both parents together (Siporin, 1980, p. 12). Zilpha Smith in 1890 urged workers not to see the people they served as "removed from family relations. We deal with the family as a whole" (Smith, 1890). Freed (1982) observed that the "sophisticated family therapy of today has its recorded roots in…these early leaders of the family movement, although credit is seldom given to them" (p. 475).

The programs of the Charity Organization Societies rapidly grew to offer more than the services of the "agent," or early social worker, who worked on a family-by-family basis. The Buffalo Charity Organization Society, for example, established an employment agency, and day care and a kindergarten to aid single-parent mothers (Freed, 1982, p. 475).

Mary Richmond

Mary Richmond emerged, about the turn of the century, as a dynamically influential leader of the Charity Organization Society movement. Her aim was to make the dream of a truly "scientific" charity a reality, by transforming hit-or-miss friendly visiting by untrained volunteers into "deliberate and constructive casework" (Leiby, 1978, p. 122). She pushed for the establishment of training courses: "We can never acquire a professional standard until we have a school" (Richmond, 1930, p. 100; quote from 1897 speech). The first social work course ever taught was on "The Treatment of Needy Families in Their

Own Homes," at the New York Charity Organization Society's Summer School of Applied Philanthropy (later the Columbia University Graduate School of Social Work).

Richmond was creative and insightful, albeit somewhat bookkeeperish in her approach (in fact, she had once been a clerk). Her *Social Diagnosis* (1917) codifies almost legalistic rules for the collection, classification, and admissibility of data concerning the case. Her legalistic bent was illustrated by her definition of *social study* as including everything about the client (Peterson, 1979, p. 590). If her workers had really sought answers to the many items in her "Questionnaire Regarding Any Family" (Richmond, 1917, pp. 378–381), including some that were insultingly intrusive, such as whether the clients appreciated the necessity of "regular action of the bowels," the family might well have decided that starvation was a better fate. But she was firmly oriented to the family, which she defined as "all who share a common table" (1917, footnote p. 134), and stated that her workers could not help people "in a truly social way without taking their families into account. Even if our measure were the welfare of the individual solely, we should find that the good results of individual treatment crumble away often because the case worker has been ignorant of the client's family history" (p. 134).

Although Richmond wrote in *What Is Social Case Work?* that "the worker is no more occupied with abnormalities in the individual than in the environment, is no more able to neglect one than the other" (1922, p. 98), she defined casework as "those processes which develop *personality* [italics added] through adjustments consciously effected, individual by individual, between men and their social environment" (pp. 98–99). Her focus was not only dualistic, but it seems clear from her own statements that her perception of "the objective of casework is people changing or, in Richmond's words, 'personality development' [and] the approach is to the individual" (Hartman, 1971, p. 412). Richmond perceived the practitioner's work with the environment as a route to developing the personality of the client, not as a goal worthy in itself, such as providing desperately needed material resources or advocating with an employer to give a job to the father of a family. Despite this emphasis on

personality improvement of clients, Richmond was later criticized by Hamilton (1958) for paying *too* much attention to the
problematic situation or circumstance: "What actually was
treated was the problem—desertion, alcoholism, poverty, or
illegitimacy—rather than the person" (p. 13).

Despite her purpose of improving clients' personalities
through environmental modification, Richmond still was indeed interested in taking action about the circumstances of the
client. She conducted one of the first social research studies on
the single-parent family, concerning 985 widows who were clients of Charity Organization Societies in nine cities (Richmond
& Hall, 1913). Pumphrey comments that Richmond and her
colleagues "would find current theory concerning the advocate
role congenial—they invented it early" (1973, p. 265). Richmond
presaged community mental health's "basic assumption...that
there is an intimate relationship between the social organization
of the community and the individual psychological organization
of its residents" (Peck, Kaplan, & Roman, 1966, p. 60). And
Goldmeier saw Richmond as an early "systems" thinker: "Intu-
itively she seemed to follow (a systems perspective). The way
Mary Richmond wrote about the interdependence of the various
forms of social work and the interrelatedness of various social
forces in family and environment certainly suggests a systems
theory outlook." (Goldmeier, p. 283). She was as cognizant of
the need for social reform (what she called the "wholesale" approach) as for individualized work with people and families in
trouble (the "retail" approach); and she was impatient with
those who saw one or the other as more important, maintaining
that both were necessary and complementary (Richmond, 1930,
pp. 215–216).

Richmond admired and copied the lawyers' method of ac-
cumulating and drawing inferences from facts, but actually she
introduced the medical metaphor in her configuration of data
collection (or "study"), social diagnosis, and treatment (Peterson, 1979, p. 587). Her *Social Diagnosis* (1917) referred to the
social worker as a "social physician." Although she considered
Freud "immoral," and feared that the interest in his ideas might
mean that psychiatry would come to dominate social work,
Richmond's configuration was ironically one of the factors re-

sponsible for the next stage in the development of professional casework—the preoccupation with the pathology of the individual based on the medical model of psychiatry, with relative exclusion of the family as a unit as well as exclusion of other social systems that were part of the problem situation.

In 1918, Francis McLean—an early community organizer whom Richmond had brought in to organize the Charity Organization Societies on a national basis and who became the executive of the American Association for Organizing Charity—asked the member agencies "whether the family or the community should be the peculiar unity of charity organization." The agencies replied that "their own interest and special competence...was casework with 'disorganized families'" (Leiby, 1978, p. 126). The organization changed its name to the American Association for Organizing Family Social Work (and, in 1930, to the Family Welfare Association, later to Family Service Association of America, and finally to Family Service America). The organization's first published organ was *The Family*; its name was not changed to the present *Social Casework* until 1946. Very evident at this period, therefore, were the family orientation and the dedication to ameliorating the situational circumstances of the poor that characterized the nascent profession. But other situational forces were simultaneously converging on social work; like most of its clients, it was caught up in circumstances not of its own making (although, like *some* clients, unfortunately it "adapted"—or succumbed—all too well to those forces).

ENTER THE MIDDLE CLASS, PROFESSIONALISM, AND FREUD

World War I brought the working-class and middle-class to social work services. The Red Cross Home Service was established, "intended to apply the principles of social casework with disorganized families to help servicemen and their families cope with the emergencies of wartime separation" (Leiby, 1978, p. 160). Hitherto, social work had been associated with poverty and charity; but the families of servicemen were not usually primarily economically dependent and felt that they had a rightful claim to help with their war-created difficult circumstances that were not of their making. These new working-class and middle-class clients and their social workers began to "construe helping as a technical service analogous to that of a lawyer or doctor" (Leiby, 1978, p. 161); and the workers began to think of themselves as the true professionals with a middle-class voluntary clientele that they emulated (especially since Flexner had delivered his oracular judgment that social work could not be considered a "real" profession [Flexner, 1915]).

The use of professional caseworkers had also begun to spread to hospitals, mental institutions, schools, probation, and parole. The startling new ideas of Freud were being disseminated increasingly throughout the well-educated classes. *Mental hygiene* became a catchword, and the child guidance movement, begun in the 1920s, brought out a "large and appealing group of clients whose problems were personal and emotional rather than financial" (Leiby, 1978, p. 183). In 1918 the first course on "psychiatric social work" was held at Smith College, and psychiatric social work came to be perceived as the most prestigious stratum of the profession. "In later years it would seem easy to dismiss this enthusiasm—the psychologies were confused, the therapies ineffective, the viewpoint politically conservative—but at the time it was liberating" (Leiby, 1978, p. 185). The new Freudian-based ideas about problem behavior as being symptomatic, not of here-and-now pathologic circumstances or interactions or lack of coping skills, but of early childhood traumata that might be exercised by a therapeutically skillful, truly "professional" social worker, were enormously exciting. There was an illuminating flash, an "ah-hah!" sensation. Not only did the adoption of the new "scientific" psychology seem to offer the hope of finally achieving the true professional status and expertise from which Flexner had sought to exclude social work—equally importantly, it offered what looked like a theory (if not according to scientific criteria for a theory, at least in the popular sense, meaning a purported explanation). And lack of a properly elaborated theoretical base had been one of Flexner's primary complaints about the infant profession. Social work was beginning to struggle with the enormous task (still unconsummated) of trying to develop a practice theory that was indeed a real, empirically validatable theory rather than merely a "perspective" or a "model," and that encompassed its focus on *both* person and situation *and* their enormously multivariate kinds of interaction—a task so complex that no practice or academic discipline has yet achieved it. It was felt by those who flocked to Freud's psychology that perhaps social work could do better for itself by borrowing a theory that, if it did not really fit the purpose of the social work profession or the problems of the great majority of its clients, at the least was increasingly accepted, prestigious in its own right (at the time, anyway), and did seem to offer illumination for some of the practice problems that social workers faced. Psychoanalytic theory seemed to explain a number of puzzling things about the sometime contrary and resistant client who passively or vigorously rejected the worker's offers of concrete services and problem-solving suggestions and advice. It seemed to explain even more puzzling things about that subgroup of clients that was suffering from true psychiatric disorder, and whose problem behavior and perceptions were part of their problem circumstances. Further, middle-class clients were more like the middle-class worker herself, and she felt more comfortable with people on her own cultural and verbal wavelength than with the uneducated poor, who were often of a different ethnic or cultural background, whose ideas about life, the Protestant ethic of deferring gratification, proper role relationships within the family, how to rear children, and so forth, were so incomprehensible, disconcerting, and difficult to "correct" toward the middle-class norm.

A major impact of the new psychology adopted by social casework was that it was focused on *the individual, not the family as a unit*. At the 1919 National Conference of Social Work, a debate took place that reflected the conceptual schism that was splitting social work. E. E. Southard, the chief of psychiatry at the Boston Psychopathic Hospital, delivered a paper on "The Individual Versus the Family as the Unit of Interest in Social Work," in which he recommended that the young profession "abolish the family as a unit of interest in social work and...replace that unit with the individual" (Southard, 1919, p. 585). Porter R. Lee, Director of the New York School of Social Work, rebutted:

No individual is wholly an individual. He is himself plus every other person whose interests and his touch.... The family organization gives to each member of the family group the right to demand certain things of other members. Treatment that considers one member alone irrespective of these demands, and the obligations which go with them, is inadequate.... Family case workers have learned by experience that the important fact of family solidarity, of inter-dependence of interests, can be capitalized to make individual treatment effective in a way impossible without. (Lee, 1919, p. 325)

This was written in 1919—30 years before the emergence of family systems theory and therapy! And it was written by a social worker.

Unfortunately, Lee failed in his plea for the family rather than the individual as the focus of social work, as attested by other papers given at the 1919 Conference by Jarrett, Spaulding, and Taft.

A paper that greatly influenced the field was "The Psychiatric Thread Running Through All Social Case Work" by Mary C. Jarrett, the Associate Director of the Smith College Training School for Social Work, who had formerly been the Chief of Social Service at Southard's Boston Psychopathic Hospital. According to Jarrett, the title of her paper was inaccurate: rather, "the 'thread' constitutes the entire 'warp' of the fabric of case work" (Jarrett, 1919, p. 587). "The special function of social case work," said Jarrett, "is the adjustment of individuals with social difficulties" (p. 587), and the case worker should "seek for the causes of conduct in mental factors" (p. 590). She was distressed that "this fact—that a majority of social cases are psychiatric problems—is probably not yet generally recognized" (p. 588).

Edith R. Spaulding's paper described the psychiatric social work training at Smith College. She confided that that school had first to answer in the affirmative "the question whether it was wise to take a group of women without medical training into the sacred precincts of the temple of psychiatric thought" (Spaulding, 1919, p. 607). She also seemed to favor a takeover of social work by psychiatry, with the worker functioning as an obedient handmaiden whose role was "to carry out in detail and intelligence the treatment which the psychiatrist indicates but which he does not have time to carry out" (p. 610).

Jessie Taft, in her paper "Qualifications of the Psychiatric Social Worker," held that psychiatric social work was not just a new specialization focusing on the mentally ill population, but "a new way of approaching all case work" that would "enable the social worker to deal with the personality of the patient in his social setting as intelligently and constructively as the psychiatrist deals with it in the hospital" (Taft, 1919, p. 594). (Modern-day readers, however, might question how "intelligent and constructive" was mental hospital psychiatry in 1919.) Taft's underlying assumptions were that psychological disorders were at the root of clients' difficulties, and that the goal of social work was to cure these disorders so that clients could be adapted to their environments: Social casework should be "that science or art of untangling and reconstructing the twisted personality, of changing human behavior so that it adapts the individual to his environment" (p. 595). No consideration was given to the possibilities that in some cases it was the environment that was depriving and dehumanizing, and that the environment therefore should do the adapting to legitimate human needs; or that in other cases the client's "twisted" personality and behavior were reasonable responses to a pathological environment; or that in yet other cases person and circumstances *both* needed to change to make possible a more constructive interaction or ecological fit.

Dr. Richard C. Cabot, who with Ida M. Cannon had started the first hospital social work department at the Massachusetts General Hospital in 1906, attempted to argue against the idea implicit in the presentations of Jarrett, Spaulding, and Taft that adapting the individual to the environment was a valid goal of social work:

> Adaptation means becoming fit. A key fits a lock so that it can rest there. The locksmith adapts it and all is well. But people can get so well adapted to their environment that they are no earthly use. Social work does not aim to produce people who are passive, pacific, contentedly and smoothly functioning in the prison of things as they are. Social work wants to enhance life and one of the things life often does is to remake and reform its environment or, failing that, to smash it.... Perfect adaptation is not a human ideal. It is a mechanical one. The ooze on the ocean floor is now adapted, I suppose, to its environment for a good many thousand years to

> come. But active life is forever choosing, constructing, destroying, reforming its environment. Not even to himself does one want to be permanently adapted. That is to settle down like a mollusc or a middle-aged loafer. One breaks up his over-perfect adaptation again and again as long as there is life in him. (Cabot, 1919, p. 365)

Despite the arguments of Lee and Cabot, however, an increasing number of social workers—especially the younger ones applying to the new psychiatric specialization in schools of social work—was rushing to cross the Rubicon to embrace the new individualistically oriented psychiatric-deficit paradigm.

CHALLENGES TO THE PSYCHIATRIC PERSPECTIVE

One "hold-out" against the psychiatric caseworker model was Ada Eliot Sheffield of Boston, who wrote several articles and delivered papers during the 1920s, but whose seminal works were a 1930 paper (Sheffield, 1931), "The Situation as the Unit of Family Case Study," and a 1937 book, *Social Insight in Case Situations*. (The 1930 paper, interestingly, was delivered to a symposium of the Section on Sociology and Social Work of the American Sociological Society—an illustration of the much closer ties that existed then than do now between sociology and social work.)

It had been Mary Richmond who first outlined the duality of social work's approach to person or to environmental situation. The pendulum has been swinging wildly back and forth since then, sometimes hovering over the person polarity, as in the psychiatric casework movement sketched above, and sometimes over the environment polarity, as in the emphasis in the 1960s on advocacy and change of institutional systems. Although the recent ecological perspective is offering some bridging concepts, this duality still plagues us; we are still searching for a conceptual integration of the two—since we recognize that in our client's actual lives they are indeed an inseparable unity and not a dichotomy.

Sheffield, who is little known to today's social workers (although she has been rediscovered by some: see Zimbalist, 1952; Siporin, 1972; Mailick, 1977; and Braverman, 1986), attempted such an integration. She politely criticized Mary Richmond as being, despite that leader's emphasis on "wholesale" as well as "retail" methods, still too focused on development of the individual's personality as the purpose of casework (Sheffield, 1937, p. 76). Sheffield was equally critical of the definitions of social casework developed by the two Milford Conferences of 1929 and 1932, as also being overly focused on the individual. The latter of these resorted to a dichotomous representation of individual and environment as representing "two poles of interest" within the case (Sheffield, 1937, p. 77). Sheffield, who had been influenced by the gestalt psychologists and by Kurt Lewin, could not understand a dualistic or segmental approach to social work practice, which she thought "makes a piecemeal advance toward understanding by viewing situation-items *atomistically* and moving additively toward a grasp of the whole, whereas a psychosocial whole operates as a *system* which like an organism conditions the very nature of its interdependent elements" (Sheffield, 1937, p. 265). General Systems Theory and cybernetics had not yet been invented, but Sheffield had preceded them in her grasp of the essential idea of *system* and its interaction with its component parts.

Sheffield saw the business of social work as changing problematic *situations*, not changing people alone, or changing their circumstances alone, or even of moving back and forth between the two. By situation she meant a total gestalt (or a system) in which various individual human actors or groups of people (called clients, or significant others, or bureaucrats, or landlords, or professional helpers) were caught up with each other in a set of reality circumstances that included time and space, material resources and deficits, physical health, the life-stage needs of individuals and families, the characteristics of the community, and the policies and procedures of institutional systems. The situation of a case was, for Sheffield, all the systemic components that were interacting in such a way that a problem for the people called clients ensued. She could not address herself to the issue of whether social workers were supposed to change clients or to change environments, because that issue did not make sense to her. What did make more sense was seeing a system of interactions as the problem; it therefore followed that it was key components of that multilevel system that had to be changed. People, of course, were represented in these key components and in the change process: Individual family members and the family as a group, the landlord, the representatives of other agencies—and now also the family social worker. The case was successfully completed when the worker had brought about sufficient change in this web or network of interactions so that the problem no longer existed, or at least was as ameliorated as much as was realistically possible. The people in the problem situation called clients were the focus of the case, in terms of their being the ones who were to benefit from the practitioner's service, and also in terms of their responsibility, to the limits of their abilities, for working on whatever needed changing in the problem gestalt, including themselves if necessary. Although work directly with the clients therefore took place (of different kinds and to different degrees in different cases), direct work with clients was not considered by Sheffield to be necessarily more important to problem solving than work with the other people and circumstances that were involved. We return to some of these ideas of Sheffield in Chapter 7, where the beginnings of a model for work with the present-day multiproblem family will be suggested.

In the 1930s, Sheffield found herself in the unfortunate position of marching to a different drummer than did the majority of social workers. She was definitely not a "psychiatric caseworker." She saw social workers, not as junior, ill-paid psychiatrists, but as autonomous professionals whose practice was substantively different from the professions oriented solely to people-changing.

In 1930 there occurred what Siporin (1972, p. 93) calls "a historic confrontation" between Sheffield's situational orientation and the newer psychoanalytic perspective. In that year, Virginia Robinson published a widely read book, *A Changing Psychology in Social Casework*, in which she "sharply attacked the 'sociological' and 'situational' orientation of both Richmond and Sheffield, and...championed psychoanalytic psychology as the valid theoretical base for social casework" (Siporin, 1972, p. 93). The (female) social work profession yearned after the status of association with the new theory of the (male) psychiatrists; social work also seemed to prefer the reductionistic, prepackaged "understanding" of problems that the new psychology offered, so much easier to apply than the sophisticated judgment and analytic thinking about multiple levels of problem variables that was implicit in Sheffield's model. Sheffield's ideas lost, and "situation theory was largely jettisoned" (Siporin, 1972, p. 93).

Our description of social casework as developing in a psychiatric, people-changing rather than situation-changing direction, is, we believe, an accurate portrayal of the professional literature of the next several decades. But those who write about a professional practice are a very small proportion of all those who are actually practicing it. Many practitioners working with individuals and families devastated by the Great Depression of the 1930s continued a sensible focus on trying to ameliorate their clients' situations, as did many later practitioners in public agencies such as public welfare and low-cost medical clinics, as well as a few private agencies such as family service, whose caseloads consisted of a heavy proportion of poor families living in conditions of social deprivation. Indeed, social work's tradition of commitment to the impoverished multiproblem family, and the development of its experience and expertise with this most important client population, was continued by social work practitioners in what were, and still are, considered as being comparatively low-prestige (because they are not "psychiatric") agencies. But in many other family service agencies and in the child-guidance clinics, casework did become synonymous with individual psychotherapy.

Bertha Capen Reynolds was one social worker who found herself caught in the conflicted currents of the time between the old philanthropy of Richmond and the Charity Organization Societies, and the newer psychiatric social work. She was "not orthodox in either social work [meaning in the style of the charity agent] or psychiatry. I could not stomach philanthropy. I did not care for the way some psychiatric social workers looked down their intellectual noses at all other social workers and lived in a rarified atmosphere of the approval of psychiatrists" (Reynolds, 1963, pp. 78–79).

The major textbooks on casework practice published in this period through the 1960s struggled to articulate a psychosocial formulation that would integrate the "two poles" of person and reality circumstances. Although they talked about "environmental modification" as an integral part of that practice, their major thrust was psychotherapeutic and "the client" was always an individual. Gordon Hamilton, author of the casework textbook that in two editions (1940/1951) became the bible of casework courses in most schools of social work, although she pointed to the economic factors in family distress and disorganization and argued powerfully that social work should retain its interest in work with poor families, was herself heavily influenced by Freudian psychology. Hartman's analysis (1971) of the textbooks of Hollis (1965) and Perlman (1957) sees both authors as locating the problem within the individual, and defining casework as a person-changing activity.

In 1980, Hollis (then a Professor Emeritus in retirement from the Columbia University School of Social Work) stated that she was "afraid that many of us teaching casework may have treated the environment as self-evident and given students the impression that understanding the personality and interviewing techniques were the really challenging and interesting aspects to casework" (p. 5). She maintained, however, that even though this perspective may have been true of her own and others' teaching and writing during this period, only a small minority of *practitioners* at the time engaged in practice that "concentrates primarily on the past to the neglect of the present, that assumes a paternalistic, directive stance toward clients, that denies the importance of the environment, or that relies on…'insight' as the main dynamic of treatment" (p. 7).

But from the end of World War II for approximately the next 20 years, when family problems were brought to most family service agencies or child guidance clinics, where the psychiatric medical model dominated, what was recognized in the diagnostic assessment as a relationship problem—meaning a problem in *group* or *subgroup* interactions—was treated as if it were the individual problem of the individuals involved. Information about other family members and family relationships was obtained vicariously if at all. Spouses were seen separately in marital counseling; mother and child (sometimes, but rarely, the father) had separate therapists in parent-child counseling. Social work followed blindly and obediently its psychiatric mentors—then, as now, the ascendant profession in the political and economic culture of mental health facilities. Even in family service agencies of the period, staffed primarily or totally by social workers, a consultant psychiatrist (almost always psycho-analytically oriented) was employed in this mentorship role. Sherman cites a 1941 article by Waite contrasting the casework of that year with that of 50 years earlier, in which Waite observed how "family casework had *moved beyond* [italics added] the older emphasis on trying to know and be in touch with several family members," because of the need to avoid the competitiveness and jealousy existing among family members, a fear of "blurring the autonomy" of the individual client, and the perception that "society has increased its emphasis on the individual even at the expense of his membership in the family and society at large" (Sherman, 1961, pp. 19–20). As late as 1968, Briar criticized that "the image of the modern caseworker...is above all that of a therapist, which is to say that for the most part he performs only a therapeutic function" (p. 7); and Rapaport observed that "somehow, social casework has come to be equated with psychotherapy" (1968, p. 225).

THE RE-EMERGENCE OF A FAMILY FOCUS

An outstanding early exception to the emphasis on the individual was M. Robert Gomberg, Executive Director of Jewish Family Service in New York City until his untimely death in 1958. As early as 1944, at the height of the psychoanalytic period, Gomberg was writing that the family as a whole was the focus of casework. He addressed such family concepts as family unity and coherence, family organization, roles and relationships, and the balance of these in the family (Gomberg, 1944, 1948). Nathan Ackerman later joined Gomberg's agency; he and other staff at the agency in their writings of the next two decades were only partially successful in their struggle to break out of the individualistically oriented psychodynamic mind-set of the time. While Gomberg had been beginning to think of the family in systemic and holistic terms, Ackerman and his colleagues were still seeing the family in terms of interacting individual personalities. The work of Ackerman and others at this agency (and later at the institute that Ackerman founded in New York) was tremendously important in the early development of family therapy; but it was not yet family therapy as we know it today.

There were, to be sure, other and sometimes contrary eddies in the flow of development of casework and of social work. The "functional" school of social casework, developed in the 1930s by the faculty of the School of Social Work of the University of Pennsylvania, disagreed with the "diagnostic" Freudian orientation of social work schools such as those at Columbia University and Smith College. Instead, the functional school preferred the "psychology of growth" of Otto Rank, an apostate disciple of Freud. The functionalists were less interested in classical Freudian traumata than they were in the client's developing personality through the way he would use the worker's help in utilizing the agency's service. But the objective was still the personality development of the client.

Reynolds, in her blunt fashion, saw the emphasis of the functional school as being not on the client but rather on the agency's function, as "the most man-made and temporary of all the social forces within which we operate" serving to "distort the casework process instead of clarifying it" (1963, p. 285). Disenchanted by this time with the psychiatric social work in which she had been trained at Smith (where she was later Associate Director), Reynolds criticized evenhandedly the diagnostic or Freudian emphasis of most schools of social work at that time as well as the Rankian orientation of the functional faction. She felt that the diagnostic school had at least the possibility of developing a scientific base for social work practice but "had lost its way in Freud's generalizations about the nature of man, which he thought valid for all times and places." And concerning the functional school: "The value which it has in helping people...is a value to be judged by the criteria of a philosophical or religious belief, not the criteria of scientific testing and comparison of cases, one with another. I did not think that the functional theory of casework had the possibility of becoming a scientific discipline" (p. 287).

Despite this judgment, it is noteworthy that two of the earliest books on casework with the family emanated from the functional school (Taft, 1944, 1948).

The psychiatric cast of casework was more characteristic of the schools of social work of the Eastern Seaboard than it was of schools in other parts of the country. According to Reynolds, psychiatric caseworkers were more interested in doing therapy with their clients than in delivering the services of their agencies, such as child welfare, financial relief, or health care. But the University of Chicago of Sophonisba Breckenridge and Grace and Edith Abbott, a well as other schools that it influenced, "resisted this trend to disregard the social work in which, after all, the majority of agencies and workers were engaged, and continued its emphasis on public welfare and on the social forces affecting the adjustment of individuals from outside themselves" (Reynolds, 1963, p. 145).

Reynolds also articulated her resistance to the emphasis on work with individuals with concomitant neglect of the family. Reynolds says that she

> began to see that it is only by an artificial abstraction that we ever think we are dealing with individuals alone. Even when social casework contributes most fruitfully to a person's better adjustment, probably nine-tenths of his problem solving is done in groups in the process of living, and it is to group relationships that he must take his released or enriched self. Family casework is group work, really. We isolate an individual for treatment only temporarily and with great risk that what we thought was excellent work will be undone in the complex of family relationships. (Reynolds, 1963, pp. 203–204)

Community organization and social group work, as companion social work "methods" to social casework, developed out of settlement houses, Y's, the Scouts, and other facilities for recreation and adult education (Leiby, 1978, p. 185). The emergence of social group work, particularly, as a subspecialty in social work might have added appreciably to the development of theory and technique for work with family groups. The literature began to fill with exhortations that caseworkers and group workers needed not only to collaborate with each other as colleagues in the same profession, but additionally to learn from each other. But caseworkers did not seem to learn one of the fundamental principles of group work: that when one is dealing with a group problem, it should be dealt with as a problem of the *group*. Group work, for its part, although it developed much expertise about all sorts of natural and formed groups, never paid much attention to the family, the template for all group process; and its contribution to family practice was accordingly minimal.

Social casework was, however, not so naive as to incorporate Freudian theory completely uncritically or without the effort to discriminatively select from it, to mold and adjust it, to social work's specific needs (Wood, 1971). The "classic" casework textbooks referred to earlier—despite their limitations in terms of their focus on the individual rather than the family and their psychological rather than social emphasis—were also scholarly and creative efforts to integrate social work's rich empirical practice experience with the only theoretical framework, borrowed from psychiatry, then available. A breakthrough helpful to social work was the contribution of the ego psychologists (Kris, 1947; Rapaport, 1951; Hartmann, 1958; and especially White, 1959). Ego psychology focused, not so much on unconscious processes or the traumata of long ago, as on the conscious efforts and capacity of human beings to both adapt to, and force to adapt to them, their life circumstances—the motivation and capacity that originally got us down out of the trees. White, particularly talked about such concepts as mastery and what he called *effectance*—the experience of being able to make an impact on one's world, rather than being only its helpless, "adaptive" victim. In essence, he was talking about a process of *interaction* between people and their situational circumstances, and of coping and problem solving. Social workers had by then become a bit disenchanted with the effectiveness of insight into early childhood traumata as a cure-all; some of the heretically less converted observed that they saw no real evidence in their cases of such etiology in the life problems of the majority of their clients. Psychiatrists—even psychoanalytically oriented psychiatrists—were also becoming disappointed with insight as a necessary therapeutic tool and goal (Hobbs, 1962).

But ego psychology, particularly its focus on coping mechanisms and effectance capacities, seemed to fit better the kinds of cases with which social workers dealt (so different from the kinds of cases with which psychoanalysts dealt). Like any borrowed theory, however, that has not been born out of the experience of its own professional practitioners, ego psychology was only partially useful. It had little to say about the family group, and little to say except by implication about the environmental *circumstances or situation* of people who were not in the ego psychologists' "average expectable environment." It addressed only the reaction of persons unfortunate enough to find themselves trapped in quite below-average environments; it did not help the social worker (or thus, the client) to figure out how to get those environmental circumstances to change closer to the "expectable" mean.

RENEWAL OF INTEREST IN THE MULTIPROBLEM FAMILY

In the 1950s, interest in the multiproblem family resurfaced, and a number of projects delivering service to this client population were undertaken. One of these was the practice-research endeavor of the St. Paul Project (Overton, Tinker, & Associates, 1957; Geismar & Ayres, 1958, 1959, 1960; Geismar & LaSorte, 1964). The ideas of the newborn family therapy movement were not yet available to the practitioners in these projects, who had to rely only on their own and the profession's rich practice experience with the multiproblem family. The work of early writers on the multiproblem family such as Scherz (1953), Regensburg (1954), Fantl (1958), and Overton (1955, 1960) were largely atheoretical, because they were, after all, confronted with practice situations for which the psychodynamic theory of the time provided few guidelines. The families they served were overwhelmed by multiple problems, and some of their basic survival needs were not being met. They were unlikely to respond favorably to requests for introspection, and instead demanded help with their material problems. Their past experience with social agencies had made them distrustful of the intentions of professional intervenors.

Family-centered and reaching-out social work as articulated in the *Casework Notebook* (Overton, Tinker, & associates,

1957) represented a break with the doctrinaire psychiatrically influenced past of the previous three decades of social work. It was, in fact, a return to a more unified approach—characteristic of the early social work—that stressed the interdependence of family positions and roles as well as society's responsibility for aiding the socially deprived. Family-centered social work generated a good many concepts and practice principles from the experiences of the leading practitioners with resistant, hard-to-reach families (Overton, Tinker, & associates, 1957).

The strongest revival of the Overton-Tinker approach to serving multiproblem families was embodied in what came to be known as family-centered, home-based services in child protection. Programs under this heading gained momentum in the mid-1970s, mainly in response to society's confrontation with the problem of child abuse and neglect (Maybanks & Bryce, 1979), and they received renewed recognition during the 1980s through services such as Homebuilders and Family Preservation units attached to child welfare services. The debt of home-based services to the St. Paul Family Centered Project is recognized in the title of Horejsi's article (1981), "The St. Paul Family-Centered Project Revisited: Exploring an Old Gold Mine." Frankel's review (1968) of the home-based services movement points to limited hard evidence on effectiveness but to a rich potential for testing the innovative ideas generated by the programs by way of well-designed and controlled studies.

ENLARGING PERSPECTIVE:
INCLUSION OF SOCIOPOLITICAL DYNAMICS

In the 1960s, the War on Poverty ideology shifted the professional perspective on child and family welfare from the family to society. A typical statement often heard representing the new orientation was, "there are no multiproblem families, only multiproblem communities." (This assertion makes the wrong assumption, of course, namely that the concept of multiproblem seeks to fix blame rather than to describe a condition.) Social work enthusiastically embraced a social-change orientation, sometimes (as illustrated in the transformation of the New

York City Community Service Society) withholding direct services from individuals and families in favor of planning and organizing endeavors at a community-wide level. Social casework came under attack as being anachronistic. Casework, which dealt with people case-by-case, was taken to task because it had not eradicated societal poverty. The expectation was that the societal changes that were just around the corner would eliminate the problems of the poor because they would eliminate poverty itself. The Vietnam War, and the struggle between "guns" and "butter" for national resources, ended that dream, although it left in place some of the better programs for the disadvantaged (such as Head Start) out of the many that the national poverty effort had spawned.

At the same time that direct social work services were being criticized as unnecessary, social agencies that dispensed such services were also being censured for having deserted the poor in favor of the middle class, who were considered more appropriate clients for the psychotherapeutic casework that was still dominant in many family service and mental health agencies. One publication that had a great impact was Cloward and Epstein's "Private Social Welfare's Disengagement from the Poor: The Case of Family Adjustment Agencies" (1965). This sort of disapprobation from within the profession itself, along with the groundswell of the War on Poverty, compelled many agencies to institute changes in their programs and policies.

Malfunctioning at the microlevel was rediscovered in the late 1960s in the wake of rising crime and delinquency rates. There as a continuing tendency to seek remedies mainly by way of broad-scale intervention such as the Model Cities programs and the Service Integration projects of the U.S. Department of Health, Education and Welfare. By the middle 1970s, with the War on Poverty having run out of steam, the family once again entered the picture. Yet, its reemergence as a focus of intervention came only subsequent to the unearthing of child abuse and neglect and family violence as problems of high priority, and after a commitment by a new U.S. President (Carter) to work for a strengthening of the American family.

The rediscovery of the multiproblem family led social workers to confront practice situations similar to those faced by professionals nearly a generation earlier. But writings of the 1970s on the multiproblem family were by and large devoid of references to earlier works on the subject. Concepts and practices known to workers in the 1950s were rediscovered and given a new terminology. Family-centered social work came to be known as "applying the systems approach." The worker-client partnership concept gave way to the term *contract*. Joint client-worker planning and problem solving was designated as goal-oriented service, and so forth.

The attention of practitioners who had persisted in working with the poor in the previous years had never been deflected from the environmental circumstances of their clients; but now the attention of the profession as a whole was brought back to the "situation" of the person-in-situation social work configuration. Stein (1960) and Hearn (1969) were particularly influential in this trend, and Hearn was one of the earliest social work writers to talk about "systems." Siporin (1970, 1972, 1975), partly drawing on the early ideas of Sheffield (1931, 1937), creatively expanded and refined the concept of the situation of the client. He defined casework as "social treatment" in which psychotherapy "is but *one* set of procedures" (Siporin, 1970, p. 17). Principles and techniques of direct work with systems environing to that of the client, such as brokerage, mediation, and advocacy, began to be codified (Grinnell, 1973; Grinnell, Kyte, & Bostwick, 1981). Other textbooks of the 1970s also addressed a more holistic view of social work purpose, and a more generalist definition of the worker's role, meaning one that went beyond the narrow role of psychotherapist only (Goldstein, 1970; Pincus & Minahan, 1973; Middleman & Goldberg, 1974; Meyer, 1976), began to be emphasized.

An *ecological* or *ecosystems* perspective uses ideas of ecology as applied to human systems (Bronfenbrenner, 1979) as a restatement of the old social work person-in-situation motif. Although it is only a perspective or "way of looking at"—not a theory or even a practice model—the use of ecological language and concepts appears to specify the social work arena of concern better than did the older term. The ecosystems framework directs the worker's attention to "the *fit* between the person and the situation with an emphasis on the interface" (Meyer 1982,

p. 56). Concepts such as adaptation, a cybernetic model of stress, the balance between perceived demand and perceived capability, and feedback of the consequences of coping efforts are utilized. Underlined is the idea of *goodness of fit* between the needs of people and the resources and demands of their physical and social contexts. Problems in living are defined as poorness of that fit, because of the individual's or family's comparative lack of skills and coping capacities, and/or the lack of resources available in outside systems or the stresses they inflict. Although different, more modern, language is being used, this is very close to the ideas of Sheffield—in fact, in her 1937 book (p. 203) she provides what today would be called an "eco-map"!

THE FAMILY THERAPY MOVEMENT

While the societal and social work events sketched above were transpiring, the new movement of family therapy was developing and its influence was beginning to be felt in social work from the 1950s on. The stage for the development of family therapy had been set by a number of events and factors. Those who early experimented with working with the total family were disenchanted with the ineffectiveness of the psychodynamic individual-treatment model for cases of schizophrenia, and also for many behavioral problems of children. The work of Kurt Lewin (1935, 1936, 1951) and the gestalt school of psychology had had an impact on some in the mental health field, as had Harry Stack Sullivan's shift of focus from the purely intrapsychic to the interpersonal—although Sullivan addressed primarily only the relationship of the child with his parents and not the family as a whole (Sullivan, 1953). According to Guerin (1976), family therapy was an "underground" activity in its early years because those who were experimenting with it feared the disapproval of their psychodynamic colleagues. It surfaced nationally in 1957, in panel presentations at the annual meetings of the American Orthopsychiatric Association and the American Psychiatric Association.

As noted previously, the social worker M. Robert Gomberg at the Jewish Family Service in New York City was writing as early as 1944 about the family. In 1951 he and Frances T. Levinson published a book, *Diagnosis and Process in Family Counseling* (Gomberg & Levinson). These writings on family therapy *predate* Nathan Ackerman's association with that agency (Siporin, 1980, footnote, p. 13). Ackerman, who developed many of his ideas about family therapy when he was associated with Gomberg's agency, is reputed as the "father of family therapy"—but the indication appears to be that it was Ackerman who learned from the social workers at this social agency as much, or more, than they learned from him. The agency's social work staff, including Sherman, Mitchell, Beatman, and Leichter, were responsible for developing some of the early formulations about family diagnosis and treatment. Frances Scherz of the Jewish Family and Community Service in Chicago was writing as early as 1954, and later headed the Committee of Midwestern Family Agencies, studying various new methods of treatment of couples and families (Scherz, 1970).

In descriptions of the history of the family therapy movement by such psychiatrists as Bowen (1978) and Guerin (1976), and even in books on family therapy in social work practice (Nelsen, 1983; Kolevzon & Green, 1985), social work's role is given short shrift—both in terms of its long history of work with families and the contribution of those such as the social workers at the Jewish family agencies in New York and Chicago who were some of the earliest theoreticians of family therapy. Virginia Satir (1967) is usually the only social worker ever mentioned as having played a role in the gestation of family therapy—although Braverman observed that "for years [Satir] denied or omitted identifying her professional training in social work" (Braverman, 1986, p. 236).

Concerning the debt the strategic school of family therapy owes to social work, Braverman observed that "although strategic theorizing is important to contemporary social work, little recognition is given to the fact that many early casework theories contributed to it" (1986, p. 234). In Braverman's article, interestingly, Ada Sheffield resurrects again when she is given credit, along with other early social workers, for their recognition of the phenomenon now known in family therapy terminology as "punctuation" of an interactional exchange (1986,

p. 237). Braverman also sees such family therapy techniques as "joining" and "positive reframing" as very old social work interventions (1986, p. 239).

Hartman and Laird also decry the lack of credit given by family therapy to social work (1983, p. 18), and note that social workers themselves participate in this professional self-abnegation: "Unfortunately, many of those social workers who have made significant contributions to the burgeoning family therapy literature tend to be identified as family therapists rather than as social workers, and their writings rarely appear in the social work journals" (p. 19).

Siporin (1980) observed that "marriage therapy and family therapy are traditional and basic social work services. Social workers have provided these services as part of the core of social work practice since the beginning of the profession" (p. 11). For many years, social workers supplied the bulk of marital and family counseling but, Siporin observed, this has declined precipitously in recent years due to "the aggressive competition from other helping human service professions and the passive responses to such competition by social workers" (p. 14). Siporin continued:

> From such a tradition of practice and education, social workers have developed a distinctive base of knowledge and values, a unique theoretical position, and a special style and mode of practice in marital and family therapy. This distinctive approach has had little recognition and has been grossly slighted, even by social workers. A great deal of reciprocal influence should be acknowledged between social work practitioners and the theorists and practitioners from other helping professions such as Ackerman, Bowen, Jackson, Haley, and Minuchin—many of whom were taught this content by social workers. (pp. 15–16)

The family therapies have attracted direct practice social workers in large numbers, but social work writings, with some exceptions (Hartman & Laird, 1983; Reid, 1985; Janzen & Harris, 1986) have been rooted in the philosophies and organizational frameworks of other disciplines. Social work practitioners have been among the most eager consumers of conference and institute presentations featuring charismatic therapists. The philosophic orthodoxy previously attached to two major social work treatment orientations (the diagnostic and the functional) has, it appears, given way to a new adherence to non-social-work doctrines that are less likely to further professional identity.

Siporin pointed out that family social work has a much more sophisticated appreciation than does family therapy of the "complex interrelationship of individual personality and social systems" (1980, p. 18). We would add that this is because social work, despite its past detours down the false trails of therapies oriented only to the individual, has as part of its professional history, legacy, and know-how created by practice experience over 100 years, always held to its focus on individual-in-family and family-in-environing systems. Family therapy has finally moved from individual-as-patient, to individual-in-family, to (often inappropriately) family-as-patient. But it has not yet recognized what social work has known for a long time: family-as-system-embedded-in-other-systems. Even though family therapists see themselves as aligned with a "systems" approach, their treatment orientation is systems focused only in the most narrow sense, namely the interaction of individuals within the family (Johnson, 1986). This is a far cry from general systems theory as formulated by Miller (1978), von Bertalanffy (1968), and others, which takes account of the hierarchical interrelationship of the system (the nuclear family), subsystems (such as psychological and biological components), and suprasystems (such as the community, the human service system, and the labor market). Johnson, in fact, concluded that "in general, family systems theorists treat the family as a closed system" (1986, p. 300).

As family therapists concentrate their interventive effort on members of the immediate family—and frequently such treatment is one-dimensional in that it revolves around a single variable such as communication, emotional distress, disengagement, or unresolved past conflicts—little attention is being given to factors beyond the family boundaries. Although one could argue that a family systems approach need not correspond to general systems theory as adopted by engineering, economics, or sociology, the utility of a closed-system approach can be challenged when it comes to dealing with the modern family, especially the family that has experienced major dislocation in society. It appears, indeed, that as clinical social work moved in recent years to get on the family therapy bandwagon it abandoned an important aspect of the traditional social work perspective, namely the genuine client-in-situation approach.

Social work, in joining the marital and family therapy movement, has come to perceive the individual client once more in the family context. But in adopting the theory of one of the many schools of family therapy, the social worker is adopting the perspective and philosophy of the other therapy-dispensing professions such as psychiatry, clinical psychology, and marital counseling. These professions, in contrast to social work, have never put a premium on rendering service beyond the confines of the family system. "The neglect of macro-system factors," states Johnson, also has led to inappropriate "therapizing" of the family, when therapists "redefine emotional distress that is environmentally generated as inadequate family or interpersonal functioning" (1986, p. 300).

Although some family therapists, such as Lansky (1981) and Minuchin et al. (Minuchin & Montalvo, 1967; Minuchin, Montalvo, Guerney, Rosman, & Schumer, 1967) have addressed themselves to the impoverished dysfunctional family, their intervention was concentrated on the internal system in general and interpersonal relations in particular.

HISTORICAL OVERVIEW

Social work lacks a tradition of historical analysis of practice theory and research. The profession tends to be thoroughly oriented to the present, dealing with issues and problems in the context of theories and practices generated or being diffused at the moment, both within its own ranks or more often by cognate fields. The absence of an efficient technology to assess the effect of intervention methods has left social work extremely susceptible to the vagaries of ever-changing theories and techniques of treatment. The profession moves with the tide enthusiastically and uncritically, rarely looking back at past ways of defining problems and coping with them.

We do not mean to create the impression that later approaches are or should be perfect replicas of their earlier ana-

logues. Time works in the direction of conceptual and technological refinement. The point is rather that the advocates of the
more recent techniques and conceptualizations more often than
not appear to be blissfully unaware of preceding efforts. Social
work's "ahistoricity" has led it repeatedly to reinvent the wheel.
There may be great joy in such independent discoveries, but
they hardly represent effective scientific procedures because
they lack one of the core elements of science, namely the cu-
mulation of knowledge.

The theory of social work generally, of social casework more
specifically, and of family casework at the most specific level,
have a long way to go yet before they can claim to be real theories
for practice, meaning not a perspective or a model or a collection of ideas but an integrated web of propositions that are
empirically validatable.

The theory of family therapy has a long way to go also. In
Chapters 5 and 6 we attempt a comparative analysis of the descriptive and prescriptive theories of family social work and
family therapy.

Chapter 5

Descriptive Theory
Family Social Work
and Family Therapy

In the preceding chapter, we offer a conclusion that the theories of both family social work and family therapy have a "long way to go" before they can be considered real theories, that is, organized sets of testable propositions. Every practice theory has both descriptive and prescriptive dimensions. The descriptive dimension of a theory concerning intervention with families undertakes to describe and explain how families function and malfunction and, as such, forms the basis for the prescriptive dimension or the recommendations for professional remedial action.

This chapter attempts a critical analysis of the descriptive dimensions of the theories of family social work and family therapy. The prescriptive part of those theories is addressed in Chapter 6.

SOCIAL WORK THEORY: INDIGENOUS OR BORROWED

Early social work practitioners working with troubled families had no real descriptive theory of the family to guide them. The only practice theories available to practitioners dealt with the individual or with groups other than families. The major theories concerning the family were those from sociology, and despite an emphasis by social work in the 1960s and 1970s on importing knowledge from the social sciences, and the pragmatic value to practitioners of such social science contributions as the developmental life stages of the family, most sociological theories concerning the family were not designed by their authors to guide intervention. Pre-family-therapy social workers therefore could do no better than to work from their practice experience of what families were like, plus whatever they could get from social science, because the psychological sciences had not yet really addressed the family. They did not have available to them an overall conceptual framework to serve as an organizing structure. The perspective on the individual of the psychologies of the time could not be translated into terms of the family group without recourse to distorting anthropomorphization. Social group work, group psychotherapy, and small group research had little to offer concerning the special group known as the family.

The 1950s social work literature demonstrates that the profession was then beginning to wrestle with the need for a descriptive theory of the family. The influence of the individualistically oriented psychological theories of the time was evident, however, in that these early attempts tended to adopt an additive strategy; that is, they tended to assume that the family was the sum of its individual parts. The fairly obvious notion of interaction among family members was not overlooked, but it tended to become obscured by what was still a partializing rather than synthesizing perspective. Beatman (1956), for example, despite the title of her paper, "Family Interaction: Its Significance for Diagnosis and Treatment," focused on "individual appraisal of the personality, character structure, defenses, and pathology of each family member" (p. 111) as these were played out in the individual's interactions with others in the family. Personality factors of individuals were therefore held to represent the substance of interaction; the importance of more systemic factors such as role assignment, internal boundaries around subsystems, power hierarchies, and other later concepts of family therapy were not yet recognized.

In 1962, Schwartz was writing about the widespread uneasiness of social work practitioners with the then-new approach of multiple-client interviews for which there was "not as yet a consistent and firm theoretical base on which to build" (p. 294). Although the present authors' bias is firmly on the side of the need for developing validatable theory to guide effective practice, it is interesting to note that the social workers of Richmond's era, a half century earlier, seem not to have felt the same uneasiness about their lack of theory: They considered that multiple-client interviews with the members of a family were the natural way to proceed. Actually, the point here is not that theory interferes with practice (the perspective advanced by family therapist Carl Whitaker, who finds all theories for practice "constrictive and constipating" [1976, p. 154]), but that the mind-set, or implicit theory, of the early workers was family oriented, whereas that of their descendants was not. The latter were "constricted and constipated" by the individual orientation they had learned; they found it enormously difficult to begin to think in other than atomistic terms. The again-family-centered approach of such practitioners as Overton in the 1950s seems therefore all the more remarkable, because they had little more in the way of family descriptive or prescriptive theory to guide them than did the workers of Richmond's time—and in addition, they were swimming against the tide of the prevalent individual orientation.

THE FAMILY THERAPY MOVEMENT CONTRIBUTION: MIXED BENEFICENCE

The family therapy movement offered a descriptive theory of family functioning and malfunctioning that moved away from individualistic personality factors to interactive systemic processes. It seemed to offer the missing theoretical conceptualizations needed to capture the complexities of family functioning.

The contribution of the family therapy movement to understanding of and effective intervention with the multiproblem family has been a somewhat mixed beneficence. In Chapter 6 we address some of the difficulties of the prescriptive theory of family therapy, such as the inappropriate and possibly damaging nature of some of its interventions for the multiproblem family. Concerning its descriptive theory, it can be said that not all of the discoveries and insights of family therapy, although couched in new language, appear to be fundamentally all that novel. The theorizing is often fuzzy, and operationalization of many of the concepts is difficult or impossible. But such deficiencies also characterize many other theories in the social and behavioral sciences, even those that have been in existence much longer than family therapy.

On balance, the conclusion is offered that the family therapy movement has added appreciably to our ability to understand and help many kinds of troubled families, primarily because it drew our attention to interaction; and many, although not all, of its descriptive ideas and prescriptive propositions are applicable to the multiproblem family.

REVOLUTION IN PERSPECTIVE:
UNANSWERED QUESTIONS AND PARADIGM SHIFT

The major contribution of the family therapy movement to the mental health field generally has been, ironically, not so much its focus on the family as the unit of attention (which indeed has some disadvantages, to be discussed later) but the extremity of the change in perspective concerning client problems that has been involved.

Some family therapists have termed this change a shift in epistemology. *Epistemology* is a term much in vogue at present; many articles have been written about the epistemology of family therapy and even the epistemology of the family. The traditional definition of epistemology is that subdivision of philosophy that investigates the origin, nature, methods, limits, and validity of what we know. More than a change in epistemological orientation, however, has been involved: Rather, what seems to have occurred was a paradigm shift, as described by Kuhn (1957, 1970)—albeit on a quite minor scale, since Kuhn seems to reserve the term for scientific revolutions of the magnitude of the change from the Ptolemaic to the Copernican view of the universe, or the reverberating impact in so many areas of human life as that occasioned by Darwin's theory of evolution. Although hardly on the same plane of importance or scope as these, for people in the helping professions, the family therapy movement did involve a shift in the paradigm or world view they brought to their professional tasks.

A paradigm expresses a philosophical position that includes cosmology (beliefs about the structure of nature and the place of humans in nature), ontology (the meaning of existence), epistemology (definitions of what constitutes knowledge and how knowledge is and should be generated), axiology (beliefs about values and ethics), the problems that are considered important, and the preferred methodology for problem solving. It should be noted that these are not the exclusive domain of the scientist or theoretician; the most uneducated person has ideas or beliefs about each of these areas. But neither ordinary people nor scientists usually explicate even for themselves these underlying philosophical assumptions, which tend to be accepted unquestionably as givens. As philosophical positions, we tend to attach ourselves to them emotionally rather than intellectually; they are convictions that we consider to be axiomatic or self-evident. They are usually reinforced by virtue of their equal acceptance by others in the scientific/professional community or other relevant reference group. Indeed, they are "received beliefs" imparted by the authoritative teachers of the particular culture involved—in the case of the helping professions, by professional mentors and training programs.

The prevailing paradigm (or paradigms—sometimes they are multiple) in a particular discipline or group of related disciplines determines the kinds of questions that are asked and the kinds of theories that are formulated as tentative, speculative answers to those questions. Every theory is based on a multitude of assumptions about cosmology, epistemology, values, and the like; it in essence reflects a philosophy. It is therefore too narrow and thus inaccurate to address only the epistemology of a particular theory such as family therapy; the epistemology involved is only one aspect of a multifaceted underlying philosophical paradigm. Paradigms are neither true nor false, valid nor invalid; they are merely more or less useful. Although paradigms involve rules, these are not hard and fast but rather loose and evolving frameworks.

Theories are conceptual boxes into which we attempt to stuff the reality we experience by our senses so as to explain it (and, we hope, ultimately to predict and control it). The conceptual boxes of theory are essential for the conduct of research and other kinds of knowledge building or understanding of the human and material world. The philosopher of science, Karl Popper (1965), once demonstrated this by ordering his students to "observe"! Puzzled, they protested that they could not do so until he told them just *what* he wanted them to observe: they first needed some conceptual boxes according to which to direct their observations. Humans are natural theorizers, natural conceptual box-builders, as Piaget recognized (Piaget & Inhelder, 1958; Piaget, 1963). We cannot conceptually deal with our reality unless we can contain it somehow in boxes; whether or not those theoretical boxes become constricting, as Whitaker would have it, depends on both the theory and the uses to which it is put. They can indeed constrict and warp the way we perceive and relate to our reality, but theories can also be freeing, mind expanding, and essential to dealing with our world. Our point here is that "you cannot *not* have a theory": Almost from the moment we are born, we are busily engaged in building theoretical conceptual boxes. The general culture and the particular professional or other subculture provide, usually outside our conscious awareness, the philosophical paradigm that directs the kinds of theoretical boxes we shall construct.

Kuhn posits that paradigms, and the theories they spawn, are accepted so long as they prove useful in solving what he calls the "puzzles" that have always intrigued and challenged us about our world and ourselves. He further suggests that the theories, or speculative explanations of observed reality, that emerge from these paradigms prove useful for a time but eventually "run dry." Increasingly, anomalies are encountered that subvert the theory because they just will not fit obediently into its conceptual boxes—actually, the boxes that are provided not only by the theory but also prestructured by the mind-set, way of thinking, and belief system of the underlying paradigm. The stage is then readied for a revolutionary process of shift in the underlying philosophical, epistemological, axiological, and methodological paradigm. Usually this is a rather slow, evolutionary process that ultimately culminates in a revolutionary change. Sometimes it happens more rapidly.

Classical physics was running dry in the early years of this century in terms of its theories: Despite their great success in empirically validating many propositions dealing with the physical universe, they were encountering more and more anomalies that could not be explained by the then-current theories—that is, anomalies that remained stubbornly outside or that contradicted the conceptual boxes provided by the paradigm of classical physics on which the theories were based. Einstein's genius was perhaps not so much that he provided new theoretical "answers" for these anomalies, but that he asked different *questions*: He recognized that he would have to move outside the theoretical conceptual boxes available, and in so doing he shifted the paradigm.

A different way of thinking, a different philosophical base in many respects, a different paradigm from older theories of practice, is involved in the family therapy movement. Psychodynamic and other theories of people and their troubles looked at persons atomistically: Even when the presenting problem was that of a troubled relationship, the assumption was that what needed treatment were personality factors of the individual partners (see, for example, Hollis, 1949). Family therapy's shift was away from this kind of atomistic, analytic, and linear Aristotelian logic to thinking in terms of reciprocal causality, interactions, and synthesis—in short, systems.

The recognition that the individualistic theories, and their paradigm, of the helping professions had been running dry was voiced by the editors (Ackerman, Beatman, & Sherman) of the very influential 1961 book, *Exploring the Base for Family Therapy*:

> The helping professions have often reached a cul de sac in the treatment of individual social maladaptation, emotional disturbance, and mental illness. The preoccupation with individual psychic processes which has characterized helping efforts during the past few decades unquestionably brought great advances in psychological theory as well as in therapeutic procedures but...it has

become increasingly clear that a major break-through in theory is
necessary if substantial further advances are to be made. (p. 2)

To be sure, as early as 1944 such innovative thinkers as
Gomberg had proposed attention to "family organization and
the different roles normally assumed by the several members of
a family" (p. 147). But the time was not right in the 1940s: Individualistic theories were in a powerful position of dominance.

THE SYSTEMS VIEW

The family therapy movement, to be sure, did not invent a
systems perspective or the move away from a linear epistemology. These changes had previously been occurring in a number
of other disciplines from which the family therapy movement
borrowed heavily.

In physics, for example, many of the propositions of Newtonian mechanics, well-established through extensive experimental research, are still valid today for many applications. But
for systems of atomic and subatomic dimensions (Kuhn's anomalies), Newton's theories do not hold and have been replaced by
quantum physics, whereas for systems moving near the speed of
light or in enormous gravitational fields Newtonian physics has
been supplanted by Einstein's formulations. Keeney (1982),
writing on the "epistemology of family therapy," suggests that
although "Newtonian epistemology is concerned with knowing
the nature of billiard balls and the forces that operate on them,"
the newer perspective is more interested in the interactional
system that all of the balls on the billiard table comprise. The
new perspective "jumps from the paradigm of things to the
paradigm of pattern" (p. 154). The metaphor (or epistemology,
if you will) that Freud used for his psychology was Newtonian
mechanics: Energy in the form of wishes and drives seeking
release, much as pent-up steam in a steam engine would behave,
but held in check by ego and superego, and utilizing the safety
valves of defense mechanisms. Although many of the early family therapists had been trained as psychoanalysts, the reductionistic, linear, and mechanical metaphor involved in this
theory was increasingly being questioned as a useful foundation

for psychotherapy. Bateson, one of the theoretical pioneers of the family therapy movement, extended the criticism further: he and his colleagues "viewed most of psychology and the social sciences as misguided. To put it more bluntly, they regarded most of social science as insane.... The source of social science's insanity has to do with its adoption of a Newtonian epistemology. The argument was that the use of an epistemology of billiard balls to approach human phenomena is an indication of madness" (Keeney, 1982, p. 155).

General Systems Theory

A major influence on the development of family therapy was the general systems theory of biologist Ludwig von Bertalanffy. A general systems theorist "understands the world in terms of relatedness. A particular entity is examined in relation to the things it affects and is affected by rather than in relation to its essential characteristics" (Hartman & Laird, 1983, p. 62). In other words, to understand the behavior of one billiard ball on the table, one would not examine that billiard ball, but would look, rather, at its interaction with the other balls, the table, the cue, and the human manipulating the cue. A primary assumption of systems theory is that the whole is not merely the sum of its parts, because simple addition leaves out the crucial component of interaction. This attention to interaction has aided the family practitioner in attending to what is happening among the human actors involved, and has led to increased sophistication in understanding of such interactional processes as communication channels and power distribution in the family. It has certainly been a conceptual improvement over early reductionistic efforts to understand the family by treating it as if it were an individual human: "If the family unit is anthropomorphized, perhaps we can better study its bisexual and asexual drives, its loves and its aggressions, the neuroses and psychoses of the unit" (Josselyn, 1953, p. 343).

Cybernetics

Cybernetics, developed by mathematician Norbert Wiener (1948, 1954) overlaps with general systems theory in that both claim to be general sciences of wholeness, although today cybernetics defines itself as "the science of effective organization" (Bullock & Stallybrass, 1977, p. 151). Both general systems theory and cybernetics claim applicability to a wide variety of fields; each considers itself transdisciplinary. Cybernetics focuses on the flow of information within and between systems, and the nature of adaptive control exerted by the system. According to Keeney, whereas general systems theory changed our conceptual lens from parts to wholes, cybernetics changed the lens from substance to form (1982, p. 155).

Ecology

Ecology, which has an obvious relationship both to general systems theory and to cybernetics, has been drawn upon not only by social work in its ecosystems perspective, but by family therapy theory as well. However, although social work has used an ecological metaphor to deal with the interaction of an individual or family with its environing systems, family therapy has given only lip service to the family system's contextual surround. A term first used in 1873 in biology to refer to the relationship between organisms and their environments, the meaning of *ecology* has been broadened (Bronfenbrenner, 1979) to include a focus on the "nature of transactions between person and environment" (Hartman & Laird, 1983, p. 70)—with the term *person* being taken to mean groupings of persons also (as in the family). Ecology therefore also deals with systems: with organisms and their environing contexts, taken as an interactional whole.

Earlier practitioners dealing with family problems, including those working with multiproblem families, were by no means unaware of the need to attend closely to such interactive processes as the what and how of communication among family members and with their world outside, how authority and power were distributed and exercised, whether the parents were able to constitute themselves as a collaborative executive team, and so forth. There is no question, however, that the family therapy movement has made for more sophisticated development of these "intuitive"—meaning either common sense or born of practice experience—perceptions of the early practitioners.

TOWARD A DESCRIPTIVE THEORY

This does not mean that the descriptive theory of family therapy has reached full development by any means. The theory, and the total field of family therapy, is characterized by great confusion, a profusion of jargon and muddy concepts, an unenlightening and sometimes angels-on-pinheads quality of argumentation, and the emotional, uncritical "true believer" attitude common to members of what quite accurately is still called a "movement." For example, Reid (1985) is one of the few authors of social work/family therapy texts who is critical of some aspects of family therapy theory; other authors writing about the use of family therapy in social work practice tend to be uncritically accepting of every concept labeled as family therapy.

But there certainly has been progress since the early days, when family therapy was characterized as a set of interventive techniques in search of a theory. In short, family therapy descriptive theory is just about where it is reasonable to expect it to be after only 30 years. But if it is ever to be transformed from a movement to a validatable theory, some real work is needed and some real problems will have to be addressed.

Two major sets of problems appear to exist for the development of family therapy descriptive theory. One has to do with the nature of its linkage with its parent theories. Another has to do with the degree to which the theory meets several criteria for the goodness of a theory that are commonly accepted by the scientific community. Primary among these criteria is testability; then follow such measures as the scope and level of abstraction of the theory, its explanatory power, the clarity of definitions of concepts, the internal consistency of the logic involved and the avoidance of logical fallacies, the operationalizability of the concepts, the parsimony of the theory, and its heuristic value.

General systems theory and cybernetics form a major part of the intellectual base for family therapy theory; and as such, they have made a rich contribution in terms of their emphasis on interactive processes. But there are difficulties involved also. Both general systems theory and cybernetics, as originally formulated, dealt with kinds of systems other than the human grouping known as the family. The claim that all of their propositions are applicable to the family may be valid, but it is an argument from analogy—one of the weakest forms of argumentation.

The Problem of Conceptualization and Level of Abstraction

Homeostasis, for example, is one of the basic concepts borrowed by family therapy. Cannon in 1932 referred to the homeostasis or tendency to equilibrium of the human body. The argument from analogy goes: If a human body is a system and it possesses demonstrable equilibrating mechanisms, and if the family is a social system, then it also must possess equilibrating mechanisms like a human body. The argument fails, however, because a human body is something real, tangible, perceivable by the senses; but a social system is an abstraction. The concept "social system" has been fallaciously reified.

Because entities are similar in some respects does not mean they are similar in all respects, and it certainly does not mean that they are the *same* thing. Family therapy theorists claim that "isomorphisms" can be identified in all living systems—that is, two or more things possessing the same structure in that their corresponding parts have the same properties and relations. But, as Bullock and Stallybrass point out:

> Whether two things are isomorphic or not depends on how they are described. It is possible to prove that almost any two things are isomorphic, if descriptions at a high enough level of abstraction are used. So talk of isomorphism without a specification of the relevant types of description is liable to be vacuous or at least slipshod and ambiguous. (1977, p. 323)

Many of the concepts of family therapy descriptive theory that include assumptions of isomorphism of the family to other systems lack this kind of needed specification.

Another serious difficulty with general systems theory and cybernetics, and with the family therapy theory that has borrowed so heavily from them, is their highly abstract nature. Some level of abstractness is not only inevitable but desirable in any theory, which attempts to abstract from phenomena perceivable by the senses so as to offer a conceptualized explanation for them. The issue is the optimal level of abstraction for a given theory. For a theory of practice with troubled families, a tremendous amount of work is needed to translate down the abstractions of the above theories to a sufficiently concrete level so as to make them really applicable by practitioners. One unfortunate result of the too high-level nature of the conceptual abstractions in family therapy descriptive theory is that some family therapists appear to become, literally, abstracted by the abstractions of the theory, to the detriment of the real people and the problems they are supposed to help. Family therapy carries the risk of becoming a pseudo-intellectual exercise for the practitioner rather than a helping endeavor with the purpose of concrete benefit to the family.

Bateson called cybernetics "the biggest bite out of the fruit of the Tree of Knowledge that mankind has taken in the last two thousand years" (1972, p. 476). He may—or may not—have been right. It may be time, however, for family therapy to withdraw some of the attention it has devoted to the high-level borrowed abstractions of its parent theories, and for both family social work and family therapy to get on with developing them into what Merton (1957) called "theories of the middle range." These are theories that focus on relatively limited problem areas—most usefully here, different kinds of families and problems—and that avoid the extremes of the too-particularized and concrete *ad hoc* explanations that on the one hand have characterized family social work, and the too abstract and ambitious general conceptualizations on the other hand that describe family therapy. Such middle-range theories will necessarily be multiple rather than one unitary overarching theory to be applied to all families and problems because almost by definition, a theory broad enough in scope to encompass every family case situation will, in its quest for grand generalizability, pay the price of overabstraction and resultant inapplicability to specific case situations. There are similarities (family therapists would insist on saying isomorphisms, which is not the same thing) between affluent, educated, insight-oriented families and impoverished multiproblem families; but the differences between them may be as or more important than their likenesses. Some of the processes hypothesized by family therapy theory may pertain to both (assuming, of course, that such processes actually exist), and it is possible that some of the same interventive techniques will "work" for both. But family therapy theory is presently plagued by its need to search for overarching isomorphisms or generalizations that apply to everything.

The Problem of Validation

The dilemma is that the explanatory power of a theory expands in direct relation to its scope and level of abstraction, but if it waxes too ambitious and attempts to explain too much, it ends up explaining nothing: The explanations become so general and amorphous as to be meaningless. To the extent that the explanations lose their conceptual meaning, they also lose their capacity to be operationalized and empirically tested. Popper (1965) discusses the problem of too-broad claimed explanatory power, as illustrated by the theories of Marx, Freud, and Adler:

> I felt that these...three theories, though posing as sciences, had in fact more in common with primitive myths than with science; that they resembled astrology rather than astronomy.
>
> I found that those of my friends who were admirers of Marx, Freud, and Adler were impressed by a number of points common to these theories, and especially by their apparent *explanatory power*. These theories appeared to be able to explain practically everything that happened within the fields to which they referred. The study of any of them seemed to have the effect of an intellectual conversion or revelation, opening your eyes to a new truth hidden from those not yet initiated. Once your eyes were opened you saw confirming instances everywhere: the world was full of *verifications* of the theory. Whatever happened always confirmed it....
>
> It was precisely this fact—that they always fitted, that they were always confirmed—which in the eyes of their admirers constituted the strongest argument in favor of these theories. It began to dawn on me that this apparent strength was in fact their weakness....
>
> In some of its earlier formulations...the predictions [of the Marxist theory of history] were testable and in fact falsified. Yet instead of accepting the refutations the followers of Marx reinterpreted both the theory and the evidence in order to make them agree. In this way they rescued the theory from refutation; but they did so at the price of adopting a device which made it irrefutable....

> The two psychoanalytic theories were in a different class.
> They were simply non-testable, irrefutable. There was no conceiv-
> able human behavior which could contradict them. (pp. 34–37)

Because of the very abstract nature of the theoretical conceptualizations of family therapy theory, it is impossible to predict how valid and useful they may ultimately prove to be when
and if they can be operationalized. It may be, for example, that
the concept of homeostasis will prove to be extremely useful for
the pragmatic realities of practice. So far, this has not been the
case. Homeostasis, defined as "a range of stability within which
the system moves" (Hartman & Laird, 1983, p. 66) is accepted by
most family therapists as something that "is," that actually exists
as an empirical entity. It may exist as a real process in social
systems, but this has not yet been demonstrated. The concept of
homeostasis is now under attack by family therapy theorists
themselves; Dell, for example, states:

> The concept of homeostasis has served as a major building block,
> if not the cornerstone, of family theory and family therapy. De-
> signed to account for the perceived stability of systems (and symp-
> toms), homeostasis is an epistemologically flawed concept that has
> repetitively been used in the service of dualistic, animistic, and
> vitalistic interpretations of systems. Accordingly, homeostasis has
> led to quirky clinical formulations and a great deal of fuzzy theo-
> rizing. (1982, p. 21)

Fuzzy theorizing it certainly has produced, as well as justifica-
tion for practitioners' failures when they could not get a family
to change (i.e., could not overcome the family's "innate" homeo-
static processes). The present trend to replace homeostasis with
the concepts of *morphostasis* and *morphogenesis* does little to correct the difficulty.

Homeostasis is an *inferred* process of a system, not an empirically observable actuality. Belief in its existence depends on
inductive reasoning. Inductive reasoning, in contrast to deduc-
tive logic, goes *beyond* the information in the data derived from
observation to a more or less speculative conclusion as to what
those data mean. The "problem of induction," recognized by
philosophers of science since Bacon, refers to the fact that many
different conclusions might be inferred from the same data.
Maybe the observed datum that a given family seems to cling
desperately to its problem although complaining loudly about

it, and to resist all interventions designed to relieve the problem, means that a hidden, nonobservable process called homeostasis is at work—but maybe it does not; maybe there is another explanation. The inferring of a covert, unobservable entity or process from observable data is a risky undertaking. It frequently tells more about the belief system of the person doing the inferring than it does about the explanation or meaning of the observed data. Psychoanalytically oriented practitioners, for example, are trained to look beyond the "manifest content" of the patient's verbalizations to their "latent content" or inferred meaning. Because this meaning is being inferred according to the conceptual boxes of the practitioner's theory, it tends to reveal more about the practitioner than the patient—it serves as a Rorschach test of the practitioner.

The existence of phlogiston, a nonexistent substance, was inferred in the Middle Ages from the observation that fire was involved in the process of combustion—a belief that persisted until the discovery of oxygen and the empirical demonstration of its role in the process.

The logical fallacies of reification and tautology are pervasive problems in family therapy descriptive theory. Nugent notes that a theory

> ...is created to represent or "explain" certain observations. Thus, the conceptual scheme of the theory must be used in such a manner that it is kept logically separate from what it represents. If it or concepts from it are equated with the phenomenon they were created to represent, then the theory being used to represent and explain certain observations *becomes* the observation and hence is representing and explaining itself. Not only is this usage paradoxical, it can also be considered a pernicious, subtle way of confirming a theory. (1987, p. 16)

Many writers on the method of science have stressed the importance of remembering that a theory should not be "regarded as a description of real unobserved underlying processes, but rather as but a convenient summarizer and predictor" (Cook & Campbell, 1979, quoted by Nugent, 1987, p. 15). In other words, the abstractions of a theory do not exist except in the minds of human beings; they have no one-to-one relationship with real, that is, concrete phenomena.

Theory is taken too seriously and too credulously by many in the family therapy field (and by many social workers, who are as much in awe of it as they were of the earlier Freudian formulations), to the point where the practitioner uses it, not as theory, but as a quasi-religious dogma. There is a tendency to forget that any theory in its formative pretesting stages is no more than a purported, and usually highly speculative, explanation for why some things are observed to occur in reality as they do. The propositions, and certainly not the mere concepts, of a theory are not knowledge; they are speculative, "suppose that," explanations. The propositions become factual knowledge only when they are tested against the empirical world of reality and are found to occur as hypothesized. A theory is not a fact, not a reality, not even a discovery. It is the invention of a human mind. Copernicus did not "discover" his heliocentric theory because there was no Copernican theory until he invented it. A theory usually, but not always, begins inductively: Someone wonders about why phenomena occur as they are observed to do, and then invents a theory to explain and organize these observations. But the theory must also be tested deductively: If its propositions and hypotheses are valid, they will occur as predicted under conditions of observation that control for bias as much as is humanly possible, and that permit replication by others. The weight of such evidence—unless and until it becomes so overwhelming that the theory can be considered as law (and laws do not exist in the social and behavioral sciences)—does no more, however, than add credibility to the theory's explanation. Another, rival, explanation might well exist for the observed phenomena. The need for caution about a too-ready acceptance of unvalidated theory is underscored by Popper's insistence that scientific knowledge grows, not by attempts to validate theories, but by efforts to refute them (1965). This is admittedly an extreme position, one that is not accepted by all philosophers of science, but it speaks to the dangers of accepting unvalidated theory as holy writ. A large number of family therapists have difficulty distinguishing between knowledge and belief.

The naive family therapist who believes that abstractions such as homeostasis exist in other than a conceptual sense will have no trouble at all in finding "evidence" of homeostasis in her observations of a particular family. But the occurrence of fire was once believed to be evidence of the existence of phlogiston.

If conceptualizations may not be treated as real in their own right, then how can we use theory that is, after all, composed of concepts and constructs of greater or lesser degrees of abstraction? At the level of *propositions*, which is where the wheat of theories is separated from the chaff. "Explanation, the *raison d'etre* for all theories, is conveyed through a series of statements called propositions. Propositions constitute the heart and substance of theories. A proposition is a statement which asserts something about reality by stating relationships between (linking) two or more concepts" (Chafetz, 1978, p. 75). Philosophical and epistemological assumptions, definitions, concepts, do not assert anything about reality (although they may assert what the theorizer *wishes* was the reality). But propositions do talk about reality: They assert that a tangible, observable link is to be found there between concept A and concept B (and possibly also C, D, and so on). Now at last we are dealing with something that goes beyond the formulation in the theorizer's head. Whether the linkages posited by the propositions of the theory will be found to exist in reality by a variety of observers is the essential test of the worth-whileness of the theory. No matter how elegant and apparently brilliant the theory's concepts and insights, if its propositions do not hold up to testing, the theory falls of its own weight.

To some, astrology seems elegant and brilliant. But the predictions of astrologers as to what will happen to public figures in the coming year are rarely verified in reality. (Of course, as Popper pointed out, there are always "explanations" offered by the astrologers as to the apparent failure of their "science," such as that the person involved did not truly follow the directives of his or her star signs; or, even better, if the astrological predictions are made vague and abstract enough, they can be made to apply to anything that happened.)

The terms *proposition* and *hypothesis* are sometimes used synonymously in the literature, although hypothesis is usually used to mean a proposition phrased in precise form for research testing. For either, however, the concepts involved must be *operationalized*, and this is a fundamental problem being faced by family therapy descriptive theory. Because of the too-abstract nature of the concepts used, and also because of what seems to be a lack of interest in empirical validation, not much effort has been put forth toward defining how the concepts are expected to operate in observable reality. What are the observable indicators of, for example, morphogenesis as a process in family systems—what can the observer expect to see when he encounters it, what is the reality "shape" of morphogenesis in operation, and why are these indicators evidence of something called morphogenesis and not of some other phenomenon?

An example of a clinical descriptive observation that might possibly be operationalized sufficiently so as to test whether it actually does describe multiproblem families is Aponte's (1976) assertion that poor families tend to be underorganized rather than disorganized. He describes underorganization as inadequacies in the "structural underpinnings" of the family's operational organization, namely, the alignments (joinings or opposition) of members in carrying out an operation; the force or "relative influence of each member on the outcome of an activity"; and the boundary, or inclusion or exclusion of certain members from the activity (p. 434). If operational indicators of the concepts alignments, force, and boundary can be developed that are both valid and reliable, it may be possible to determine empirically whether lack of a coherent and consistent organizational structure is characteristic of no impoverished multiproblem families, or a small proportion of them, or a large proportion, or all of such families. Weltner (1985) makes much the same clinical observation concerning the impoverished family with multiple problems, and attempts to match diagnostic assessment of where the family "is" to differential choice of interventive strategy. The clinical observations of family therapists such as these are interesting and provocative, and may turn out to be extremely important and valid pieces of descriptive theory for understanding the multiproblem family. But at present these observations are only practice wisdom, which is not the same thing as theory. Many practitioners confuse the practice wisdom of well-known leaders with theory, or even with validated knowledge. Practice wisdom is a tremendously valuable resource in any practice profession, because it serves as a breeding ground for the inductive generation of theoretical propositions which then need to be tested. But practice wisdom must undergo quite a few more steps before it can become theory, let alone validated knowledge.

Translation of Concepts into Propositions

The descriptive theory of family therapy contains an embarrassment of riches of conceptualization and clinical observation, and a poverty of propositions. The conceptualizations and clinical observations may be interesting, thought provoking, of heuristic value possibly—but their validity remains an unknown until they can first be translated into operational terms, and then further translated into propositions to be tested empirically.

Many of the same conceptualizations of the descriptive theory of family therapy are expressed in different language by different writers. It is therefore difficult to assess whether the explanation for family problems offered by the theory is sufficiently parsimonious. Parsimony of a theory is defined by Chafetz (1978, p. 81) as "the smallest number of variables and propositions necessary to explain the dependent variable" (of family functioning and dysfunction). Further work on conceptual clarity and operationalization of concepts is necessary before a judgment about the parsimony of the theory can be made. Only attempts at empirical validation will reveal whether the propositions are insufficient in quantity to actually explain family phenomena or, conversely, whether some are overlapping or superfluous.

The prescriptive theory of family therapy—how the practitioner ought to intervene in particular practice situations—by its nature lends itself more easily to operationalization, because the prescriptions involved are usually rather concrete and are variations of the propositional "if...then" format ("if the practitioner does X, such-and-such will ensue"). The quality of the prescriptive theory of family therapy is addressed in more detail in Chapter 6. It can here be suggested, however, that translation of the abstractions of the descriptive theory into propositions and hypotheses needs to be a high-priority issue for the field.

As long as the vague abstractions of descriptive family therapy theory remain unoperationalized and therefore untested, even with further research on the prescriptive aspects of the theory the gap between descriptive and prescriptive theory will continue to grow. Descriptive theory is the basis for diagnostic assessment: It tells the practitioner what to look for and what sense to make of what he observes. Descriptive theory also serves as the basis, the "why," of the interventions recommended by prescriptive theory. If the prescriptive interventions of family therapy cannot be solidly grounded in its own descriptive theory, then family therapy will indeed be "a set of techniques in search of a theory" and inadmissible as a scientifically based professional endeavor.

Problems with Family System Approach

The interest of family therapy in systems and interaction rather than with the individual components of the system has resulted in a heuristically novel and valuable way of looking at problems of people-in-interaction. The systems focus, however, has had some problematic side effects. The family system itself can easily be anthropomorphized—reification again. To assume that a nonhuman entity can think, or be goal-directed, or take action to equilibrate itself is the additional logical fallacy of teleology. The *people* who constitute the system are the only ones who can perform these actions.

Reification of the family system has led, ironically, to the same kind of anthropomorphism represented by earlier attempts to apply psychoanalytic formulations about individuals to the family group (Josselyn, 1953). It reflects an implicit fallacious animism and vitalism. Such anthropomorphization distorts the way the practitioner relates to the family's human actors; their tangible reality and humanness can be lost in the preoccupation with an abstraction.

The assumptions of family therapy theory concerning causality represent one of the most serious practice and ethical problems the theory has engendered. Family therapists tend to eschew words like *causation* or *etiology*, maintaining that causation is *always* reciprocal rather than linear and that these terms are therefore meaningless. Dell goes so far as to assert that "the concept of causation is an epistemological error. All causal accounts of phenomena are fundamentally flawed and erroneous" (1982, footnote, p. 21).

But the notion of causation has not been dispensed with in family therapy. It has been shifted from a linear understanding to a circular, reciprocal one—but the idea of causation is still here. The a priori diagnostic assumption of many family therapists has been that, whatever the problem, something in family interaction is responsible and needs to be changed. The symptom of an individual member is necessarily the function or product (the result) of dysfunctional family processes (the cause). According to family therapy theory, if one billiard ball displays "symptomatic" behavior—wobbling rather than rolling true—this is due to the interaction of all the components of the billiard game "system." To diagnose the problem, one would examine that interaction rather than looking to see if the individual ball might be defective in some fashion.

This unexamined and empirically untested dictum of family therapy descriptive theory has led too often to misdiagnosis and severe iatrogenic damage to already-hurting people. The attempt to treat schizophrenia by family therapy is the most dramatic example. The earlier ideas of pre-family-therapy psychiatrists such as Fromm-Reichmann (1948) and Sullivan (1962) identified the "schizophrenogenic mother" as the noxious etiologic influence. Lidz, Parker, and Cornelison (1956) included an equally pathogenic father in their theory of the etiology of schizophrenia. The family therapy movement expanded these ideas of causation further to include pathological patterns of communication and interaction within the total family (Bateson, Jackson, Haley, & Weakland, 1956; Lidz, Cornelison, Terry, & Fleck, 1958; Lidz, Fleck, & Cornelison, 1965; Bowen, 1960; Jackson, 1960; Wynne, Ryckoff, Day, & Hirsch, 1958; and Singer & Wynne, 1965).

The onset of schizophrenia in a family member has been treated by attempts to correct assumed etiological pathogens in family interaction. Despite the assurances of the therapist that the intent was to help rather than to blame, the family still heard the clear message that in some mysterious way they were responsible for the terrible disorder that had struck their loved family member. Torrey observes that "the magnitude of this guilt and blame is enormous and has led to depression, divorce, and even suicide" (1983, p. 94). Terkelson (1983) in retrospect criticized his own attempts over 10 years of experience to do family therapy with families of schizophrenics, the therapeutic belief system he had been taught:

> I was trained in a tradition that assumed madness to be an inter-personal affair, and so in family meetings I listened to the parents talk about life with the ill person, abstracting from their reports those interactional phenomena that I thought suggestive of parental pathogenicity. I then set out to alter that pathology. Typically I would fail in that endeavor, only to explain the failure as a manifestation of tenacious, pathological resistance to self-disclosure....
>
> Inherently appropriate questions regarding the nature of psychosis and important practical management issues would go unaddressed or addressed apathetically. (p. 192, quoted by Johnson, 1986, p. 302)

The evocation of intense emotions by the family therapy approach was frequently additionally iatrogenically damaging to the schizophrenic member, not to mention the authoritative advice of some therapists that the schizophrenic person should not take his psychotropic medication because he was not, after all, "sick."

A theory of family-interaction etiology of schizophrenia ignores the growing and persuasive evidence that this disorder is basically organic (Torrey, 1983; Howells & Guirguis, 1985). Johnson takes to task family therapists who express "contempt for well-validated and replicated research that contradicts cherished beliefs" (1986, p. 302) by such proclamations as that of Haley:

> The trouble with the biological or genetic theory of schizophrenia is not only that *there is no evidence to support it* [italics added by Johnson, 1986] but that the mad young person's problem is defined as being in the medical rather than the parental domain, and so the therapist has no leverage to restructure the family hierarchy. (Haley, 1980, p. 21)

Any family with a member exhibiting troublesome behavior will become "disturbed" to greater or lesser degree. The family may or may not have been disturbed before. Its group dynamics may or may not have been involved in the creation of the individual's problem. Although one of the functions of a family may be seen to be to tolerate and provide means for expression of some degree of "craziness" of its members (where else can we afford to be a little crazy?), extremely disturbed behavior of the symptomatic member obviously will have a negative impact on other family members, with quite possibly widening ripples to many aspects of family interaction and functioning. Family therapy has tended to confuse an effect with its cause—another example of the risk of the fallacy of teleology implicit in a monocular insistence that causation is always circular and interactive.

INDIVIDUALIZED AND DIFFERENTIAL ASSESSMENT

In some cases, careful diagnostic assessment may reveal that the original cause of the problem is something awry in family systemic processes. The usual example of this is the child who acts out whenever the parents' submerged marital conflict appears on the verge of erupting. In other cases, the family was not the original cause of the problem, but has become caught up inadvertently in exacerbating it. Here the example might well be the relatives of a schizophrenic who because of their lack of information about the nature of the disease are unwittingly behaving in ways that exacerbate rather than ease the problem. In additional other cases, the family has played neither of the foregoing roles but might well, with professional support and guidance, be a major resource for the troubled member. This applies to many, although not all, families of delinquent youngsters (Geismar & Wood, 1986). In still other cases, what originated as the troubles of a family member may have a severe impact on functioning of other members and of the total family group, especially if the index member plays an important key role in the family system—an obvious example would be the impact of the breadwinner's unemployment. And in yet other cases, the problems of an individual are highly personal, related to his or her internal or extrafamily experiences rather than to anything that has happened or is happening within the family, and the family has no role to play in their resolution other than support and empathy (assuming it is even appropriate for the family always to know about intensely private concerns of its members).

Although there undoubtedly still are family therapists who attempt to treat organically based problems of individuals by "therapizing" the family, the field as a whole—faced by overwhelming evidence of the ineffectiveness and iatrogenic damage of such an approach—has stepped back from some of the wilder claims of what family therapy can do. It is now felt by many responsible family therapists that a more useful approach is the less "sophisticated" one of education and support of the family, especially if it is the family rather than the professional delivery system that must play the role of ongoing health care provider. This now goes under the rubric of the *psychoeducational* approach. It used to be called ordinary casework, as practiced for example by social workers in health care settings who for many years have helped patients and families to understand and deal with the concomitants of illness.

Assumptions of Causation and the Ethical Dimension of Family Therapy

The less than admirable record of family therapy in its attempts to "treat" schizophrenia and other organic disorders by treating presumed intrafamilial causative pathology is disturbing in its ethical dimensions, for two reasons. It points to an antiempirical stance on the part of many in the field, a preference for abstract—sometimes almost mystical—theorizing to the detriment of careful attention to the data of the case. It is an antiintellectual stance as well, a substitution of the packaged thinking of the theory for one's own analytic processes and good sense (linear logical reasoning?).

It would undoubtedly be manifestly unfair to conclude that the therapists who engaged in these abortive and damaging attempts did not care about the clients who were involved; the therapists, it must be believed, were possessed of ordinary amounts of compassion and were truly trying to help. From this perspective, they were no more ethically at fault than were the physicians of past centuries who tried to treat anemia by bleeding the patient. Honest mistakes, based on the incomplete information available at a given time in any profession, are not unethical.

But from another perspective, there was a serious ethical dereliction of professional responsibility. That has to do with the therapists' preference for the generalizations of their theory over the more accurate information about the nature of the problem that *the clients* themselves were trying desperately to communicate to the therapists. To repeat Terkelson (1983): "Inherently appropriate questions regarding the *nature of psychosis* and *important practical management issues* [italics added] would go unaddressed or addressed apathetically" (p. 192). These were important issues recognized and raised by the client families, but their perceptions and concerns were ignored. Sometimes clients know more than their professional helpers.

The intellectual problem of family therapy theory referred to earlier—its predilection for vague and unvalidated generalizations—becomes therefore not merely an intellectual (or epistemological) concern, but a tangible, real-life ethical problem that has negatively affected real people. Although an increasing number of family therapists are tiptoeing away from their earlier claim that they could cure organic disorders, the continued naive credulity of the field concerning its theory remains a major problem that has ethical as well as intellectual aspects.

The still-continuing "movement" aspects of family therapy are apparent to those who teach or supervise beginners, whose obsession to be admitted to the hallowed company of family therapists appears almost like a religious-conversion experience. It also has intimations of personal-status needs rather than an altruistic motivation to help fellow humans in trouble. A movement is swept along by the ideological fervor of its members. Perhaps family therapy's continuing to be more a movement than a solidly based therapeutic approach to families in trouble should not be so surprising. Other historical movements in the helping professions have demonstrated the same characteristic in their early development, from the movement for "moral uplift" of the poor in the 1800s and early 1900s, to psychoanalysis as the new religion of the 1920s and 1930s. But a major reason for the diminution of psychoanalytic thought in more recent times has been that it could not operationalize its concepts so that they could be tested. Lack of validation has never, of course, deterred true believers. But the clients of family therapists have been socialized to expect competent professionals, not true believers.

Family Interaction with Environmental Context

A final difficulty with the descriptive theory of family therapy will be addressed only briefly here, and examined more fully in subsequent chapters (Chapters 6 and 7) concerning prescriptive interventions. Although family therapy theory, in its borrowings from General Systems Theory, cybernetics, and ecology, addresses the *total* system of individual-in-family-in-environmental-context, in actuality the theory highlights the internal dynamics of the family system with incomplete or totally absent attention to the family's environmental context and its interaction with relevant external systems. Earlier we quoted Johnson (1986) concerning the destructive impact of "therapizing" a family for its presumed internal pathology, when the pathology is actually located in environing systems.

The most important contribution of family therapy—and it is an outstanding and very important one—has been to direct the attention of mental health professionals to the previously relatively ignored crucial element of *interaction*. The descriptive theory of the field has made progress in partializing so as better to develop conceptually what is meant by this extremely complex idea. It may be time for family therapy to move beyond the quantity of the provocative ideas it offers to the quality of these conceptualizations, and to the issue of validation on which the theory will stand or fall. Olson's observation of 1970 still obtains that the field has not developed a solid theoretical base and that its practice principles remain untested.

CHOICES FOR THE FUTURE DEVELOPMENT
OF DESCRIPTIVE THEORY

Our call for work on developing the descriptive theory of troubled families so that the propositions of that theory can be empirically tested is, we recognize, characteristic of those who still adhere to a linear, Aristotelian epistemology. There are many kinds of research, and approaches such as ethnomethodology may prove useful in studying and attempting to validate both the descriptive and prescriptive dimensions of family practice theory. But whatever the research methodology, a linear epistemological stance is evident in any question about the validity of theory.

Social work practice research has been criticized by some (Heineman, 1981) for clinging to an "obsolete scientific imperative" as its underlying paradigm. But no law has ever been passed that only one paradigm can hold sway at a given time; it is entirely possible to have coexistent multiple paradigms, and such do indeed exist in several disciplines.

In the best of all possible worlds, their multiplicity would be enriching; in the world of reality and the way that we humans tend to react when the cherished beliefs of our underlying paradigms are challenged, that multiplicity is seen as only confusing and as provocation for scholarly squabbles as to who owns the one and only truth. But whereas the new paradigm of modern physics has partially replaced that of Newtonian mechanics *for areas in which the new paradigm serves better*, the Newtonian paradigm has by no means been dispensed with. There are still many phenomena in our physical world that are better understood and explained by Newtonian than quantum physics. The issues are the knowledge-building capacity and what Kuhn (1957, 1970) called the "puzzle-solving" capacity of a given paradigm, at a given time *and for particular issues*. For the issue of the validation of theoretical propositions, no one has yet come up with a better way of going about it than the procedures of scientific research.

The critics of the paradigm of traditional research and knowledge building do no more than criticize; they do not present any alternative strategy by which we can differentiate between validated knowledge and mere opinion, speculation, philosophy, or practice wisdom. Those who object to the scientific paradigm must carry the burden of fashioning a better alternative. Until they do so, the research process identified in this chapter is the only way we have yet developed to validate our practice knowledge.

For family therapy, the issue of validation of practice knowledge would seem to be a choice between whether it will become an astrology or an astronomy.

Chapter 6

Prescriptive Theory
Family Social Work
and Family Therapy

Although a logically linear progress of theory-building in practice professions would entail the development of descriptive theory first, leading in turn to prescriptive propositions for practice that are based on that descriptive theory, in the field of family problems the reverse pattern has obtained. Like the family itself, the interaction between descriptive understanding and practice prescriptions has been, not circular, but rather spiral in nature. Prescriptions for practice predated a descriptive theory of the family, in both the family social work of decades ago and in the family therapy movement. A few people tried heretically innovative ways of intervening, and sometimes found that these seemed to "work." Descriptive theory was only later developed in an attempt to explain why.

PRACTICE PRINCIPLES, THEORY, AND VALIDATION

Prescriptive theory also arises out of the coalescing of the practice experience of many professionals into principles of practice. In Chapter 5 it is observed that the practice principles distilled by the aggregate practice wisdom of many practitioners are not the same as tested knowledge, and are not even yet a

105

theory. Theory requires that practice principles and other concepts be tied together within a conceptual framework. We also noted that in practice professions, knowledge building often takes place from the ground up, that is, from the discoveries and innovations of practitioners in their workplaces, rather than from an elite group who begin with abstract generalizations. This is probably the most useful start for the theory of a practice profession, because it is better able to produce what Glaser and Strauss (1967) call "grounded theory." It is the way family social work started, with Mary Richmond analyzing the practice experiences of her workers (although it could be argued that social work did not move quickly enough to construct an adequate conceptual framework for those practice principles). It is the way family therapy started, with the risk-taking practice innovations of pioneers (although it could be argued that family therapy then moved perhaps too precipitously and prematurely to attempts at constructing a "grand" theory to explain why these innovative interventions seemed to work, and that the field of family therapy might have been better off if it had continued to collect and analyze data before moving to abstract generalizations that were not grounded in sufficient data).

Practice principles are hypotheses. The practitioner applies them in a case in a kind of "quick and dirty" research—research at a more primitive level than the elegant designs and elaborate controls against bias that are usually considered requirements for research. But if the practitioner is aware that her practice principles are no more than hypotheses, what she is doing is experimenting with them in the case to see if they "work" as predicted (Wood, 1978, 1980). The evidence as to their efficacy would of course be even more solid the more the practitioner attempts to apply research canons designed to improve objectivity and accuracy, for example by use of $N=1$ methodology (Hersen & Barlow, 1976). But even if the practitioner has never heard of $N=1$ research, and would perhaps be surprised to hear that she is engaged in hypothesis testing, in effect this is what she is doing. If, however, she views the practice principle as a certainty, then she will not be looking for data in the case that either support or disconfirm the principle, and will continue to forge ahead despite evidence that she is not being helpful. Absence of a need for certainty and for intellectual closure seems to be a requirement for responsible practice.

The history of human affairs is littered with now-discredited hypotheses that remained alive too long because their hypothetical nature was not clearly acknowledged and they were considered to be self-evident.

Sometimes there will be a good deal of rough evidence from the accumulated experience of many practitioners as to the validity of a particular practice principle. For example, the correlation with effective helping of the helper's qualities of warmth, empathy, and genuineness had received much corroboration from the experience of practitioners before they were finally operationalized sufficiently enough so that harder research evidence could be accumulated. Sometimes practitioners know from their empirical practice experience that something works, but it is impossible for them yet to know why. An example here is the experience of the 19th-century physician Ignaz Semmelweiss, who observed that requiring doctors to wash their hands in an antiseptic solution before attending an obstetrical patient reduced the incidence of the deadly puerperal fever in his hospital. Pasteur had not yet developed the evidence for his germ theory of certain diseases, and Semmelweiss therefore could not know that invisibly small organisms were being transmitted by physicians from sick women to those still healthy. But his practice principle of medical cleanliness worked.

Sometimes practice principles become part of an uncritical group-think phenomenon: Everyone assumes they are true because everyone else thinks so. But, despite the enthusiastic faith placed in them by practitioners, they turn out to be dead wrong. Examples here would be the practice principle at the turn of the century that what the poor needed was moral lectures by the practitioner; or the practice principle of family therapy that what the schizophrenic and his family needed was family therapy aimed at exorcising the family-process demons that had caused his illness.

Reid (1985) is one of the few writing on the use of family therapy ideas and techniques in social work who has addressed the issue of whether the practice principles and treatment techniques from family therapy that he details have any empirical evidence as to their validity or efficacy. Because little such evidence exists, he presents his readers with this caveat. Reid stands out because few other writers, in family social work or in family therapy, view practice principles as hypotheses or seem aware of the unvalidated efficacy of the interventions.

Cognitive-behavioral therapy is an exception to the many other treatment approaches in the mental health field, including both family social work and family therapy, in that its developers have paid close attention to empirical validation of their propositions (see such writers on the use of behavioral principles with families as Gambrill, 1981; Patterson, Reid, Jones, & Conger, 1975; Mash, Hamerlynck, & Handy, 1976; Hersen, Eisler, & Miller, 1978). This does not mean that cognitive-behavioral approaches are necessarily the best for all problems of all families; our only point here is that, in contrast to family social work and family therapy, more effort has been expended by the behavioral school on empirical validation.

More often than not, however, in the development of practice professions, the level of as-yet-unresearched practice principles is where a profession "is" at the moment, and this seems to apply to both family social work and family therapy. As with a client, one has no alternative but to begin with where the client—or the profession—"is."

Family social work before the family therapy movement was not able to move much beyond unorganized collections of principles for work with families; a conceptual framework into which to place these principles was not well formulated because the frameworks that existed had to do with individuals. The same can be said for the development of prescriptive theory in family therapy. In family therapy there is a proliferation of intervention techniques (many more than were available to early family social workers); and an equal proliferation of different schools of family therapy, each with its own perspective and preferred interventions. This is quite different, it should be noted, from the middle-range theories advocated in the preceding chapter. There we recommended development of multiple minitheories, each focused on specific different kinds of families and problems. The multiple schools of family therapy do not at present, however, represent these kinds of middle-range theories focused on specific client populations. Rather, each lays claim to being a grand theory applicable to all families and problems.

Some students of the family therapy field feel the confusion of this rich diversity is more an advantage than a disadvantage at the present time, heuristically leading as much to creativity as it does to artificial demarcations and partisanship. Some work has been done in attempting to synthesize the contributions of various schools toward development of an integrated model (Birchler & Spinks, 1981; Feldman & Pinsof, 1982; Pinsof, 1983; Nelsen, 1983), but emergence of a comprehensive and truly integrated formulation of family therapy prescriptive theory may not be expectable for some time to come.

PRACTICE PRESCRIPTIONS OF FAMILY SOCIAL WORK AND FAMILY THERAPY

Chapter 5 did not address a detailed comparison between the descriptive family theory of family social work and that of family therapy, because such a theory does not actually exist in any formulated fashion. It is a different story, however, with prescriptions for practice: Both family social work and family therapy have at least articulated some of their assumptions about practice with families and principles for that practice.

This chapter therefore attempts a comparison of the prescriptions of family social work and family therapy, as these specifically pertain to the multiproblem family.

The work of Overton, Tinker, and associates (1957) at the St. Paul Project will be used as an exemplar of pre-family-therapy family social work with multiproblem families. This is meant not to slight other early social workers who also developed practice principles for work with such families—indeed, Overton and Tinker drew heavily from them. Their almost-book-length *Casework Notebook* (Overton et al., 1957) serves not only as an account of their practice experiences with multiproblem families, but also as something of a distillation of the insights and prescriptive recommendations of practitioner-writers before them. A fairly complete but necessarily selective list of practitioners who published on the multiproblem, or at least the impoverished, family would include of course Richmond (1899, 1907, 1917, 1922, 1930), as well as Sheffield (1922, 1923, 1924, 1931, 1937), Breckenridge (1934), Lowry (1936, 1948, 1957), Taft (1944), Younker (1948), Wiltse (1954, 1958), Regensburg (1954), Hallowitz, Clement, and Cutter (1957), Henry (1958), and Hill (1958). Helen Harris Perlman (1957) was a consultant to the St. Paul Project.

Overton and Tinker were familiar with the very early work concerning families done by Ackerman, Gomberg, and staff members of the New York Jewish Family Service, because their bibliography lists citations to Ackerman (1954), Behrens and Ackerman (1956), Gomberg (1958), and Scherz (1953). Ackerman and his colleagues were major figures in the early development of family therapy, but it was at that time not yet really family therapy as we know it today. Coyle, a leading social group worker of the era, observed that although the Jewish Family Service team alluded to the whole family as a group, actually they were referring only to relationships within subsystems smaller than the total family (marital, parent-child, etc.). "The theory used to underpin this development is largely psychiatric and is concerned in large part with the intrapsychic elements in family relationships.... No additional concepts about the family as a group are used in this type of practice except as the significance of these intimate family relationships for each individual family member is given greater importance" (1962, p. 348). This intrapsychically infused model of early family therapy was *not*, however, the one used in the St. Paul Project; Overton and Tinker were quite unpsychiatric in their approach. The work of Overton and Tinker therefore seems to represent a relatively pure exemplar of family social work, not yet adulterated by the later developments of family therapy.

Assumptions and Approach to Practice

Certain assumptions underlie and direct prescriptions or principles of practice and represent their rationale. These are usually value positions that—in contrast to the propositions of a theory—by definition are untestable as to validity. They can only be accepted or not accepted. Their only test is how useful they prove to be in directing effective practice.

A basic assumption of family social work was that the multi-problem family wants to function better and is capable of functioning better. Family social workers were of course aware that something was very much awry with the multiproblem family, but they did not start with a perspective on pathology. They assumed that there were good reality reasons why the family was not functioning better. Their approach was therefore an optimistic one oriented not to the treatment of pathology but to health, learning, coping, and successful functioning.

Psychotherapy research has indicated that such "non-specific" factors as personal characteristics of the practitioner play a very large role in the effectiveness of treatment—quite possibly as important as, or in some cases more important, than the specific interventive techniques employed (Truax & Mitchell, 1971; Bordin, 1974; Gurman & Razin, 1977; Parloff, Waskow, & Wolfe, 1978). Double-blind studies are used in medical research to test the efficacy of new therapeutic drugs because of the recognition that, if the dispensing physician knew to whom he was giving the experimental substance, his hope for its effectiveness might subtly be communicated to the patient and bring about a false placebo effect. A salubrious placebo effect of sorts may well have been partially responsible for the high degree of effectiveness empirically demonstrated by such family social work as that in the St. Paul Project (Geismar & Ayres, 1959).

Overton and Tinker in fact went so far as to say they had "a *bias in favor* of socially inadequate families" (p. 65). In contrast to the frustration evoked in many practitioners who attempt to work with these hardest-to-reach families, the family social workers experienced work with their families as challenging, surely, but also more exciting and satisfying than practice with more stable middle-class clients. They preferred working with this client population whom they found deserving of admiration and respect. The practitioner was prepared for early hostility, defensiveness and resistance, but she was gambling on her assumption that if she could patiently insinuate her way past these self-protective behaviors she would find ordinary people struggling the best they could in a bad situation. The assumption that individual and family strengths were hidden under the initial hostility of the families and the multiplicity and severity of the problems, was a necessary precondition for the worker's even looking for such strengths, let alone finding them. We conjecture that the caseworker's real liking and respect for her clients, rather than her specific techniques of joining, were what convinced the families that although she had come to their homes uninvited she was there "to stand *with* people against their problems" (Overton et al., 1957, p. 13).

Part of what happened between the social worker and the family was that this assumption of the worker enabled her to objectify the family's problems, and in turn helped the family to do so as well. This applied even when part of the problem was the attitudes or behavior of family members. Objectification meant that dysfunctional behaviors and relationships were not seen as inherently and therefore unchangeably lodged within personality traits. The objectification of problems was in itself a forceful beginning intervention, counteracting the internalized messages the family had long received from other social authorities as to their inherent inadequacy and impotence. When this was accompanied, as it was, by the worker's honestly addressing the problems that the community was requiring that the family work on, and a supportive but persistent demand that the family begin work, the demoralized family began to believe that perhaps they were the kind of competent people that the worker insisted they were.

Not every modern-day family therapist starts from a presumption of pathology, and there are undoubtedly many who would subscribe to the earlier generation family practitioner's hopeful assumption that the multiproblem family wants to and can function better. But it is not inaccurate to characterize the family therapy field as a whole as preoccupied with pathology of internal family dynamics. The presumption of pathological processes in the family is often made by a family therapist before the first contact; to call on a medical analogy, the diagnosis is made before the patient is even examined.

The assumption of family social work was on the side of morphogenesis rather than morphostasis (although of course the older practitioners had not even heard of those terms). They assumed, simply, that dysfunctional behavior was the family's

attempt at solution of their problems, and they began by convey-
ing respect for the struggle to cope that such an attempt represented despite its ineffectual outcome. Seen as an attempt to
cope with external or internal problems, the corollary assumption was that the motivation and energy to cope better was there,
available for direction by the worker into more successful efforts. It was years later that Watzlawick, Weakland, and Fisch
(1974) wrote of the common human tendency to get stuck in our
attempted solutions, which then become more problematic than
the original problem they were designed to solve. In some cases,
what appear to be the dysfunctional attempts at solution by an
impoverished multiproblem family may indeed not be dysfunctional at all, but rather the only response possible for the family
in the face of massive social and environmental pathogens. To
the middle-class practitioner who is naively ignorant of the
jungle-like communities in which such families live, it is easy to
judge the family's response to its noxious environment according to middle-class standards that assume the ego psychologists'
"average expectable environment," but that are simply inappli-
cable to the situation of the family.

Another assumption was that partnerships between practitioner and client family was not only possible, but was a better
model for practice than one of "therapy." The practitioner and
the family had different responsibilities in their joint work on
the family's problems, but the relationship was a collaborative
one. The first professional task of the practitioner was to relate
to the family in the first encounters in such a way that their
initial distrust and sense of threat began to give way to a perception that the worker would work with them on the goals that *they*
wanted to achieve. Family therapists call this process *joining*,
and it is a good term. Joining is defined in family therapy as "the
act of entering a client's system in order to fully understand all
the nuances of the client's world so that the therapist can influence the client to change," but at the same time "keep(ing) sufficient distance to maintain...maneuverability" (Braverman,
1986, p. 238). Braverman traces this concept to a social worker of
the 1920s who wrote about the necessity for the practitioner to
identify with the client but also to be able to engage in the
mental sleight-of-hand required to simultaneously "withdraw to

a vantage point" (Dexter, 1926, p. 180, quoted in Braverman, 1986, pp. 238–239). Note that the family therapy definition of joining assumes that changing the family is necessarily the goal of treatment. As used in family therapy, joining refers usually to "getting a foot in the door" with the family so that the practitioner can get down to the real work of changing the family's pathological internal processes. In contrast, family social work saw joining as a process that characterized the entire time span of the case. The worker "stood with people against their problems" by forming a team relationship with the family. The family's contributions to the assessment and resolution of the problem were treated as respectfully as would be contributions from the members of a team made up of professionals. The experience of multiproblem families at the hands of paternalistic, intrusive professionals has rarely been that of being treated with this kind of respect and confidence; just the assumption of the worker that family members were the kind of people who could engage in collaborative problem solving was another powerful intervention in itself.

The family social worker also assumed that even the most limited of family members in the most disorganized family could engage in straightforward, rational (linear?) problem solving. Ego psychologists would say that she reached for the healthy aspects of the personalities of individual family members, and for the need and ability of the family to plan and work together, based on their group bond and mutual commitment. She helped them to cognitively understand their problem situation and what could be done about it. Some of the same assumptions and cognitive techniques were later to be used in such therapeutic developments as crisis intervention, rational-emotive therapy, and cognitive-behavioral therapy. Family therapy has used change of cognitive perception of the problem in its techniques of reframing and positive connotation but, as these are described in the literature at least, they sometimes have about them an air of a not-for-real ploy like the opening gambits of a door-to-door salesman. The family social worker really believed that changed cognitive perception by the family of their problems, in the direction of making the problems seem more workable, was the first step in a problem-solving process of linear rationality that was not only appropriate and useful in attacking the problems but also a process in which the family, with help, was competent to engage. Family therapy's dislike of linear rational and logical processes has led to a relative disregard of when and how these can be effectively utilized.

In the majority of the cases studied in the St. Paul Family Centered Project, the families were able to use the worker's help in rational understanding and planning toward problem solving. Sometimes the worker's faith was naive—or, rather, her naivete consisted of her not recognizing in time a particular family's investment in an irrational, that is, emotional but pathological, process of their own. In an analysis of the failure cases of the St. Paul Family Centered Project (and it is rare in the mental health literature to find failures reported on, let alone analyzed for the purpose of learning from them), Tinker (1957) concluded that a major factor in ineffectual outcome of some of the minority of cases with which they failed was that the parents could not engage in problem solving because it would threaten the dynamics of the marital relationship. One of two kinds of marital system pathology was identified in these cases: either a dysfunctional distribution of power in which one partner was dominant and controlling and the other subservient and helpless, or one where the partners took gratification from their pervasive and persistent marital conflict. The St. Paul workers did not have available techniques later developed by family therapy for intervention with "stuck," rigid system dynamics like these (although changing such relationships today is still extremely difficult and no known family therapy techniques have guaranteed efficacy). The point here, however, is that according to the research evidence of the St. Paul Project, many more of the families were able to utilize a rational problem-solving approach than were not (Geismar & Ayres, 1959).

That professional helping services should be "family-focused" was an important assumption of early social workers going back to Mary Richmond. They meant something different by this, however, than the way the term is used today by family therapists who assume that change of family systemic dynamics should necessarily be the focus of treatment. Family social workers included in their definition change of dysfunctional family processes to the extent that the limited descriptive theory available to them at the time enabled them to identify such processes clearly, and to the extent that their prescriptive theory provided them with interventions so oriented. But they used the term in a much broader sense. Family social work was for the benefit of the whole family (in contrast, for example, to the model of child welfare at the time which focused primarily on the child's needs). Family-focused also meant engaging the family as a group in collaborative teamwork with the caseworker on the problems that were affecting the whole family, in contrast to the pattern current at that period of working with only one member or separately with several members. Overton, Tinker, and associates (1957) recommended that "in work with a family the choice of the person or persons to be worked with should be based on group need rather than individual need. If we really believe that our social purpose is to strengthen the family, this is the prior consideration" (p. 158).

GOAL SETTING AND CONTRACT

Multiproblem families usually come to the attention of social agencies because some community standard has been violated: child neglect or abuse, family violence, substance abuse, or delinquent behavior of the youngsters or adults. The practitioner is mandated to draw to the family's attention these violations of community norms in a nonjudgmental but clear and honest way. In the beginning of the St. Paul Family Centered Project, the social workers were fearful that being straightforward with the families about the reasons for the community's concern would interfere with building a good relationship. The workers learned, however, that they

> ...could be more open and direct with their clients most of the time. We have constantly searched our work to see where and why we became evasive, cloudy or circuitous. Progress has come through the steady discipline of holding ourselves to pointed as well as warm relationships with our clients, and noting how much better people respond to clarity. We are no longer afraid to tell parents the dangers we see. We no longer need to gloss over reality. But we have never confused honesty with hostility. (Overton et al., p. 158)

Some schools of family therapy, on contrast, advocate a manipulative, shock-tactics, "paradoxical" approach to the family (for example, Haley, 1976; Selvini-Palazzoli, Boscolo, Ceccin, & Prata, 1978). Such techniques may well be warranted in situations in which the *evidence* of the case indicates that symptomatic behavior or dysfunctional relationships will be refractory to more straightforward interventions. The use of paradox and other manipulative techniques with the multiproblem family is addressed later in this chapter; let it suffice here to observe that the great majority of multiproblem families (and indeed, we suspect most other families) do respond well to a more honest and up-front approach to their problems. Particularly in the case of the multiproblem family, where it is imperative that the family early be helped to begin to take positive action concerning problems that are placing them in conflict with the community, the family needs to understand cognitively and unambiguously the problem area that needs work.

Multiproblem families are used to being treated in evasive, confusing and buck-passing fashion by the service-delivery system. It would seem to be especially important for these families that the contract with the practitioner spell out in specific and unambiguous terms the goals that are being set, and the respective responsibilities of worker, individual members of the family, the family as a group, and other helpers and services. (A contract need not, of course, necessarily be written, although this may be useful in certain cases; but whether written or oral, it should be clear.) A hidden agenda on the part of a practitioner who is only giving the appearance of helping with reality problems, but whose real interest is in changing the family dynamics unbeknownst to the family members involved, does not appear to be useful with these families.

Family therapists have relearned, the hard way, the old casework dictum: "Begin where the client is." In the early years of family therapy, practitioners convinced (and in some cases, perhaps quite accurately) that the acting-out behavior of a child was functional, in that it deflected the parents from arguing about their marital problems, attempted to shift the problem too prematurely to the marital issue. The result was frequently that the case aborted. Family social workers were aware that the beleaguered and often demoralized multiproblem family, un-skilled in insight into their own processes or sophisticated analysis of their problems, could usually only see their need for some concrete and immediate resource. The worker began by directly discussing the problems that she and the community saw, but then moved to asking the family members what they saw as troublesome for them. The family's response was characteristically in terms of a concrete need. "A concrete service often has more meaning than an early attempt to deal with feelings and attitudes....If a family can see that we can do something besides talk, if they can have an actual demonstration of helping, they will trust us with other matters" (Overton et al., 1957, pp. 49–50). The preoccupation of a family therapist with fascinating internal dynamics of the system can mean both failing to recognize when some resource is indeed urgently needed, and also missing the opportunity to utilize the symbolic meaning to the family of the practitioner's concern with their material lacks and basic needs.

Goal setting in family social work was seen as a collaborative process of negotiation, based on mutual discussion of what was wrong, why, and what could be changed. Workers demonstrated respect for differences between themselves and the family, and differences among family members. If the family had been able unaided to diagnose its own problems accurately and set feasible goals for problem change, it probably would have been able to take constructive action previously. The family worker recognized that the multiproblem family needed help to begin to apply these skills. But she treated with respect the ideas and perceptions of all involved, realizing that unless she did so the family would not treat her suggestions with equal respect. In this sense, the family casework of the St. Paul Family Centered Project resembled much more social group work and group therapy than it did family therapy.

The practitioner's aim, in encouraging expression of different perceptions, was severalfold. She knew that if differences remained covert, the family members would work to sabotage her and each other. She was also modeling for the family that disagreements did not necessarily mean conflict or personal rejection, and that they would be listened to respectfully and honored for their contribution to the polyocular view of the situation. Like the group worker, she knew that this phase had to precede the coalescing of a sense of group bond. And finally, she was learning about the family's perceptions, beliefs and values so that she could fit herself and her interventions into their frame of reference.

Partnership with the Family

Family therapy is moving toward recognition of some of the insights of the family social work practitioners. DeShazer, for example, maintains that it is not a technique such as paradoxical intervention that brings about change, but rather "the *fit* or isomorphism between the family pattern and the intervention pattern" (1982, p. 82). The family social worker was helping the family members to see not only the basic fit among themselves in terms of their common goals, but also the fit between the family and herself and the fit between the problem(s) and the interventions. She did not use terms like *isomorphism*, but that is what she meant.

The St. Paul social worker was aiming throughout toward the creation of a sense of partnership and teamwork. There was no intimation that the worker knew better than the family about the nature of their problems, their internal motivations and family processes, or the necessarily best way to resolve the problems. It was a mutually responsible relationship of adults, rather than a parent-child or therapist-patient relationship. Today's family therapists sometimes take on the responsibility for solving a family's problems for them by use of paradox or other techniques that place the family in a one-down, passive, childlike position. The family social worker was aware of the childlike needs of some of her very immature and limited parents and was willing to respond to these; but she focused on whatever areas of maturity existed or were a potential for growth by gently insisting that the parent(s) begin to engage with her in problem solving in an adult and responsible fashion. The empirical evidence of the research done on this project indicates that even immature parents were usually able to respond to an approach that reached for whatever areas of maturity they possessed rather than a maternalistic relationship that further infantilized them.

Prioritization of Problems

Sometimes the only problem the family was able or willing to recognize was the intrusion of the worker into their lives. If so, the worker equably began with that by discussion with the family of what they thought they needed to and could do to make the worker's presence unnecessary. Often the family was aware of its multiple problems but found their multiplicity and severity overwhelming. Then the worker began by teaching them how to partialize, suggesting that they and she could work together on only one or two things at a time and inviting the family to choose the issue they saw as the most urgent. If the family's choice was clearly unrealistic or dangerous, the worker assumed the responsibility to point this out and to decline to participate in a plan that would mean further trouble or another failure for the family. But otherwise, even if the family's selection of their priority issue did not match the worker's diagnostic sense of what was most important, the family social worker went along with the family. In the colorful phrase of Overton et al., she was seeking to "hitch [her] treatment wagon to the family's motor" (1957, p. 51). She knew that if she and the family could experience some success in working on the priority problem of the family's choosing, the family would not only begin to feel more hopeful about doing something about their other problems but additionally would be more able to accept the worker's suggestions, since she had accepted theirs. The family therapy literature is now advising practitioners who work with "easier" voluntary client families not to wander too far afield from the family's sense of urgency about the presenting problem; if the therapist does not stay within the family's frame of reference, they are likely to resist her interventive efforts or to abandon therapy.

Considerations of Time and Capability
to Change in Goal Setting

Family therapy tends to be a therapy in a hurry. In terms of the time span of a case, this is undoubtedly an improvement over earlier psychodynamic therapies that assumed that the client had to be in treatment for a long period before improvement could be expected. Extensive therapy may indeed be required for certain kinds of individual and family problems. But Hartman and Laird criticize "the assumption so often made in psychotherapy that if a little intervention is good, then more must be better" (1983, p. 333). The assumption also goes against the research finding that, in most cases, if some progress has not begun to occur in the early stages of a case it is less likely to occur later. Our point here concerns the relationship of time to goals. It is not reasonable to expect most severely troubled multiproblem families, beset by environmental inadequacies as well as whatever internal family problems may exist, to totally resolve or even to appreciably ameliorate all their compounded problems in a very short time span. But the urgency of their problems and the threat of punitive community action weigh as heavily on the practitioner as on the family, creating a pressure for rapid resolution. Family social workers such as the St. Paul group were aware that they had a limited time span in which to work and they were as subject as are practitioners today to community demands for quick cure of the problematic family. But they learned to make haste slowly, to set goals with the family not in terms of dramatic and sudden major change but rather in terms of small incremental chipping away at the problem or problems selected for work. They knew that small success experiences were first necessary before the family could risk more major changes either within itself or in its transactions with the world outside.

Some family therapists take from their theory an expectation that one or a few dramatic and surgical interventions are all that is needed for family "cure." This may be so for some kinds of family problems, but it does not apply to the multiproblem family (or, we suspect, for most other families). The family social worker knew also that she had to gear her expectations or goals just a little beyond what the family thought they were capable of.

She "began where the client is," and she remained close to the family's perceptions and motivations, but she did not stay there—she moved out in front, just an inch or so, and beckoned the family on.

DIAGNOSTIC ASSESSMENT

The family social worker did not start with a theory as to why the family had not been able to function better. She was required to develop information or data from the case itself on which to base her selection of a differential diagnosis. It might have been that it was beyond the reasonably expectable capacity of any family to withstand the kind of destructive environmental forces to which it was being subjected (plus possibly the well-meaning but also destructive intrusions of other professional helpers; see, for example, Auerswald, 1968, and Hoffman & Long, 1969) and that what was needed was not therapy of the inner workings of the family but whatever power the worker and her agency could muster to combat these external pathogens. Alternatively, or in addition, it might have been within the family's latent potential to fight off or neutralize these outside forces, but they did not have the knowledge or the skills to do so; what was needed in terms of intervention was focused teaching by the worker, and possibly linkage of the family with other families in the same situation, thereby expanding the power base of each. Alternatively, or in addition, the family might have needed to change in one or several ways. Key members might have needed to learn crucial skills, such as how more effectively to discipline their children, or how to care for an infant, or how to go about getting job training. Or family members might have had a deficit in skills of communication and conflict negotiation. Or the demoralized parent(s) might have needed help, from the worker and/or from extended family or formed support groups, in establishing an executive subsystem for the family. Or the family might well have known that they needed to change some things about themselves, but they could not clearly see what these were. or they might have been well aware of what changes were required, but did not know how to start. Or they might have been so fearful of the worse reality that change of the painful (but, at least, known) present reality might bring, that change seemed impossibly dangerous. Or they might have needed to take responsibility to begin to change destructive "solutions" to their problems, such as the retreat of substance abuse, or withdrawal into enmeshment, or helpless acceptance of family disintegration and disengagement of the members from each other.

Social Work's Assessment "Balance Sheet"

Diagnostic assessment in family social work was concerned with constructing a "balance sheet" of family operations, in which specific identification of family strengths was as important as recognition of the deficits and problems. The worker was gambling on her assumption that even in the most troubled families there were reserves to draw on, if she could just locate and stimulate them, of individual fight and motivation for a better life and flickering hope, and of family loyalty and mutual caring and need.

Weltner (1985), writing in the family therapy literature on "matchmaking" between the appropriate type of therapy and various "levels" of family pathology, offers an interesting (but as yet unvalidated) diagnostic taxonomy of these family dysfunctioning levels. Using the analogy of house construction, he sees the problems of families at Level I as being concerned with issues basic to the survival of the family and its members, namely physical nurturance and protection. Usually, in these families, there is insufficient executive capacity in the adult parental system to provide nurturance and security. Weltner advises identifying resources available to shore up the faltering executive system, and enable the parent(s) to begin to function more competently. These resources may exist within the family itself, for example in what Weltner suggests can be a "cabinet" of older teenage children, or someone from the extended family or another system. Weltner recognizes that such an interventive strategy blurs generational boundaries, but points out that the survival crisis the family faces warrants such temporary crossing of generational boundaries. Level I families represent trouble in the "foundation" of the house, whereas the problems of Level II pertain to the roof and the framing, namely authority and limits. Again, the difficulty is with the parental system that is either not clearly communicating behavioral expectations to family members, or is in such a position of powerlessness that the expectations are not enforced. Here also the interventive strategy begins "with a survey of strengths and resources and the welding of a coalition strong enough to offer sufficient authority" (p. 44). Weltner colorfully calls this looking around to see what "troops" the therapist can call upon to help out the beleaguered parental executive(s). He suggests that the interventions can be quite straightforward and are usually gratefully accepted by families in these dire straits: "A drowning man will grab any rope" (p. 46). Level III families are better organized but have developed dysfunctional patterns, often relating to triangulation of a family member and/or violation of generational boundaries. Intervention consists of structural and strategic work to reshape the family's "internal architecture until everyone has an appropriate space and appropriate amounts of access and privacy" (p. 47). Families at Level IV are concerned with "the fine art of living," and their own "inner landscape" (p. 47). For these families, existentially oriented therapies are most appropriate.

Multiproblem families are obviously not at Level IV, but if Weltner's admittedly rough diagnostic classification scheme is accurately descriptive, they could be found at any of the other levels. His general point is an important one: The therapy must be tailored to the needs of the family as determined by careful assessment; the choice of interventive strategy should not reflect the predilection of the practitioner for one or another school of family therapy, or her fondness for particular interventive techniques.

The cohesiveness, or group bond, or sense of "familyness" of a family is of course an old observation of novelists and poets and ordinary people. An evaluation of the degree to which family members felt a commitment to their group, and the family's capacity to function as a unitary group, was included in the diagnostic assessment of family social workers. Sometimes the family was found to be too united, too enfolded in on itself

(today's family therapists would say "enmeshed"). Family isolation has frequently been noted by observers of the
multiproblem family; unfortunately, the instinctive boundary-
tightening reaction of many such families serves both to cut
them off even more from environmental resources and to increase the environment's contemptuous perception of them as
strange and queer. The family social worker's task was then to
find ways to utilize the energy that was keeping the family cower-
ing together as a way of warding off a hostile environment, to
help the family use their group bond in more constructive problem solving. Other families were disorganized, with an insufficient sense of family bond, the members centrifugally flung off
into space in individual isolation from each other. Here the family worker's task was to help them to begin to see their mutual
self-interest in group participation in the problems that plagued
the family as a group.

The "balance sheet" of strengths and deficits required of
the workers in the St. Paul Family Centered Project meant not
only these as they applied to family operations, but also in the
social situational context. In comparison with family therapy,
the older social work tradition was more sophisticated in its
sense of the family as a system in interaction with a hierarchy of
other systems. Although terms such as *systems* and *hierarchy* were
not used, clearly this was the understanding. One of the primary differences between family social work and family therapy
is the better recognition by the former of the family as embed-
ded in a neighborhood, a community, a cultural group, and a
web of institutions. Although some family therapists still dis-
courage attention to anything outside the family system (Haley,
1980), others are beginning to criticize this tendency to equate
the term "system" only with the family system (Pinsof, 1983).

Intrafamilial and Extrafamilial Processes

Family social work was nowhere as sophisticated as is family
therapy in its diagnostic understanding of internal family processes, although, on balance, the family social workers did not
do so badly with this either. They did not have available for use
constructs such as boundaries, the hierarchical distribution of

power and authority in the system, or metacommunication processes; and they perhaps would have done even better with their cases if they had had available this conceptual arsenal. But perhaps not: Perhaps, like many family therapists today, availability of the more abstract of these conceptualizations might have led them to intellectualized conjecture about unknown covert processes, forming "a fog over the actual complexities of a case, obscuring rather than illuminating its realities" (Reid, 1985, p. 86).

Family social workers viewed the family as a system, although they did not use that term: "We had often tried to build a family diagnosis simply by adding various individual diagnoses together. This did not work...a family is quite different from the sum of its parts" (Overton et al., 1957, p. 16). They emphasized that information about family relationship patterns is better obtained by observation of family interaction than by either direct questions or interviews with individual members. They felt that the practitioner could get a more accurate picture of family interaction in the home, the natural habitat of the family, than in office interviews. They assessed family functioning in terms of the developmental life stage of the family group and of its individual members.

The research instrument used in the St. Paul Family Centered Project (the St. Paul Scale of Family Functioning) made use of systems concepts by measuring the performance by family subsystems and the total system of socially expected tasks, including its interaction with the community. Diagnosis therefore included *both* "family operations" *and* the family's interaction with its relevant environing systems. This encompasses an enormous amount of information because, in addition to the complexities involved in understanding a family, "environment" is "everything left over after some client system has been isolated" (Reid, 1985, p. 246).

A focus was needed around which to organize diagnostic information—and this was, not the family system in vacuuo as is often found in modern family therapy, but rather the problem(s) chosen for work mutually by the worker and the family. This was tantamount to Sheffield's (1937) idea of the problem situation as the focus of the case. Extrafamily systems were therefore naturally included in this diagnostic assessment to the extent that they were relevant to the problem. Other information might be fascinating, but it was disregarded if its saliency concerning the problems was not clear—if it could not be *used* for understanding of the problems and the task of problem solving.

Too often in today's family therapy, information is sought about family history and internal dynamics whose pertinence to the problem at hand is, at best, obscure; or information about the family is gathered according to some theoretical schema with relevance to the problem not being considered. Overton, Tinker, and associates warned against either snap judgments and blind spots based on insufficient information about the family and its troubles, or on the other hand trying to know too much or gathering data which could not be put to use (Overton et al., 1957, p. 82). The family social workers were not interested in gathering an overabundance of information on the family history, and in this they presaged the structural and strategic schools of family therapy while they contradicted the Bowenians. Family social workers were interested in the etiology of the family problems only to the extent that a clear link could be made between this information and action to resolve the problem. They were much more concerned about what seemed to be going on in the here-and-now that was maintaining the problem.

Family social workers were certainly aware that a family cannot "run" without an executive subsystem. As noted earlier, they learned from their failures that the quality of the marital relationship was often the key to the outcome of the case, because serious conflict between the parents as marital partners often blocked their ability to act cooperatively in their parental or other family-executive roles. They attempted to involve fathers as early as possible; and the approach to the father was direct, not via the mother. They insisted on interviewing parents together, even if this meant evening home visits. They resisted the temptation to remove a child from the home, except in situations of immediate and serious risk, as well as the temptation to take the child into individual treatment as a way for the worker to retreat from, rather than deal with, the resistance of the parents.

Family social workers over several generations emphasized the importance of searching for and specifically identifying family strengths and inner resources, as well as resources outside the family. This would be a refreshing development in family therapy, which tends to be so pathology-focused.

Although the worker shared with the family only whatever in her own diagnostic thinking the family could use (to change something changeable), diagnostic assessment was seen as a product of worker-family interaction. This diagnosis, it should be noted, included not only facts, but also attitudes and feelings of individual members and the family group as another category of factual reality. The family participated in the "social diagnosis" of their problems: in analyzing what was keeping the problem going and in deciding what was changeable. In some instances, the family read or even participated in the writing of the worker's recording! Diagnostic assessment was itself utilized as an intervention, an instrument of change, because not only was cognitive understanding of the nature of the problem seen as a basis for problem solving, but also throughout every helping process in the case ran the clear thread of family-as-partner.

Theoretical Framework for Assessment

The diagnostic assessments of the family social workers might well be perceived by family therapists today as unsophisticated and simple. But in a recent book on social-work family practice, Reid advocates that diagnostic assessment should be data-centered "in terms of specific identifiable behaviors, beliefs, interactions, and the like. Following the rule of parsimony, these data are organized and analyzed with a minimum of assumptions. Simple, 'obvious' explanations are favored over complex interpretations based on notions of hidden processes" (1985, p. 84). Reid's insistence on specifiable data, he recognizes, "may be difficult to meet for hypotheses of covert processes and for high-order theoretical constructs, especially in complex cases. Consequently, practitioners may gravitate toward more obvious explanations and simpler ideas" (p. 86). But in Reid's view, simplicity of diagnostic formulations "is as it should be: It is better to work with limited knowledge than with false knowledge that masks ignorance" (p. 86).

In Chapter 5 we raise the issue of whether family therapy descriptive theory adequately meets the criterion of parsimony or if in fact it is suffering from a glut of conceptualizations. We suggest there that this question cannot be well answered until further work is undertaken on the operationalization of the concepts and constructs. The prescriptive theory of family therapy, however, does seem to be extremely unparsimonious in its recommendations for what constitutes adequate diagnostic understanding of a family case. The amount of practitioner and family time and energy spent on, for example, construction of genograms may or *may not* be relevant to understanding of the present problem and decisions concerning how to go about changing it. Additionally, attention may be deflected from the relevant work that needs to be done, and the family may be confused rather than helped by raising issues from the past. It may indeed be better prescriptive advice for the practitioner to proceed with the most obvious and simple explanation of the problems in the case, at least for "openers"; and not to move on to more convoluted diagnostic hypotheses unless clearly specifiable data emerge to indicate that something more complex is occurring than was initially envisaged.

Despite the fuzzy abstractness of many family therapy conceptualizations, some do represent an improvement over the vague semantical labels the family social workers had available to deal with phenomena of great complexity, for example *relationship, conflict,* and *cooperation among family members.* The term *boundaries* would have been useful as a way of expressing the understanding of the family social workers of necessary divisions among generational and other subsystems of the family. The St. Paul Scale of Family Functioning, which the workers utilized to gather the research data on the family, did, in effect, use the concept of *boundaries* without employing the term itself. The family social workers observed that social authority systems invaded with impunity the impoverished multiproblem family in a way that would not be attempted with middle-class families, and they recognized that the family needed assistance in warding off unhelpful invaders. The construct and term *boundaries* would have had utility here in sharpening the understanding of what was happening. They observed also that some families responded to external assaults by becoming isolated, too much turned in upon themselves. Today they would be called *enmeshed* or *fused*, which may be better semantical terms for describing this phenomenon.

Family therapy's more sophisticated understanding of authority and power distribution within the family today adds to earlier practitioners' intuitive understanding of these processes. They would have better recognized, for example, that the powerlessness of the member labeled by the family as weak or incompetent sometimes can be wielded by that individual as a kind of power, forcing others to assume the individual's roles and tasks and enforcing payment in the form of the guilt and/or resentment of other family members.

Overton, Tinker and associates' (1957) written accounts of the St. Paul Project give the impression that they and their workers tended to view the community service agency network as invariably benevolent and well functioning, with their focus restricted to helping the families utilize the agencies' resources. Perhaps they only wrote this way out of consideration of the politics of agency relationships, and privately held less positive opinions of the community agencies of that time and place; or perhaps in that particular community, reputed for its social progressivism, agencies did function better and collaborate better than is usually the case. (However, 6 *years* of work with community agencies, to ensure collaboration, took place before the opening of the project.)

Concepts of power distribution and power negotiation developed by family therapy would have been helpful to the St. Paul workers in expanding their recognition that a large part of what they were attempting to do was empowerment of the families to effectively resist or outmaneuver the bureaucracy when appropriate, or to negotiate successfully for agency resources. It might have helped the workers to avoid the common pitfall of becoming triangulated between the family and some external powerful agency (although this must have been obviated to some extent by the agreement the project insisted on, in advance, that its workers carry the coordinating role concerning the work of other agencies with the families). The family social workers would have had to make some translation of these family therapy concepts to the interface between the family and the surrounding bureaucratic systems, because family therapy tends to restrict its discussion of processes concerning power to the interior of the family. An outstanding exception is Hoffman and Long (1969)—whose article, however, reads much more like "unglamorous" family social work than it does family therapy.

Similarly, the work of family therapy theoreticians has added appreciably to the understanding by practitioners of communication and metacommunication. Such understanding helps the modern practitioner to attend as much to the process of communication as to its content.

INTERVENTIVE TECHNIQUES

Rational Problem Solving

As noted, the earlier practitioners' approach of engaging the family in a primarily rational problem-solving process (albeit with great attention to emotional factors and in an atmosphere of warm support) presaged later theoretical developments in fields other than family therapy such as crisis intervention, rational-emotive therapy, and cognitive-behavioral therapy. There is some research that supports the efficacy of this approach for various kinds of family problems (Jacobson, 1977; Jacobson & Margolin, 1979; Robin, 1981; Woodward et al., 1981; and Geismar & Wood, 1986). Reid's *task-centered* model, now expanded to work with families, also utilizes rational problem solving (1985). Reid argues against the family therapy dictum that all problems are necessarily "rooted in system dynamics that family members are unaware of and [are] unwilling to disrupt" and that call for dramatic techniques to unbalance the system (p. 99). Rather, he proposes:

> The stress on therapist-initiated system change, and the consequent subordination of the family's participation in problem solving, is based on a *morphostatic* view of the family as a system. A

system controlled by morphostatic processes is highly resistant to change.... The assumption that family systems, even disturbed ones, are generally governed by change-resistant morphostatic processes is open to question, however. *Morphogenic* processes, that account for systems change, are always present even in systems that appear to be stable. (pp. 99–100)

The effectiveness of Reid's problem-solving or task-centered model, based on principles such as these, has received considerable research support as to its usefulness with a wide range of client problems (Reid, 1985, pp. 80–83).

Reframing

Although problem solving was the thrust and major focus of family social work as practiced in the St. Paul Project, the practitioner intervened in a variety of other ways both within the family and in its dealings with its environment.

Related both to the cognitive element of their problem-solving approach and also to the emphasis on the strengths of the family as much as its difficulties, the family social workers did a good deal of what is today called *reframing* in family therapy. This is a very old social work principle: More than 60 years ago Lucy Wright (1924) referred to it (cited by Braverman, 1986, p. 239). Reframing was used, however, by family social workers not as a ploy or technique but as a sincere attempt to call the family's attention to a more workable perception of their problems, and also to the strengths of the family and the positive motivations that might underlie even problematic behavior of individual members.

The Worker's Role with the Family

Teaching and *modeling* were used not only for problem-solving skills, but also for such relationship areas as ineffective communication among members. The worker directly taught specific skills, and, through her own behavior in interaction with the family, modeled teamwork, joint planning, differential assignment of responsibility, and conflict negotiation.

The workers could be firm and assertive as well as supportive: They intervened to block destructive interactions in a session or even terminated the interview when necessary. They were creative and skillful in what they called the "supportive use of authority," based on Studt's (1954) seminal work on this aspect of practice. Parental authority and responsibility were strongly supported. The family social workers did not use the term *triangulation*, but they were aware of the risk of being "forced into the role of referee or into taking sides" (Overton et al., 1957, p. 112).

Work with Family Subsystems

Not all sessions were conducted with the total family; when appropriate, the worker worked for a time with particular subsystems of the parents, or of a parent and child, although they were cautious about a major emphasis on work with individuals, seeing this as the practitioner's retreat from the difficulties of maintaining focus on using the family group itself as the primary problem-solving medium.

Emphasis on Action

The use of *home visits* meant that the family social workers was in a position to observe and to actively intervene in problematic family interaction as it actually occurred — what family therapists would today call a directive to the family in an office session to "enact" here and now the quarrel of last night that they are only verbally describing.

Problem solving with the family meant much more than discussion: The emphasis was on planned action. Responsibilities were assigned to the worker, to individual family members, to the family as a whole, and to helpers from other agencies whose efforts the family social worker was coordinating. The problem-solving work assignments to the family were the precursors of family therapy's "directives" or "homework"; and the action requirement was a beginning semblance of later behavioral therapy techniques.

Bridge Building to Other Social Systems

The family social worker, despite her interest in the functioning of the family, was equally focused on the nature of the family's transactions with the outside world—because, in many cases this is where at least some, and often much, of the problem was located. She provided emotional warmth and support to the family but was aware that she had to avoid becoming the major source of such support, always a temptation when dealing with very needy persons. Her interventions focused on finding or creating other support systems, within the family, with extended family and neighbors, and with community resources. She saw her role as building bridges between the isolated and hostile or demoralized family and their social systems.

Behavioral, Role-Play, and Family-Sculpting Techniques

Family social workers would have benefitted from knowledge of later-developed behavioral techniques such as *contingency contracting*, teaching parents *positive reinforcement, time-out, operant extinction*, and *conflict negotiation* (Blechman & Olson, 1976; Patterson et al., 1975, 1976; Jacobson & Margolin, 1979; Stuart, 1980; Gambrill, 1981). Although more research evidence is needed, findings to date indicate that a behavioral approach within a family systems framework is more effective than nonbehavioral family therapy at least with families of delinquent adolescents (Geismar & Wood, 1986).

Role play might have been used by the St. Paul workers, because it is not a new technique, but it is not alluded by Overton, Tinker, and associates. Role play may well be a very useful technique with the multiproblem family in helping to work through family relationship problems or, possibly, in preparing key members for interviews with school or welfare personnel (Shaw, 1980). A family not oriented to self-insight or to understanding of others' motivations and feelings may learn about their relationships through the action of role play, whereas they could not do so by verbal discussion. People unskilled in dealing with authorities or the intricacies of community bureaucracies may well need to learn how to deal with these frightening realities in the safety of role-play rehearsal.

Family sculpting (Papp, 1976; Constantine, 1978; Jefferson, 1978) is a technique of family therapy that may be useful for some multiproblem families, if a clear rationale for its use exists other than the interest of the practitioner in the drama of the technique itself. The experience of family members' portrayal of their perceptions of their own and each other's roles within the family through a frozen or moving tableau can be an emotion-laden and eye-opening experience. It may be useful for uneducated or inarticulate families who find action a better means of expression than words. The emotional and uncovering nature of family sculpture, however, may render it "too much too soon" for some families; and good diagnostic assessment of the family and practitioner judgment are required as to what the family can constructively use.

Paradoxical Techniques

The use of the family therapy technique of paradox with the multiproblem family is problematic. The use of an intervention such as paradoxical directives would have horrified the family social workers of past decades. Use of *paradoxical techniques*, apparently at least, contradicts their emphasis on honesty of the practitioner toward the client family and use of rational approaches. Indeed, there are those today who consider use of such techniques as manipulative, "sneaky," and arrogant.

A somewhat more detailed exploration is devoted to this technique than to the other interventions of family therapy, for several reasons. First, the term and its usage are frequently misunderstood. Further, the experiences of reading the family therapy literature and listening to its practitioners creates the impression that paradox is extremely fashionable at present and is sometimes applied indiscriminately to every client family. Use of paradoxical techniques calls for diagnostic perspicacity and appreciable practice experience of the practitioner; in the hands of a beginner these techniques can be dangerous. And last, it is extremely doubtful that use of these techniques should represent a major strategy of intervention with a multiproblem family, although they may have some place with certain cases and under certain circumstances, especially in their milder forms.

The term *paradox*, from the Greek, means contrary to opinion or expectation: a paradox is a seemingly self-contradictory statement that yet can have a surprising kernel of truth. The usual example of a technically "correct" paradox is the statement of Epimenides of Crete, "All Cretans are liars." Because Epimenides is himself a Cretan, the statement can be true only if it is false, and it is false even if it is otherwise entirely true. It is the logical fallacy of paradox because it confuses the logical levels between a class and members of a class.

Dell points out that the label of paradox "is currently applied to such a wide range of therapeutic and interactional phenomena that the meaning of the term has been blurred and corrupted almost beyond usefulness. Today, any unconventional therapeutic intervention is likely to be called a paradox" (1981, p. 37).

Ascher and Efran (1978, p. 547) give a definition of a paradoxical task as one that "requires clients to perform responses that appear to be incompatible with the goal for which they are seeking assistance" (quoted by Reid, 1985, p. 238).

Instructing an insomniac to try to stay awake is a paradoxical directive, based on the diagnostic hypothesis that the client's solution, that is, his desperate attempts to fall asleep, has become more of a problem that the original difficulty. Or a quarrelling family might be instructed to fight about a certain issue only "by appointment": at a specific time and for a specified period. The family then finds that they cannot fight in the same old way because it is no longer spontaneous; additionally, the therapist has become an invisible presence in the fight scene since the family is obeying her directive, and just that presence changes the nature of the conflictual interaction.

The purpose of paradoxical or other unconventional interventions is to dramatically startle the individual client or family out of their unproductive "logic" about the nature of the problem; and/or their equally unproductive and rigidly repetitive solutions, which are now maintaining the problem; and/or their need to resist and defeat the therapist. Selvini-Palazzoli et al. (1978) go so far as to claim that anything predictable is therapeutically ineffective. This may perhaps obtain for the kinds of families treated by her Milan group, but it seems an overstatement if applied to the great majority of troubled families who come for help. Especially with a multiproblem family, it seems more sensible to start with an assumption that the family's resistance is due to fear of what the authoritative practitioner may do to them (such as removing their children), rather than to some need of the family system to remain stuck in its pathological groove because this is performing some survival function for the family. The latter may turn out to be the case; but, if so, there is no reason to fear that the practitioner will not eventually stumble across such a dynamic—the family can be counted on to give abundant *evidence* of its existence in the form of resistance intractable to any other approach. A major difficulty with the current a priori assumptions of many family therapists that every family needs paradoxical intervention is that there is often *no evidence from the case* to support such a diagnostic assumption.

The term "paradox" has now been expanded to encompass 180-degree reframings of the problem, for example that Johnny's hyperactive behavior at home and his failing work at school are his good-hearted attempts to prevent his parents from fighting over their marital issues, or to keep his mother stimulated enough so that she does not become depressed. In some cases, this diagnostic judgment may well be correct; in other cases, Johnny may be suffering from an undiagnosed organically based learning disability or attention-deficit disorder, in which situation the therapist's intervention will inflict severe iatrogenic damage on both the child and the family.

Fisher, Anderson, and Jones, in their discussion of indications and contraindications for the use of paradoxical interventions, point out that these techniques are inappropriate when careful diagnostic assessment indicates that support, information, guidance, or direction in solving the family's problems are what is needed (1981, p. 33). These authors specifically exclude from use of paradoxical techniques families that they classify as chaotic, childlike, and impulsive—all of which may be found in the population loosely known as multiproblem—as well as the less pathological family (but also found among the multiproblem) that "needs a setting in which to work issues through a professional support and direction in solving their own problems" (p. 33). The focus of work with the chaotic family is more usually on helping them establish some internal organization and stability rather than on the elimination of a specific symptom. The childlike family, according to Fisher et al., is often also too "loose" and without sufficient cohesiveness for paradoxical interventions to be effective, and will often perceive such interventions as if they were rejection. Use of paradoxical techniques with an acting-out, overtly conflictual, impulsive family may well escalate antisocial behavior. These authors decry the frequent misuse of these potentially powerful procedures that often are employed as "excuses for lack of skill or insufficient diagnostic study" (p. 34). Reid, who presents a very clear discussion of the meaning of the term *paradox*, the possible indications for its use, its limitations, and the paucity of research evidence for its effectiveness (1985, pp. 236–244), also emphasizes that use of these techniques must be based on accurate diagnostic assessment of the dynamics of the family and the perceptions of its individual members (p. 239).

Use of some milder forms of paradoxical techniques might, however, be useful with some multiproblem families. Asking a family to try to have again, right now in the session, the fight from last night that they are describing, is a paradox of sorts because it asks the family to temporarily continue the behavior they want to change. Gentle support and encouragement are usable by most families to help them deal with the fear of the unknown that change may bring; but if a family is frozen by its sense of fear and threat, and this does not give way to more conventional techniques, "joining the resistance" by suggesting they have been changing too fast and ought to slow up a bit may be more productive than arguing or exhortations (which of course are never productive!). With a family that is really stuck in its own "paradoxical" rigid solutions or games, a counter-paradox by the practitioner aimed at dramatically highlighting the nature of their self-imposed dilemma may be the only intervention powerful enough to free them.

But paradoxical techniques are not for practitioners who are diagnostically inept or insensitive to the people they are serving, or who have a personal ego need to cure every family problem with one dramatic, slashing intervention. Family therapists of this ilk should not be allowed near multiproblem families particularly, who are especially vulnerable to practitioner malpractice and who need a helper much more in the mold of the earlier family social workers.

ACHIEVEMENT AND FUTURE GOALS

To paraphrase Braverman (1986, p. 239), the early pioneers and later practitioners of family social work, before the family therapy movement, planted important seeds. Indeed, some of the "new" concepts, practice principles, and interventive techniques of family therapy were not just acorns but full-grown oaks in the time of these early practitioners. Both social workers and family therapists do themselves an intellectual disservice when they disregard this legacy and the rich practice experience of social work that still has much to teach us today.

A disadvantage this earlier generation is under is that they wrote so simply. They did not use big words like *isomorphism* and *morphostasis*; they preferred plain English and down-home metaphors. They just do not sound sophisticated enough to be credible today. Although the polysyllabic terms of family therapy often serve only to obfuscate meaning, language that seems too simple can also obscure meaning. The reaction of a reader who turns to Overton, Tinker, and associates' *Casework Notebook* may well be disappointment: It is written at such a simple, primer level. Indeed it was intended to be just that—an easy-to-use little book for professional beginners, not experienced practitioners. But the senior author of the present volume, after many years of practice experience, still learns something new every time she picks it up. There is some quite sophisticated stuff in there, hidden away under the simple language.

The other disadvantage of the previous generation of social workers is that they had names like Alice and Bertha and Ada. They sound so quaint and, well, *feminine*. Real experts are supposed to have male names. Their names alone conjure up images of lace-gloved little old ladies having a tot of elderberry wine after a hard day of making home visits. And perhaps they did have a little tot of something or other; they deserved it. But they were not lace-gloved by any means. Tender-hearted they may have been, but strong-souled, hardheaded, and tough, too.

They were as tough and smart as those other ladies with the quaint names in the early women's rights movement (and many of the early social workers were active in that also).

The family therapy movement deserves accolades for the revolution it has wrought in the mental health field. It has, additionally, indeed added valuable insights, conceptualizations, practice principles, and novel interventions to our repertoire.

If the best of the two traditions, family social work and family therapy, could somehow be married, each would gain from the contribution of the other. That is the overall intent of this book, and in Chapter 7 we attempt specifically to achieve such a union, in terms specific to work with the multiproblem family.

Chapter 7

Treating the Multiproblem Family
A Framework of Practice Principles

Several reviews have been conducted of the research on effectiveness of family-oriented treatment in general, that is, with regard to a variety of client populations and problems (Wells, Dilkes & Trivelli, 1972; Wells & Dezen, 1978; Gurman & Kniskern, 1978; DeWitt, 1978; Masten, 1979; Wells, 1981). Although the quality of the research has improved in recent years, studies are still plagued by methodological problems—some avoidable and some unavoidable—rendering it difficult to arrive at a definitive conclusion about the overall effectiveness of family treatment as compared with other interventions that do not focus on the family. Wells (1981), however, seems to express the best conclusion that can be drawn from the empirical evidence so far when he states cautiously that "family treatment on behalf of children and adolescents, in specific areas and through identified techniques, can be justified" (p. 296).

An insufficient number of studies has been conducted on work with multiproblem families, making it also difficult to assess what goes into effectiveness of professional intervention with this client group. Some, such as the study conducted at the

St. Paul Project (Geismar & Ayres, 1959a,b) and a later one in
New Haven (Geismar & Krisberg, 1967) have demonstrated that
service to the multiproblem family can have a positive impact.
But other studies find mild or no effect of the intervention
(Brown, 1968; Mullen, Dumpson, & associates, 1972; Phillips et
al., 1980; Jones, 1983).

The reasons for this discrepancy are undoubtedly multiple,
including both problems of the research methodology and
problems of the interventions that were employed. There is a
wide variation in the independent variable, that is, the actual
practice that was involved under the global terms *intensive service* or *family-focused intervention*. In order for research results to
be comparable across studies, the experimental variable of the
intervention employed needs to be, if certainly not identical in
every project, at least consonant with what the professional community considers at a given time to reflect canons of good practice. The impression from the research literature is that there
has been great variability from one study to the next in the
quality of the professional practice, that is, in the degree of
adherence to what the practice literature at present proposes as
principles of good practice with multiproblem families. A difficulty for practitioners and researchers alike is that statements of
these practice principles are dispersed throughout the literature, and do not appear to have been organized in a systematic
fashion.

The intent of this chapter is to pull together major principles of practice with the multiproblem family that are considered important at the present time. The number of what could
be called practice principles is, of course, legion. In the purview
of a brief chapter, our selection of certain principles has to be
somewhat arbitrary, and the reader may disagree with the inclusion of some and the exclusion of others. We hope however that,
taken as a whole, these practice principles can be considered as a
set of guidelines reflecting the best knowledge presently available about professional practice with the multiproblem family.
Perhaps they are also even a "framework." But their organization must at this time be so loose, and the degree of empirical
validation for them singly or in the aggregate so spotty, that we

cannot present them as a "model." At the best and taken as a whole, they may represent a beginning step toward an ultimate model for practice with multiproblem families.

DERIVATION AND VALIDATION OF PRACTICE PRINCIPLES

Some of the practice principles derive from the family casework of social work's early years; some are from later social work with multiproblem families, primarily Overton, Tinker, and associates (1957), but from others as well during this "middle period"; and some are from modern family therapy. In this manner we are attempting, if not yet a marriage of the older and newer traditions, at least an introduction of one to the other.

There is empirical evidence supporting the validity of some of these canons or practice principles, and when we are aware of such empirical support it will be cited. Most of the principles of what is considered good practice are, however, still in the realm of untested practice wisdom. Some may appear to have a face validity, or common sense quality; but caution is still needed concerning their too-facile acceptance.

We do not attempt to present all of these practice principles in testable propositional form; but, as we observed in Chapter 6, on prescriptive theory, the "if the practitioner does X, a certain effect is likely to ensue" quality of practice prescriptions tends— with various degrees of difficulty or ease—to render them capable of translation into ultimately testable propositions. This translation needs to be done so that the individual propositions and their aggregate, which is our beginning framework, can be tested under practice conditions.

We first address practice principles concerning the personal characteristics of the practitioner, and then move on to various phases of the helping process. Although there will inevitably be some overlap, in that posited principles of practice in one category will have implications for the professional task in another category, we endeavor to deal with them as if they were discrete. In actual practice, of course, they are interwoven.

PERSONAL CHARACTERISTICS OF THE PRACTITIONER

There is research evidence that certain qualities of the helper are as important, and perhaps more important, than the particular interventive techniques employed. Jones, Magura, & Shyne (1981), in their review of research studies of protective and preventive services, found that the quality of the worker-family relationship played an integral role in outcome. Wells summarizes the research findings in this area in his statement that "there is reason to believe that *who* the therapist is—in respect to a cluster of important qualities—may be much more important than many of the niceties of technique, or the knotty issues in theory, or the many other questions that so often absorb our attention" (1981, p. 295).

In addition to the classic warmth-empathy-genuineness triad, Overton and Tinker emphasized real liking and respect for these families whom so many others find unlikeable. Those authors had a *preference* for working with multiproblem families over middle-class families with less serious problems, because they found them admirable in their struggle and responsive to help. This attitude of the practitioner is conveyed to the family in everything that happens in the interaction between them, and in itself is probably the most powerful intervention that can be brought to bear. It not only conveys hope that the family can better handle its problems, it also begins to change the low self-esteem and demoralization of family members, and begins to help them feel that they are worthy of the respect they are receiving. Without the communication of this attitude, it is doubtful that any mechanistic techniques will prove helpful.

Implicit in Overton and Tinker's stance was the lack of need to perceive the people in the family as if they were children. Their insistence that the family could engage in a *partnership* with the worker implied an expectation that the adult members could engage in an adult relationship with the practitioner. Some parents in multiproblem families may indeed be very immature in certain respects, but Overton and Tinker emphasized reaching for the more mature aspects of what are complex and multilevel personalities. There is no empirical evidence one way or the other, but the hypothesis is suggested that a well-meaning but maternalistic and condescending attitude by the practitioner evokes further childlike behavior from the clients. Such an attitude is implied by some of the literature on multiproblem families (Chilman, 1966; McKinney, 1970; Clark, Zalis, & Sacco, 1982).

What might be called a kind of beginner's naive optimism seems to be more useful in work with very dysfunctional families than does the cynicism of the long-experienced practitioner, who has had enough failure cases to have learned to guard herself against the possibility of future failure by eliminating at the outset clients whose chances of improvement seem dim. Perhaps a better way of putting it is the practitioner's willingness to risk herself, and her lack of need to be always successful. Equable acceptance of her own imperfections and variable record of professional success has its counterpart in the practitioner's ability to accept the clients' equally human imperfections, backsliding, and faltering steps toward better functioning. The practitioner who needs to be successful will pressure her families to be successful for her, not for themselves. The practitioner's willingness to take a chance on herself and risk ending up being unsuccessful, with its concomitant feelings of inadequacy and stupidity, in itself encourages the family to risk the possibility that their efforts at change of the situation will prove unsuccessful. The practitioner whose self-esteem is dependent on what Ellis (1973b) calls the "irrational belief" that making mistakes or failing means that one is totally incompetent, will in effect be granting to the client family power over her own sense of personal integrity—because it is the family that controls whether they will be cooperative or resistant, and they therefore indeed do control whether the practitioner will succeed or fail with the case. It is important for the practitioner to be clear about what she is responsible for and what she can control (which, in the last analysis, is only herself); and what the family is responsible for and what they control. The practitioner who fears ego-bruising failure at the hands of the family will probably need to maintain a degree of social distance that is counterproductive to establishment of a helping relationship, and/or an equally counterproductive mind-set in which the family is her adversary who must be defeated before they defeat her. Overton and Tinker talk about the necessity for the practitioner to deal with her own resistance to the family, meaning her fear of failure and rejection, before she can deal skillfully with their resistance to her (Overton, Tinker, & associates, 1957, p. 65).

Learning and Training Principles Involving Personal Qualities

In Chapter 8, we address how the agency culture can create or exacerbate unprofitable attitudes in its practitioners by its insistence that the success record of the organization be upheld, by lack of sensitivity to the personal needs of its staff, by too-rigid a hierarchical administrative structure, and/or by an atmosphere of competition rather than professional collaboration. For now, let us suggest that, given a belief structure of the agency that is consonant with productive attitudes on the part of the staff, and given practitioners with ordinary amounts of decency and compassion, practitioners can be trained by the agency in the attitudes and perspectives outlined here.

The practitioner's "naive" optimism, even in advance of meeting a newly assigned family, that the clients want to function better and that she will find untapped resources within them to do so, is, on reflection, perhaps not so naive. Rather, it would seem to express some of the personal attitudes referred to above: a stubborn "belief in people" (Rich, 1956) despite the horrendous problems in the case; a gambler's daring to bet against the odds; and willingness to fail but not until she has tried. These value positions would seem to have a pragmatic payoff, in that they serve, in the practitioner's mind, to "de-pathologize" the family and render them more like ordinary people and therefore more potentially helpable. Family members tend to be viewed more as people doing the best they can, however inadequately, than as cases bearing hopeless diagnostic labels. The practitioner is less likely herself to feel fearful, pessimistic and hopeless—emotions that it would be difficult not to communicate to the family, with iatrogenic destructive effect.

Partnership with the Family

Closely allied is the practice principle that the practitioner not assume she knows best how to solve the family's problems, or that her role is to impart to them this superior knowledge. Rather, the relationships is characterized more by a "we're all in this together" atmosphere, struggling mutually to find options for problem solving, which will vary from one family to the next despite the similarity of the specific problems involved.

The terms *therapy* and *therapist* mean different things to different people. A therapist working with families may indeed possess the attitudes or mind-set identified above. But *therapy* is a medical term, the dictionary definition of which is "the treatment of disease or other disorder as by some remedial or curative process" (*Random House Dictionary of the English Language*, 1968). The term therefore implies attempts to cure people of their disease or disorders, in a healer-patient relationship that is characterized by sociopsychological positions of superior and inferior, active giver and passive recipient. What seems to happen in effective work with multiproblem families is the exact converse of this: It is a relationship of partnership.

To our knowledge, Overton was the first to use the term *partnership* to describe the relationship of practitioner and family (Overton, 1956). Overton and Tinker explicate this view:

> In the early days of social work, we thought up plans that were good for people and often told them just what to do—kindly—but in terms of our ideas of what their objectives should be.... Later on, we began to appreciate that it does no good to help people off to a start of our choosing. They have to move under their own power and in a direction of their choice.... There was no intention to be autocratic here, just a mistaken notion of our professional role. The worker was seen as helper, the client as recipient—what was lacking was a full give and take between them. (Overton et al., 1957, p. 21)

Practitioner and family, according to Overton and Tinker, are working associates:

> As we go along, we review what we are doing together and look at the reasons for any gains or losses the family has made. To give the families a sense of "being in on the deal," we show them copies of letters we are writing to the court about them and parts of the case

record. In a few instances, parents have been invited to participate in inter-agency conferences about their situation. Also...we have asked our working associates to give us their observations on our social work methods. Here is a valuable source of learning what people find useful (or the reverse) about our techniques. (Overton et al., 1957, p. 22)

The concept of partnership has been rediscovered by modern practitioners working with the multiproblem family, for example Kinney, Haapala, and Gast (1981) and Kaplan (1986).

The practitioner who needs to see herself as a therapist rather than a helper working in partnership with the family may not be the best choice to work with multiproblem families, who tend to see efforts to therapize them as underscoring their inadequacies and further lowering their self-esteem and sense of competence. It seems especially important, with multiproblem families who have previously usually had experiences of being "treated" by a number of professional agencies, that the practitioner communicate, in Harry Stack Sullivan's famous phrase, that "we are all more human than otherwise."

Practitioner Role and Needs

Considered important also are the practice principles that the practitioner must feel more in control of herself and a chaotic family situation than the family does; that she be able to utilize both the authority of professional competence and the authority of her societal mandate; and that she "lend her vision," in Schwartz's (1971) phrase, to helping the family to understand their problems and to plan action. But none of these principles is the same as the practitioner's "coming on" to the family as an all-knowing expert who in effect takes over responsibility for the situation, and thereby negates the possibility of a partnership relationship with the family.

Need on the part of the practitioner to be an expert therapist may also lead to a misplaced faith in the potency of technological interventions, a belief that effective outcome depends only on the right technique. Schon (1983) writes of the "limits of rational technology" in all professions, in the sense that the practitioner must always creatively adapt and modify the technology to the needs of the unique practice situation. The practitioner who believes that skillful practice is a matter of "applying" techniques to clients will, in effect, be attempting to handle or manipulate people. This is more likely to inspire resentment and resistance than collaborative engagement.

Flexibility

Flexibility of the practitioner is usually mentioned in the literature as a necessary qualification for practitioners in all varieties of psychotherapy. In the context of work with the multiproblem family, it is perhaps better translated as the practitioner's comfort with being unsure—about both her own capacities and about the hole-riddled theory upon which she has to draw. The practitioner who is emotionally uncomfortable with the unavoidable uncertainty, ambiguity, and lacunae that characterize our repertory of knowledge and skills, will be driven to intellectual closure via choice of one "theory" or philosophy of helping that seems to offer all the answers. True-believer identification with a particular school of (unvalidated) thought relieves her not only of uncertainty but also of the requirement to think for herself in the case; she can substitute a prepackaged approach. We suspect that this is not helpful for any clients or families; with the multiproblem family, where it seems to be so important to help the family begin to engage themselves in their own problem solving, a mechanistic "book" approach is probably especially unhelpful. Further, because of the multiplicity of the problems encountered in these cases, a wide variety of interventions will probably be necessary, a variety not encompassed by any school of therapy to date.

Flexibility as a practice principle also seems to imply an awareness that for any specific problem there rarely is only one solution, or one problem-solving course of action. Many options for action usually exist, available both to the practitioner and to the family. An insistence on the rightness of the therapist's solutions, arising either from her own personal rigidity or from her dedication to a particular approach, deprives both practitioner and family of the opportunity to explore various ways of working on the family's problems and thus expanding their problem-solving skills. Papp (1976) has observed how frequently families surprise practitioners with the creativity and feasibility of their own solutions, better than any that had occurred to the professional. Overton and Tinker emphasized that the practitioner should give assurance to the family that they need not agree with her, and that it is safe for them to say "no" to the worker's ideas or suggestions (Overton et al., 1957, p. 68).

Persistence and Commitment

A sense of commitment and willingness to reach out persistently is another attitudinal practice principle highlighted by Overton and Tinker. The practitioner must be willing to "go all out and stay with your family" (Overton et al., 1957, p. 66). These authors point out that multiproblem families are often multiagency as well, in terms of their having been involved with many helping resources, not only because of the multiplicity of the families' problems but also because of the lack of commitment of the agencies to which the family has been exposed, and their readiness to close the case at the first sign of family resistance. "Persistent reaching out to distrustful, disorganized families is a 'must.' To do this requires conviction about our right to intrude, reduction of our own resistance, and more skill in meeting the resistance of the family" (Overton et al., 1957, p. 159).

ENGAGEMENT AND JOINING

Joining with a family, especially a suspicious and hostile family such as is often found under the category of multiproblem, does involve some technical practice principles. In a broader sense, however, effective engagement seems to depend more on personal characteristics and attitudes of the practitioner—on who she is—than on what she does. Put another way, the practitioner will tend to behave professionally in accordance with her attitudes and belief system.

In the beginning of the St. Paul Family Centered Project, the practitioners sent letters to referred families setting up appointments. The professionals assumed that the common courtesy of advising the families when they would come to call would be seen as a mark of the respect they wished to communicate. They found, however, that a letter served only to raise the family's apprehensions; and that it was better just to go to the home to ask when it would be convenient to come back. Often the workers were invited in right then. Apparently, at that time, few of the impoverished St. Paul families had telephones. It may be that a preliminary contact by telephone (which today are probably owned by many of even the poorest clients) would be less threatening than a letter, but better than showing up unannounced on the family's doorstep. Several approaches to preliminary contacts with multiproblem families need to be experimented with, and data collected and analyzed.

Use of Authority

A clear understanding of the concept of authority, and comfort in its use, are perceived as important practice principles. Overton and Tinker distinguish between the practitioner's societally mandated authority, and the authority of competence. The first relates to the community's authority and responsibility to intervene when family problems are seriously endangering the welfare of family members or of others in the community. The worker's representing this social authority makes her an "agent of social control," and Overton and Tinker were comfortable with that phrase. They felt they had not only the right, but that they owed a responsibility to the family, to be honest and direct with them about the problems that were concerning the community. When this was accompanied by recognition that the people in the family had been doing the best they could, in their own way, the great majority of the families accepted the workers' clear statement.

Overton and Tinker were aware, however, that the practitioner could carry out her role of social authority only through her personal "authority of competence." They point out that a probation officer, for example, who is also vested with social authority, has to rely on his authority of competence to effect changes in attitudes or behavior on the part of his clients (Overton et al., 1957, p. 138).

The practice principle related to engagement seems to be that the St. Paul practitioners were not defensive or embarrassed about their authority role, and did not see it as conflicting with a therapeutic role. In fact, their relaying the community's message that change had to occur in the family's problems was used creatively as the opening wedge in engagement, because it was accompanied by sensitive recognition of the family's feelings about the problem and community disapprobation, a willingness to listen to their side of the story, and an offer to work in partnership with them to make things better for the family so as to make unnecessary the pressure from the community. Kniskern and Gurman (1979) noted that research has indicated that the directness, clarity and self-confidence of the practitioner are related to good case outcome.

Engagement of Total Family

Implicit in the above principles of practice concerning engagement with the family, but needing to be explicated, is the idea that it is *the total family* with which the worker must engage. It is easier for the practitioner to engage only the mother, since she is more likely to be available at home during the day. This still obtains today, despite there being many mothers in the workforce. From the earliest family social work through modern family therapy, the practice principle is emphasized that it is important to involve all relevant members of the family, and particularly the father or father-surrogate if he is geographically accessible and plays any salient role at all. Overton and Tinker advise approaching the father directly, not via the mother (Overton et al., 1957, p. 99), as a way of behaviorally communicating his importance and also counteracting any impression that the children are considered the mother's responsibility only.

Today's family therapists would advise holding one interview with all members of the family, including very young children who cannot participate verbally, for diagnostic purposes at least. Some even advise including the family pets—because the way various family members interact with the dog, and the dog with them, can provide some understanding of family roles and patterns. Animals, in order to survive, indeed do learn to be quite good "diagnosticians" of their human owners and their interactional patterns. But all those people in the family old enough to share in the group problem solving, at whatever level is consonant with their ages and abilities, need to be included to the extent that their participation is relevant to the particular problem(s) being worked on. The practitioner, from her very first contact, behaviorally demonstrates her focus on the family as a group.

The practitioner may indeed be conceptually viewing the family as a system, but she needs to remain aware that what she is dealing with are individual people and their specific roles and relationships vis-a-vis each other and their individual and mutual outside worlds, the totality of which makes up the system. She is not working with a conceptual abstraction called "the family system." She is working with Mrs. Rodriquez and her live-in-boyfriend, and Mr. Rodriquez who lives elsewhere in town, and the children, and Mrs. Rodriquez's mother who tries to help out when she can, and the welfare worker, Juan's teacher, the boyfriend's probation officer, and so forth. Work with the multiproblem family is family centered in the sense that the family constitutes a major (but not the only) *work group* for problem solving. Group processes, and the combined strengths and capacity of the group, are tapped. To paraphrase Bertha Reynolds (1963), it is group work, really.

Three overriding principles appear to apply to the process of engagement. First, the worker relates to family members in such a way as to help them to begin to feel safe and supported. Sometimes verbally, but more usually behaviorally, she sends the message that she will not shame or hurt or blame or embarrass. She is careful to communicate the most exquisite courtesy and respect. She does not infantilize; she relates to strengths rather than inadequacies. She lets family members know that she appreciates and admires their struggle and the strength that that struggle shows. She assumes, and lets them know of her assumption, that even their conflicts do not necessarily mean evil intent on their parts toward each other, but rather frustrated and frustrating attempts by each member to make the others listen to his needs. She is aware that, if each member does not feel that the practitioner "hears" his needs, she will heighten their sense of threat and even, in some families, escalate the possibility of violence.

Second, the practitioner is honest and up-front about the community's concern that has necessitated her presence in their lives. She begins by this focus on the most immediate issue as perceived by the community, but then rapidly follows up that she is just as interested in what the family members see as their most pressing and important problems.

Third, she relates to them as a family work group, whose task, as a group, is to work with her in a relationship of partnership on finding ways to improve their situation.

DIAGNOSTIC ASSESSMENT

What is meant by diagnostic assessment is one of the most troubling aspects of practice for the practitioner, because it is so variously defined. It is a term that has long been used in individually oriented psychotherapies to mean clinical diagnosis of the personality, the quality of ego strengths, and the like. With the introduction of family therapy, it has now come to mean diagnosis or assessment of internal family dynamics and processes. The ecological approach expands assessment to include the nature of transactions of the family with its environing context.

Despite, or because of, these changing definitions of assessment, it is still difficult for the practitioner to get a "handle" on the kind of information she needs to gather for the purpose of assessment. She lacks an organizing focus for the overload of data concerning individuals, the family system, and their various environments. If the practitioner were to gather all the information about family processes that is recommended in family therapy texts, it would be weeks before intervention could actually begin—and even then, she could never understand fully the complexities of the interior of the family. And, as Reid observes, the environment is everything else in the case besides the people labeled clients (1985, p. 246): *What* aspects of the environment are relevant to assessment?

The Problem "Situation" as the Diagnostic Focus

Several writers see the concept of *system* as the organizing framework. Hartman and Laird, for example, recommend that the "unit of attention" should be "that complex ecological system which includes the individual, the family, the salient environment, and the transactional relationships among these systems" (1983, p. 69). But this is still impossibly complex: Which aspects, specifically, of that global Gordian knot shall the practitioner include in her "unit of attention"?

It may be useful to resurrect Sheffield's old idea (1937) about the *problem situation* being the focus of the case. The problems chosen for work, either mandated by the community or voluntarily chosen by the family, become the focal point of the case. As one set of problems is ameliorated, and practitioner and family move on to something else, the problem situation shifts and another kind of assessment is needed.

The advantage of Sheffield's concept of problem situation is that it offers the needed "handle" for selection and organization of data. It restricts the choice of information to be included to whatever is relevant to the *problem(s)* being worked on. Fascinating information about any of the subsystems involved in the problem situation—individual, interpersonal, or transactional—are deliberately excluded unless they have demonstrated relevance to the particular problem. The practitioner may note them and file them away in her head as possibly indicators of other problems that may need work later; but the principle of practice seems to be that assessment and intervention should remain focused on the problems contracted for work.

Overton and Tinker, although they do not seem to have been aware of Sheffield's contribution, also recommended that the problem situation should be the unit of attention or focal point for the case. They described the necessity for the practitioner to see the family:

> as a whole in relation to its social situation and in relation to the problems to be dealt with. But just how do you do this with a family? You cannot possibly appraise all the ties within the family and those connecting the family with the world around it. You can best examine those which have the most immediate bearing on the *key spots of trouble* [italics added] in the family. (Overton et al., 1957, p. 15)

Auerswald, in his classic article "Interdisciplinary Versus Ecological Approach" (1968), in effect spoke to this concept of the problem, with all its individual, family system, and environing context ramifications, being the focus of the case. He describes a mental health worker who adopts an "explorer" role, following the problem wherever it leads and using the information gathered in this focused journey as the basis and rationale for creative interventions.

Reid's task-centered model, developed for use with families as well as with individual problems, also seems to be expressing the same problem-focused emphasis in both assessment and intervention. This model first requires a clear contract with the client system about the changes desired in a very specific problem area. Given this agreement, clients and practitioner analyze the nature of the problem and what can be done to solve it—by the clients, the practitioner, and relevant others. Each party assumes responsibility for specific problem-solving tasks relevant to his or her role. Beyond the preliminary problem analysis, which is a joint process of both practitioner and clients, further information about forces that are maintaining the problem are developed through assessment of what Reid calls "obstacles" to the problem solving. Reid recommends that the kind of information gathered by the practitioner should be

> primarily determined *by the target problems* [italics added]. From these focal concerns, the practitioner branches out into other areas of the family's functioning and situation. The intent is not, as in some models of practice, to gather and sift a large body of information about these areas to serve as a basis for determining what the client's difficulties are. Rather, the practitioner's purpose is to secure information that will provide guidance in work with problems whose essential outlines have already been determined, not on the basis of what is "wrong" from a theoretical perspective but on the basis of what is troubling the family. (1985, p. 21)

Reid does not propose that the problems targeted for work are

> simply arrived at or fixed. They are constructed from complex, interrelated, and shifting realities. It is always a challenge to extract entities called "problems" from these realities. As the family's involvement and the practitioner's understanding grow and as events take place, original problem formulations may change. (1985, p. 40)

Similarly, Schon (1983) describes the essence of the practitioner's skill in any profession as that of extracting solvable problems from what he calls "messes." The practice situation facing the professional is a "mess" because it is characterized by "uncertainty, complexity, instability, uniqueness, and value conflict" (p. 17). Every profession brings to its own practice situations an armamentarium of practice principles and professional technology, of greater degrees of empirical validation (as in professions drawing from the physical sciences, such as engineering) or lesser degrees (as in the various psychotherapies). But the skill of professional practice is not in the mechanistic application of these principles and technology. Rather, according to Schon, the skill and the craftsmanship inhere in the professional's ability to first extract a solvable problem from the messy situation. He does this by the operation Schon calls "problem setting":

> When we set the problem, we select what we will treat as the "things" of the situation, we set the boundaries of our attention to it, and we impose upon it a coherence which allows us to say what is wrong and in what directions the situation needs to be changed. Problem setting is a process in which, interactively, we *name* the things to which we will attend and *frame* the context in which we will attend to them. (p. 40)

Work with the multiproblem family, so goes the practice principle, should be *family-focused*. The term is troublesome, however, in that it is frequently defined in very different ways. Too often, it is taken to mean that the focus of assessment needs to be on what is wrong with the family, and the focus of intervention on efforts to change the family's internal processes. Even those modern social work books and articles on family practice that highlight the ecological approach or attention to the environment, frequently spend many more pages on assessment of family processes and techniques oriented to change of those processes than do they to environmental assessment and intervention.

The definition of *family-focused* or *family-oriented* that we are using here is in terms of the family being perceived as a work group for problem solving. It may be that individuals may have to engage in trying to change some of their beliefs, attitudes or behaviors; or it may be that family subsystems or the system as a whole may have to change something in their processes of communication, boundary setting, power distribution, and the like—if such are identified as what Reid calls obstacles to problem solving.

Selective Use of Theory

Using the problem situation as the focus, or unit of attention, of the case frees the practitioner from having to use any particular theory as her lens and enables her to use theory selectively—as her tool and not her master. The practitioner does not have to force the data of the case into some theoretical Procrustean bed, but can differentially select, from the theories that are available, whatever helps to illuminate the nature of the problem and the obstacles to its resolution. The term *eclecticism* too often means a disorganized hodgepodge of various and often contradictory concepts and techniques from several theories, disorganized because there is no focal framework. Sheffield's "problem situation" as the focus, now brought up to date by writers such as Reid and Schon, offers the focus according to which the practitioner can "pull out of" various theories and approaches what seems relevant to understanding and resolution of the problem(s) selected for work. The practitioner is not really eclectic; *pluralistic* is a better term. She is freed from the necessity to choose one, and only one, theory or approach from what Havens in 1973 termed the "babble of voices" in the psychotherapies—a babble that, if anything, is even more confusingly noisy today. Theory does not straitjacket assessment and intervention; various theories are used only as they are relevant to the focal problem.

Involvement of Family in the Diagnostic Process

A family orientation means that the family is involved in assessment. Family and practitioner, together, agree on one or a few problems for immediate work; and, together, they try to construct a map of the problem situation. In Schon's terms, they "name" and they "frame" the components of the problem: what is making it up, what is keeping it going, what seem to be key elements to change to resolve it, and what factors are accessible to change efforts. These components of the problem-situation system may be in any one, or all, of the three subsystems involved: individual family members, family processes, or environing systems.

The worker does not start with a theoretical assumption as to the "location" of the problem, within or in the transactions among these three systems. Such assumptions, deductively drawn from theory without consideration of the actual data in the case, lead to such disastrous interventive efforts as the attempt to cure schizophrenia by therapizing the family, referred to in Chapter 6. Incorrect location of the problem will inevitably lead to dislocated targeting of intervention and, just as inevitably, to ineffectual outcome.

The practitioner may or may not agree with the accuracy of the assessment of the problem(s) by individuals or the group, and she is aware that their hurt and defensiveness may make them misperceive the nature of the problem or its actual location, for example, that their problems with the school over their child's behavior are "located" in the malevolent intent of school personnel. But she listens patiently and respectfully, not only as a way of getting the family engaged as a group in examining the problem, but also because she is truly interested in obtaining as polyocular a perspective as possible. She is aware that there are probably many Rashomon-like "truths" about the way the problem can be perceived, and that there is likely to be at least a germ of truth in the family's perceptions. The school personnel, for example, may indeed have treated the child and the parents in a disrespectful or hostile manner, although that is not the whole story of the problem. In other situations, the family's perceptions of the nature and location of the problem may be very accurately on target. The practitioner is aware that, because the family is living the problem, only they have access to certain crucial information about it.

Reframing the Problem

The practitioner's task is to work with the family on extracting out of the various assessments of the problem a "problem

definition" that renders it at least potentially workable. Watzlawick et al. (1974) point to how problems are maintained by
defining them in ways that render them unsolvable. Problem
definition involves locating key components of the problem in
"places" that make them accessible to change. Locating them,
for example, within the personalities of people or obscurely
conceptualized family processes moves them out of the reach of
those trying to change them.

What we are here calling definition of the problem is referred to, in family therapy parlance, as the technique of reframing or positive connotation. Problem definition goes
beyond a technique, however; it is the essential first step in making the problem *seem* workable so that it *can* be workable. The
problem definition, and the change goals that emanate from it,
are better framed in terms of positive actions than in decrease
of negatives. This is a practice principle established by the behavioral therapies. It is easier for people to think of making
some small constructive behavioral changes than it is for them to
suddenly stop a habitual behavior pattern. It is important that
the definition of the problem, put together by the practitioner
out of the various definitions she has heard from the family, be
couched in terms that are face-saving for the people involved,
yet not so diametrically different from their definitions that they
will reject the reframing effort.

Parsimony

Reid proposes that his task-centered model for practice
with families is "more data-centered than most in its emphasis
on spelling out problems and goals in terms of specific identifiable behaviors, beliefs, interactions, and the like" (1985, p. 84).
Reid goes on to articulate what we suggest is a very important
principle of assessment, one that is directly contrary to the current trend toward more and more convoluted theoretical diagnostic assumptions. He insists that the rule of parsimony be
observed in assessment, that the data be "organized and analyzed with a minimum of assumptions"—and that "simple, 'obvious' explanations [be] favored over complex interpretations
based on notions of hidden processes" (1985, p. 84).

Extrafamily Elements

A principle of assessment is that the existence of extra-family elements of the problem be very deliberately examined. When the practitioner is with the family, she sees the family and not a vague environment outside: The risk therefore exists that she will see the problem only in terms of the people in front of her. In work with the multiproblem family, where so often extra-family deficits and pathogens are part of the problems with which the family is burdened, it is especially important to take special care that these environmental elements be included in the assessment. Use of an eco-map as recommended by Hartman and Laird (1983, pp. 158–169)—or as suggested by Sheffield many years ago!—can be a very useful device in that it requires the practitioner to develop information about how environing systems may be part of the problem or, alternately, represent resources for its amelioration.

Overton and Tinker emphasized strongly that assessment must include a careful appraisal of the strengths and resources in the situation. Because both practitioner and family are naturally focusing on the difficulties and what is wrong in the situation, it is difficult for them to give equal time and attention to what is right: the strengths and resources that may be tapped for problem solving, individually, intrafamilially, and/or environmentally. Perhaps construction of *two* eco-maps would be useful. One map would diagram the elements that are involved in the creation, exacerbation, or maintenance of the problem; a twin eco-map would detail as carefully the strengths and resources that are presently available or that might be constructed (for example, development of a support group).

The family may well be able to be involved in development of these eco-maps, which would have the advantage of very concretely naming and framing the problem for them in its constituent elements. When any of us, not only multiproblem families, are caught up in worrisome problems, it is commonly very difficult to see the forest for the trees: Participation in making the two eco-maps helps the family to understand better what they are dealing with and suggests change targets and strategies.

Assessment and Therapeutic Approach

The last point bears repeating as another principle of practice: The assessment, whether verbal or in diagrammatic form, should have clear implications for change efforts. Assessment cannot be merely an exercise in "psychologese" for the practitioner; it cannot exist in isolation from change goals and the strategy of change. It should be parsimonious in that it includes only information relevant to the selected problem; and it should be sharply focused on that problem. It will probably need to be changed as new events occur that become part of the situation, or as obstacles to problem solving emerge that represent other problem-maintaining forces; but these modifications can be seen by family and practitioner as elaborations and corrections of the original assessment.

Another way of looking at assessment that is, however, not inconsonant with the above approach and principles, although it is directed more to the practitioner's understanding than understanding of the problem shared with the family, is the *transactional risk model* of Cicchetti and Rizley (1981), which particularly pertains to child abuse and neglect. These authors, in a manner somewhat similar to Lewin's "field of forces" (1951), suggest analyzing the risk factors in the family versus the protective factors. Risk, or vulnerability, factors can include long-term conditions or attributes that serve to potentiate maltreatment. These can include biological factors (e.g., a child with a difficult temperament or health problems that make child-rearing difficult); historical (e.g., a parent with a history of being maltreated); psychological (a history of poor impulse control in various areas, or the presence of psychosis); and/or sociological (high stress of the family's social situation, poor neighborhood, inadequate social networks, etc.). Shorter-term risk factors may include loss of a job, physical illness, legal difficulties, marital problems, or the child's transition into a more difficult developmental period. Counterbalancing these risk factors are protective or buffering factors. Again, these are seen as being long term (e.g., good health, intelligence, the parent's history of past good parenting, a good relationship between the parental partners), or short term (the parent's finding a desired job, periods of marital harmony, the child's transition out of a difficult developmental period).

Whatever the framework used, the practice principle seems to be that the practitioner's assessment must include an analytic comparison of pathogenic factors against problem-ameliorating factors. Overton and Tinker, in their simpler language, called this a "balance sheet" that seeks to answer the questions, "What's the trouble? How come? What can be done about it?" (Overton et al., 1957, p. 81).

GOAL SETTING AND CONTRACT

As noted earlier, with the involuntary family for whom the community has mandated intervention because of serious problems, the family has the right to know the reason for the practitioner's entrance into their lives, and the practitioner has an obligation to state clearly the problems the community sees and the changes it requires.

However, it also seems to be not only a practice principle, but also a truism, that people will work only on issues and toward goals that seem important to them. The practitioner's task and skill in the early contacts is in getting family members engaged in a consideration of what seem to them the most important changes *they* wish to see made. Haapala and Kinney observed that "if the clients are not progressing, frequently it is because we are not working on the problem of highest priority for them. Usually, it is an assessment issue...not a motivational issue" (1979, p. 253). These authors warn that professionals "have the potential to elicit more feelings of helplessness and inadequacy [in the family]. Taking too much responsibility for restructuring and redefining how their lives ought to be can make the family less certain and more confused, and even less able to work constructively" (1979, p. 253).

Overton and Tinker, in describing plateaus in progress when the family seems to stop working and loses motivation, made the same point 20 years earlier. They suggested that the practitioner has been "expecting [the family] to move ahead too fast and [has] taken too active a part in deciding on next steps"

(Overton et al., 1957, p. 120). They recommend that the practitioner gear her expectation for the family "a little beyond, but not too far ahead of what they expect of themselves" (p. 121).

Provision of Material Resources

Very often, the first change the family wants is having some concrete needs met. If possible, the practitioner attempts to help them to get these provisions for themselves, with the practitioner playing a brokerage role. In many situations, however, and especially early in a case, the family cannot yet do this; and indeed access to the resources they need may well be blocked by ungiving environmental systems. Then the practitioner must undertake advocacy on behalf of the family.

We have earlier alluded to the symbolic meaning provision of material needs can have for family members. It is also a means for the practitioner to "put her money where her mouth is," that is, to demonstrate by action and not just words that she has not only the intention but the capability to be helpful to the family. Many multiproblem families may need this demonstration by action before they can really begin to trust the practitioner and be willing to work with her, beyond being only the recipient of the resources she obtains for them. The other rationale for early attention to the family's request for concrete help is that the family is probably quite correct in their assessment of their needs: Very pragmatically, getting the electricity turned back on or emergency food on the table must realistically take precedence over all other issues. The family cannot focus on other problems when they are hungry or cold, or worried where the next rent payment will come from.

One reason for the failure of some projects with multiproblem families may have been that the practitioners were more interested in therapeutic counseling concerning inner feelings of the clients than they were in their clients' material needs (Brown, 1968). This unfortunately still seems to be the situation today: In 1987, Pelton observed that agencies serving the multiproblem family still tend to focus on counseling, although the families express a need for concrete services (1987, p. 438).

Clarity of Contract

Maluccio and Marlow (1974), Seabury (1976), and Compton and Galaway (1984), among others, have written of the practice principle, with any client system, of negotiating a clear agreement or contract on the problems to be worked on and the goals to be sought. The contract should also contain a clear and very specific delineation of the tasks for which each participant agrees to assume responsibility—family members or subsystems or the family as a whole, the practitioner and/or other members of the intervention team, and extrafamily resources. The multiproblem family perhaps especially needs the clarity provided by a contract (not necessarily written, although this may be helpful in certain cases); the family may also need the basis for accountability that the contract represents. It is a practice principle that accountability under the contract applies to all parties participating in it. The practitioner is to be held to account for how well she carried out her part of the bargain, as much as the family is accountable for their responsibilities. Setting up, in advance, a "report card" session, in which some time is devoted to practitioner and family each giving the other an evaluation of how well each has been holding to the contract, can be helpful. To be not only permitted, but encouraged, to criticize the professional is a new experience for the multiproblem family and serves to foster the sense of partnership that the worker is striving to achieve. Most families, of course, will be overly polite rather than critical, especially if they have come to like and trust the practitioner; but they probably will still give her some important information about what they are perceiving as helpful and not helpful. From the practitioner's end, report card sessions concerning the family's carrying out of its responsibilities can help her to identify emotional, cognitive, skill-deficit, or systemic barriers to progress.

INTERVENTION

A major practice principle concerning intervention with the multiproblem family is that the strategy of intervention, and actual interventive activities and techniques, must be hand-tailored and fine-tuned to the needs of each individual family, as indicated by the ongoing problem assessment. There is no overall interventive plan that is applicable to the needs of every family. Again, the practitioner who is the disciple of a particular school of therapy will find herself very constricted in the interventive options available to her.

In addition to "fitting" the problem, the interventions chosen must "fit" the family's ethnic or other culture, as well as their values and belief system. If the intervention is perceived by the family as too alien to the family style, they will reject it. In some situations, the practitioner may identify that something in the family's values or belief system is part of the problem and needs to be changed. If so, it seems to be important as a principle of practice that she be straightforward about this, on the assumption that people cannot be permanently changed in terms of closely held values and beliefs without their knowledge and against their wills. In some cases, it may be that a counter-paradoxical delineation of the dilemma the family has created for itself between its values and the goals it wants will clarify the impasse that the family must resolve. But the counterparadox does not resolve the dilemma; it merely brings its existence dramatically to the family's attention, and the family must then make some decision about how to resolve it. If its values or beliefs are in conflict with its goals, the family will have to modify one or the other.

Interventive Creativity

It is interesting that the *Casework Notebook* of Overton, Tinker, and associates devotes very little attention to techniques of intervention. They talk more about partnership, engaging the family in work on their problems, and staying close to the family's goals for themselves. They seem to assume that, if these basics are in place, practitioner and family together could come up with a variety of different and creative ways to bring about change in the problem situation. Haapala and Kinney later express the same view:

> We emphasize compassion as opposed to deification of procedures. Over-technologizing is becoming more common in our

profession and sometimes results in the "handling" of clients. Handling a client refers to the practice of going rigidly by a prescribed therapy rule at the expense of the client. The relationship is most important and we are not likely to learn how to "do" therapeutic relationships according to any set procedures. (1979, p. 254)

These authors term *process skills* the practitioner's behavioral expression of the attitudes we discussed earlier. They contrast this with the use of techniques in therapy, which they see as being

much more separate from an individual's style. They are obvious and cumbersome, such as charting, family meetings, and family sculpturing. In this way, we may think of process skills as techniques to do away with techniques and to get us down to a more basic and human level of interaction. (Haapala & Kinney, 1979, p. 256)

In the view of the authors of the present volume, there may be a place for such activities as family sculpture, and certainly for family meetings in work with multiproblem families. But we tend to agree with the thrust of the practice principle being enunciated by Haapala and Kinney, that helping families to change their problematic situation is not a matter of finding the right magical technique or of following slavishly the approach of some therapeutic school of thought. We would suggest a practice principle that the practitioner *should* know as many techniques as possible, but she cannot escape her professional responsibility to assess when and how they should be used; and that use of techniques cannot substitute for use of herself.

There are probably quite a few different interventions that might bring about the same result in a given practice situation. The practitioner needs to have the personal comfort, and the administrative freedom, to experiment with a variety of interventive options and be ready to "switch gears" when feedback from the case indicates that something different is needed.

Problem-Specific Intervention

It is not contradictory to Haapala and Kinney's point to suggest that a variety of behavioral interventions may be extremely useful with these families concerning intrafamily conflict, child discipline, and other issues (see, for example,

Gordon, 1970; Thomas & Carter, 1971; Alexander & Parsons, 1973; Mash, Handy, & Hamerlynck, 1974; Gilbert, 1976; Beezley, Martin, & Alexander, 1976; Jeffrey, 1976; Jacobson & Margolin, 1979; Stuart, 1980; Gambrill, 1977, 1981). In fact, Haapala and Kinney heavily utilize behavioral interventions. The advantage of behavioral approaches is (in addition to the empirical support that many of them have garnered) that they are specific and concrete.

Specificity and concreteness of the approach appears to fit the style of many multiproblem families much more than does vague discussion. Another advantage is that a behavioral approach to relationship issues "locates" the problem outside of the personalities of the people involved, and relates to behavior rather than to character. Frequently it also moves the problem from its location inside one person (for example, the rebellious child) to the interaction between the child and parent(s). The practitioner needs to develop specific information about the frequency, severity, antecedents and consequences of unwanted behavior before instituting a behavioral intervention; and this in itself sometimes helps family members to see the problematic behavior in more perspective. The practitioner, however, needs to be sensitive to the value orientation of the family: Some families, for example, are just not comfortable with rewarding a child (positive reinforcement) for behavior that he "ought" to engage in. In such instances, the practitioner must be flexible enough to switch to another interventive option.

Teaching of Skills

Some of the obstacles to amelioration of family problems may be identified as skill deficits in any of a number of areas, ranging from illiteracy, to lack of knowledge of child development and skill in parenting, to communication skills, to conflict negotiation, to lack of assertiveness, to difficulty in handling an interview for a job or at the welfare office. If people cannot handle well these roles or tasks because they do not know how, it is obvious that the intervention needs to be focused on helping them to learn. The practitioner may serve as the direct teacher of some of these skills. For others, a homemaker may be placed in the home temporarily, or the resources of the community utilized for special programs oriented to skill development in specific areas.

Changing Family Dynamics

Although family therapy techniques are appropriate with the multiproblem family *if the emerging data of the case indicate* that change in family organization and/or processes is needed, these techniques tend, in general, to be less sharply focused than behavioral interventions. Also in contrast to behavioral approaches, family therapy interventions are often based on the assumption of covert, undemonstrable, internal systemic processes. The task of the practitioner using family therapy approaches is, first, to demonstrate empirically (that is, by data from the case) that specific dysfunctions of family organization or process are involved in the problem in a major way; and, second, to adapt family therapy interventive techniques to make them more sharply focused and specific to the identified problem.

Environmental Intervention

As part of her ecological stance, a family social work practitioner is expected to be expert in her knowledge of community institutions and resources. This includes information about the informal as well as formal structure of community agencies, for example, that the worker on rotating intake duty on Tuesdays at the mental health center sees his job as screening out as many applicants as possible. The family member being referred is then advised to contact the mental health agency on any day except Tuesday.

Because environmental intervention is usually such a major, needed part of the total interventive strategy with the multiproblem family, the practitioner needs to have highly developed skills in brokerage, mediation, and advocacy (Grinnell, 1973; Grinnell et al., 1981). Hoffman and Long (1969) mention another environmental-intervention skill not often cited in the literature, that of cutting out of the action or keeping at bay an unhelpful community professional.

The experience of the Family Life Improvement Project in the 1960s showed that in a community with inadequate and disordered services, family and practitioner could make little headway against the family's problems (Geismar 1971; Geismar, Lagay, Wolock, Gerhart, & Fink, 1972; Geismar & Lagay, 1985). The family and the practitioner have to have resources with which to work. The practitioner has a responsibility to point to lacks and dysfunctions in the community service system, and to participate in the process of community change, but she cannot, alone, "cure" community or societal systemic pathology.

Given, however, the basic minimum of community resources and a fairly well-functioning service-delivery system, a major role of the practitioner is what Overton and Tinker called the coordinator of services. This seemed, however, to go beyond mere coordination: The worker served as a central conduit for services the family, or its individual members, were receiving from other agencies. We return to this issue in Chapter 8, where administrative arrangements for service to the multiproblem family are addressed. Here, in terms of our discussion of practice principles, it can be suggested that the role of bridging the gap between family and community is an important element of the practitioner's role repertory. Kaplan describes the "mutual withdrawal" between the family and the community:

> When a family is failing and feels rejected and ostracized, it withdraws by behaving in a manner that is unacceptable to society. It is then rejected again, and the cycle continues. Society and its institutions withdraw from the multiproblem family, not only because it is failing, but also because it appears to be unresponsive to help. When society labels a family as unreachable and impossible and withdraws its involvement, chronicity is the tragic result. (1986, p. 5–6)

The practitioner stands in a bridging location between the family and the community, aware of what Schwartz (1971) called the reciprocal need of each for the other, and helping each to reach out to the other.

Multiproblem families often are so fearful of approaching community agencies that control the resources they need, based on their past experience with these facilities, that they need help and coaching from the worker in the skills of negotiating these complex systems and representing themselves effectively. Assertiveness training and role playing are two interventive techniques that may prove helpful.

A major principle of practice involves the practitioner's finding or developing other helping systems for the family. Extended family is represented high on this list, unless there is clear evidence that their influence is deleterious. Even in very deteriorated neighborhoods, neighbors are often an important source of help and support especially for crisis situations. The practitioner may work to create a support network for individuals in the family, or subsystems, or the family as a whole.

Timing and Pace

Timing and pace are important practice principles in work with any client system, but may be especially important in practice with multiproblem families. Family members may have severe deficits in skills, and/or be so demoralized and frightened that they can make progress only in very small steps. Goals of change need to be set up as minute enough that the individuals or family almost cannot fail, and can thus be reinforced by their small successes. The practitioner needs to be sensitive to the meaning to the clients of these success experiences, subjectively and emotionally, as well as being aware that this does represent progress. She cannot be so focused on the final goals of improvement of instrumental functioning that she fails to appreciate that many small incremental successes may be needed before family members really begin to believe that they have the capacity to change whatever in their situation is within their power.

Intervention-Plan Design

The practitioner is following *the data of the case*, not some theory, in constructing with the family the plan of intervention. She is carefully attuned to feedback from the data of the case itself as to whether a particular problem-solving effort is "working." Families get stuck in their efforts to change their situations or themselves, and become frightened and feel helpless and inadequate. Then the practitioner needs to process, with them, what Reid (1985) calls these obstacles to task completion and problem solving. (Reid's task-centered approach, it is suggested, although designed for use with many kinds of family problems, is highly relevant to the needs of the multiproblem family.) The overriding practice principle concerning intervention appears to be that the family itself is involved in the design of the interventive plan as much as possible, rather than being the recipients of the practitioner's therapy. The family has responsibility for its part of the interventive strategy that is arrived at. Throughout, the concept of partnership means that practitioner and family are working together.

In Chapter 8 we present some ideas about the arrangements that appear to be necessary to have in place, both administratively in the practice agency and in relationships with other community services, to ensure that the principles of good practice with the multiproblem family are implemented. In that final chapter we also discuss briefly some considerations for the agency that is conducting research on its practice with these families.

Chapter 8

Research and Administrative Considerations

RESEARCH CONSIDERATIONS

The research evidence that exists is suggestive that in-home, intensive services to multiproblem families, that are conducted in consonance with the practice principles outlined in Chapter 7, can be effective for a large proportion of multiproblem families (Geismar & Ayres, 1959b; Lagey & Ayres, 1962; Geismar & Krisberg, 1967). This is still suggestive, however, and there is available insufficient well-done outcome research to warrant a definitive conclusion. Even more lacking is research that attempts to integrate measurement of case outcome with examination of process variables. Admittedly, designing such research is methodologically difficult. The alternative, however, seems to be a recourse to faith that the principles of practice wisdom discussed in Chapter 7 are indeed valid. Without empirical evidence, a degree of risk exists that these principles may be invalid, resulting in futile service at best to families desperately in need of effective help, or at worst the well-meaning infliction of further damage.

The families cannot afford service offered without the protection of a built-in research component, any more than they could afford to take an experimental new medical drug or treatment without close research monitoring and their informed consent. This means that agencies offering service to multi-problem families cannot afford to construct or continue programs that do not routinely include a strong and well-designed research component. There is a serious ethical issue involved. It is understandable that service agencies, out of their concern for the plight of these families, wish to rush into action programs. But the question arises as to whether they have an ethical right to do so without examining, in an objective fashion and according to canons of scientific research, the effects of their programs. If the programs are not effective, the families will have failed to receive the help to which they are entitled. At the worst, they may be further damaged by well-meaning efforts; there is evidence of deteriorative iatrogenic effect for some—small, but still too large—proportion of recipients of all varieties of psychotherapy and counseling.

Cicchetti and Toth, in describing the built-in research in their program oriented specifically to young children of high-risk families, discuss the unfortunate schism that has existed for years between practitioners and researchers. They point out that clinicians have perceived their role as being in the medical model, emulating physicians who treat organic disorders. In contrast, most researchers come from academic settings and emulate, not the physician, but the physicist; and they have tended to apply to clinical areas research methodology developed for the physical sciences. These authors, however, believe the picture is changing, at least as far as the relationship between academic and clinical psychology is concerned:

> Fortunately, in recent years a confluence of factors has lessened the separation of disciplines...so as to allow for the combining of the skills of the academic psychologist and the clinician in the person of the developmental psychopathologist. We believe that the use of research in normal developmental processes, in combination with work with emotionally disturbed children, can be integrated to guide a theory of intervention with dysfunctional families. (Cicchetti & Toth, 1987, p. 2)

We hope that it will come to pass that the definition of a modern and high-quality service agency will begin to include the requirement that research concerning its program be a routine and expected part of its function, that is, that testing of the presently accepted practice wisdom and development of new knowledge will be seen as objectives coequal with service delivery.

The research that is reported about services to multi-problem families too often is not well designed or implemented. Minimal requirements include the use of a control, or at least an appropriate contrast, group; well-designed instrumentation that captures reliably and validly objective measures of the improvement or deterioration of the identified problem(s); and gathering of outcome data not only at case closing but additionally at an appropriate follow-up period after the cessation of service.

The research process with multiproblem families should also define and apply operational criteria for accepting client families for service (Chapter 2 lays out criteria for evaluating outcome that are equally applicable to decision making in the screening-in process). The research endeavor should, furthermore, furnish formative (providing continuous feedback for program management) as well as summative (final program outcome) evaluations. Systems analysis, addressing the impact of the special service on the network of community agencies, should also be included in the research program.

The expenditure of time, effort, staff resources, and money that is involved in study planning, instrumentation, and the gathering and analysis of data is wasted unless these research activities are competently carried out. It is not sufficient, therefore, for an agency to call "research" any kind of data-gathering operation. It would be a better expenditure of resources to call in a research consultant to help the agency plan well-designed research.

Service agencies, and often funding resources, are usually more interested in implementing what sounds like an exciting new service program than are they in studying whether and how it works. Solnit observes that "policy makers are always hoping to find some intervention which will serve as an inexpensive, one-shot 'immunizing' agent" (from the foreword   Provence & Naylor, 1983, p. viii).

There is reason to believe that the numbers of high-risk families are growing, resulting from the continuation of damaging economic policies, the neglect of the inner cities, lack of housing, racism, and a host of other societal factors. Multi-problem families, whose major problem is frequently their poverty, are found in every racial group and every part of the country, but racial minorities and inner-city residents are disproportionately represented. Concerning black families alone, the National Urban League was reported by *The New York Times* (Bernstein, 1988) as citing statistics for 1987 that "25 percent of all black households are affected by crime; the rates of drug use, crime and violent deaths are exponentially higher among blacks than whites; and 40 percent of black children are raised in fatherless homes. The rates of teenage pregnancy, infant mortality, and youth unemployment mark the continued deterioration of the old ghettos." This news story quotes sociologist William Julius Wilson as stating, "After [Martin Luther] King's death, little attention was paid to the growth of a ghetto underclass that was particularly vulnerable to changes in the economy, such as the periodic recessions that led to massive unemployment" (Bernstein, 1988, p. 1).

The New York State Department of Health reported that one out of every 61 babies born in all five boroughs of New York City in December 1987 carried antibodies to the AIDS virus; and in the especially deteriorated neighborhoods of the Bronx, the ratio was 1 in 43 infants (*New York Times*, 1988, p. 6). The AIDS antibodies were transmitted by the mothers, and it is estimated that 40% of the children may develop the lethal disease, in addition to the probability that their mothers will die at some time during their early childhoods. The "welfare hotels" of not only large urban centers, but also suburban communities, are exploding with homeless families, an increasing proportion of whom were full-time employed working class people before they lost their apartments or their jobs. No family can be "functional" while living in the degrading circumstances of a welfare hotel, with no cooking facilities, nowhere for children to play, nowhere for the parent(s) to get away from the cranky whining of several children cooped up in one room, and often surrounded by drug dealing and violence.

These are additional problems that did not confront the multiproblem families or their practitioners of earlier years. The numbers of adolescent mothers have increased, some proportion of whom have severe deficits in parenting or household management skills and do not have effective help from extended families or the usual community institutions. The pressure of the sheer number and the urgency of these problems makes it understandable that agencies feel driven to implement action programs as quickly as possible, and that they are attracted to any new approach or model that seems to promise effectiveness. We suggest again, however, that they cannot afford to do so without the essential component of research.

It may seem to some of our readers that our admittedly rudimentary framework of practice principles with multiproblem families offers such promise. It may. It should not be implemented, however, by agencies that are looking for an immediate "answer." It should be tried out by agencies who recognize as much as they do their responsibility to help their desperate clients, an equal responsibility to test the framework of practice principles toward results of either their invalidation or their improvement and refinement. The agency must be willing to take the chance involved in experimentation, knowing that efficacy cannot be guaranteed in advance, and with the attitude that such experimentation is a challenging and exciting opportunity. It would of course be tragic to fail with the families, tragic for them and for the serving agency. But whatever the outcome results—success, failure, or something in between—they would still be an important contribution to professional practice, and assurance of protection against well-meaning but ineffectual service for the next cohort of clients.

There are more pragmatic reasons, to be sure, for an agency to be as research-minded as it is service-minded, beyond a scholarly interest in expanding knowledge. These are usually referred to under the heading of accountability. Cicchetti and Toth, writing of their program focused on abused and neglected children and their families, observed that

> in times of fiscal austerity, human services in general, including social and psychological services to maltreated children and their families, come under the scrutiny of budget-conscious govern-

ment administrators and legislators. Increasingly, service providers are asked to document the beneficial impact of their service efforts. The inability to provide documentation through evaluation research reports and the like makes the services in question more vulnerable to the budget-cutter's knife. (1987, p. 8)

Ironically, funding sponsors of intervention projects tend to put research studies of the effectiveness of the projects in a classic "catch-22" position. They insist on rigorous evaluation of results as a condition of funding; but—as is increasingly the case today—when funds for the whole endeavor are curtailed, it is the research component that must be reduced or eliminated. The failure, then, to engage in rigorous evaluation is cited as a reason for refusal to lend further support to the project.

ADMINISTRATIVE ARRANGEMENTS

There probably is not any one ideal administrative arrangement for delivery of service to multiproblem families. A number of different agency structures, foci, and auspices have been reported in the literature.

Whatever the form of the administrative structuring, we can suggest that it should be such that certain objectives have a reasonable chance of being achieved. Primary among these objectives is reduction of the confusion and frustration families experience when they attempt to deal with the disorganized and uncoordinated mass of services that characterize the service delivery system in many communities:

Few programs possess the integrated resources needed to impact on these dysfunctional [family] systems. Rather, it is more common for families such as these to receive a host of services offered through various community agencies. In fact, it is not uncommon for a single family to have various members simultaneously involved with individual therapists in different agencies.... This lack of cohesion among treaters often contributes to the overall disorganization of the family system. Unless coordinated, focused services are made available to these multi-risk families, an immense cost in terms of both human suffering and depletion of community resources will continue to occur. (Cicchetti & Toth, 1987, p. 8)

One administrative arrangement that seeks to decrease the exposure of the multiproblem family to a disorganized service-delivery system is that which centralizes as wide a variety of services as are realistically feasible under the auspices of one agency. Such a structure characterizes many of the programs affiliated with the National Center for Clinical Infant Programs. These programs, found in most states of the nation, are often affiliated either with a hospital or a university research program on child development. They are staffed with a team of medical and psychiatric personnel, psychologists and other professionals in child development, early childhood education specialists, social workers, and frequently also paraprofessionals such as homemakers. Even though no agency can of course offer every needed service, the centralization of many kinds of help under the roof of one auspice reduces to some extent the risk of further splintering and disorganization of the high-risk family. A degree of centralization also characterizes programs operating out of settlement houses and community service centers.

Comprehensive programs are quite expensive, but may be more cost-effective than duplication of services in the uncoordinated and often contradictory fashion that characterizes many communities. The costs alone are sizable when many agencies repeatedly open and close the same case around recurrent crises, because each agency's lack of outreach and follow-through with the individual or family are correlated with the clients' failures to continue.

An advantage of centralized programs is that they usually have a multidisciplinary staff, based on their recognition that multiproblem families often need more than what any one profession or its practitioner can deliver, but rather call for the cumulative knowledge and specific skills of a variety of disciplines.

Lacking a structure for centralization of delivery of multiple services, an agency offering service to multiproblem families will have to work with other community agencies whose services the family also needs. (In the most centralized and comprehensive program, this necessity of course still exists but to a lesser extent: Family members must still interact with the welfare system, school system, legal authorities, etc.)

It seems to be crucial that an agency serving multiproblem families be in a position to exert some reasonable control of the case vis-à-vis other agencies involved with the family. Families can be lost between the cracks created by the competitive territoriality or lack of coordination of community agencies. Because these families tend to be multi-agency as well as multi-problem, they may be known to a number of agencies simultaneously, often without each agency knowing what the others are doing, and sometimes with different agencies trying to take the family down diametrically opposing paths.

Prior to the initiation of the St. Paul Family Centered Project, six years of work went into achieving a clear agreement with other community agencies that the project social worker would assume the role of coordinator and conduit concerning all other services being rendered to the family. This was necessary to avoid the family's being confused by contradictory directives or advice from other agencies, such as the public welfare agency, child welfare, probation and parole, or mental health facilities. If the child welfare agency, for example, felt they had to remove a child because of continuing neglect or abuse, they agreed to at least confer with the project worker before taking action.

In effect, the other community agencies agreed to give the project social worker a chance to see what she could do before taking authoritative action, and to collaborate with her on a plan of overall service to the family. In addition, the role of the project practitioner was agreed upon by all the community agencies involved as the coordinator and "switchboard" of all services to the case. It is important to note that this was a role with considerably more power than the case-manager role found (sometimes appropriately) in many agencies today; an agency today that tries to replicate the St. Paul experience would have to ensure that the practitioner assigned to the case has a great deal more input and authority than does the usual case manager concerning what services the family is receiving from other community agencies.

Our framework of practice principles is based on an assumption that a not necessarily optimal but at least adequate level of services exists in the community. Both the family and the practitioner must have resources with which to work. If the level of service in the community is seriously substandard, it becomes much less likely that a family in need of such resources can appreciably improve its functioning. The "fault" then is not the family's nor the practitioner's, but rather that of the dysfunctioning of the community service system.

The Family Life Improvement Project of the 1960s (Geismar et al., 1972, pp. 70 and following; Geismar & Lagey, 1985) offers, in fact, an example of how referral of clients to inferior community resources can have a more *negative* impact on client functioning than no referral at all (especially when this project is compared with others using identical outcome measures).

It would be ideal if the agency specializing in serving multiproblem families could obtain an agreement that its families would be given priority consideration for relatively scarce community services, as long as this priority did not violate legal eligibility requirements or basic fairness to other applicants— for example, priority admission to alcohol and drug abuse inpatient or outpatient services, or consideration for low-cost housing. Although all individuals or families applying for these scarce services need them, we would argue that the need of the multiproblem family is more desperate and the repercussions more severe if the family cannot obtain the help it needs in a timely fashion.

The administrative structure, and the culture, of the agency specializing in the multiproblem family need to be such as to support the implementation of the practice principles outlined in Chapter 7. An agency climate characterized by superfluous bureaucratic straitjacketing of professional staff would not permit the practitioner the flexibility and right to make her own professional decisions called for in the practice-principles framework. Private agencies can be as heavily bureaucratized as public ones, so the choice of where the program for multiproblem families shall be lodged depends more on the characteristics of specific agencies—although it is probably more likely that, in most communities, private agencies will be less subject than a state agency to bureaucratic pressures. The private agency may also be less vulnerable to political influence than state-administered facilities, in many communities at least.

Also inconsonant with the framework is an agency insistence on loyal adherence to one therapeutic approach rather than pluralistic diversity.

If several professional disciplines are to staff the agency so that it can expand the pool of knowledge and skill available to families, the agency will probably have to do a great deal of "homework" on its own group processes. A real team approach can operate only in a group atmosphere where differences are respected, and where ongoing attention is paid to what is happening in the group process of the team. In some health and mental health facilities that supposedly use a team approach, the term is a misnomer. Frequently one person, either the most powerful in terms of personal characteristics or because he represents the dominant profession (usually medical) is the decision maker, with team members relegated to carrying out his directives. Or sometimes team process breaks down over lack of clear communication and territorial infighting among professional or other subsystems. It should be noted that these dysfunctional group processes also characterize some multiproblem families; in order to learn how to help the families, the agency administration and staff may need to practice, first, on their own dysfunctional group processes.

The St. Paul Family Centered Project utilized only one practitioner for a case. It is possible, however, that a small team of professionals and paraprofessionals would offer some advantages over the lone practitioner—so long as the team is not so large as to confuse the family, and assuming that the team has done its own homework concerning its group processes as suggested above. (See, for example, Brieland, Briggs, & Leuenberger, 1973; Eiduson, 1964; Kane, 1975; Sherwood & Hoylman, 1977; Compton & Galaway, 1984, for discussion of use of teams.)

Paraprofessionals, particularly if they are from the same ethnic, cultural, and/or socioeconomic group as the clients, have reportedly been used with multiproblem families advantageously (Epstein & Shainline, 1974; Kaplan, 1986, pp. 49–50). Proper use of a paraprofessional, however, in our judgment, does not consist of dumping a caseload on her with instructions to "do something" about difficult cases of multiproblem families. The lower salaries paid to paraprofessionals will not pay off to the agency in terms of effective service under these conditions. With supportive supervision, and membership on a team, the paraprofessional may offer dimensions of help to the family that cannot be provided by the professionals.

In some communities, development of a new agency devoted to serving the multiproblem family may be more feasible then lodging the program in an already-existing facility. This was the path chosen by the St. Paul Family Centered Project, which not only received grant funding but also staff resources in the form of its workers being "loaned" to the project by their employing community agencies which continued to pay their salaries. This route has another advantage in the "halo effect" that is likely to attend a new enterprise. This was indeed a powerful factor in activating the St. Paul Family Centered Project. However, its relatively long operational tenure (about five years) can be basically explained by the control of Community Chest and foundation funds by project administrators and effective and charismatic leadership by Alice Overton at the service level.

On the other hand, a temporary agency can also be disadvantageous in that such an arrangement cannot be permanent, and also because early enthusiasm about an exciting new project tends to wear off in time. The halo effect may lead to false-positive results of the research data on outcome, in the sense that such effects would not be secured in an ongoing agency where enthusiasm is perhaps not so high. The need of the community, ultimately, is for services to the multiproblem family that can become a solidly ensconced and permanent constituent element in the community-service system.

Whichever route a given community chooses for lodging its service to multiproblem families, creating the necessary supports and climate within the agency presents a challenge to the skills of the agency's administrators, with whom the responsibility rests. A good deal has been written in the professional literature recently about the phenomenon of professional *burnout*; some of this literature gives the impression that the risk of burnout is innate in the nature of the work (as with multiproblem families) or in the practitioner's deficit of skills in handling stress. Our own view is that working with multiproblem families does not necessarily lead to the frustration and demoralization of staff encompassed by the term burnout, nor does it necessarily reflect staff's personal inadequate coping with stress. Practice with multiproblem families can of course be tiring, worrying, frustrating, fraught with small and large failures; but it can also be a source of great professional and personal satisfaction, exciting, and intellectually stimulating. We suspect that burnout is a direct result of inappropriate and insensitive administrative practices. Fields points out that the feelings evoked in staff by insensitive and bureaucratically rigid administrative structures and procedures are those of

> personal and professional inadequacy, incompetence, dissatisfaction, anger, helplessness and despair. Painful as these feelings are in themselves, the lack of their validation by administrators and supervisors can lower staff morale further. And it is often the case that overwhelmed administrators and supervisors, responsible for the overall program, feel criticized when negative feelings are voiced and therefore discourage their expression. (Fields, 1987, p. 10)

Fields observes that "clinicians' responses to the institutions in which they work are similar to the feelings of hopelessness, helplessness, anger and despair expressed, usually behaviorally, by the families they treat" (Fields, 1987, p. 10).

It is frequently recommended that service needs to be available to the families on a 24-hour-a-day, 7-days-a-week schedule (Maybanks & Bryce, 1979; Bryce & Lloyd, 1981). The experience of agencies who offer this kind of accessibility is that 2 a.m. emergency calls are relatively infrequent, as the families begin to trust that the practitioner or team will indeed be there for them, and as they begin to develop better skills in dealing with crisis or intrafamily conflict. Providing this level of accessibility would probably require use of a team rather than a single practitioner. Contact with the family, preferably via home visits, needs to be several times a week in the early stages of the case; by definition, these are not families appropriate for the 50-minute-hour scheduled office session. Practitioners must have the flexibility, and the time, to work very intensively with a case at periods when this expenditure of time is needed. Provence and Naylor write of the need to individualize each case:

> Individualizing services is essential.... Not everyone needs or uti-
> lizes all components of a program in the same way or on the same
> timetable. Yet planners tend to assume a uniformity about the
> needs of "the poor" or "the disadvantaged" and their use of ser-
> vice. This assumption may result in poor practice.... If individual-
> ization is not valued and planned for, it is unlikely to occur. Even
> arrangements made by the strongly motivated to deliver high-
> quality services have a tendency to become routinized and rigid
> unless they are continuously watched over. (1983, p. 151)

The issue of the length of service is at present a controver-
sial one in the field. Some programs are set up to deliver short-
term crisis intervention, oriented usually to prevent placement
of a child or institutionalization of an adult family member. The
case is then turned over to regular community services, if
needed, after the crisis is resolved (see, for example, Kinney,
Madsden, Fleming, & Haapala, 1977). This short-term model
may indeed be appropriate for fairly well-functioning families
caught up in a temporary crisis. The multiproblem family, however, has chronic crises and a multiplicity of interlocked problems. It is questionable whether sufficient help can be given in a
very short time span; and it is equally questionable whether the
usual community agencies are able to deliver the ongoing and
coordinated service needed after the crisis team departs. Furthermore, a good deal of "slippage" in the referral process to
other agencies can occur if the professional is not there to ensure follow-through.

Some families will develop enough resources to be able to
"go it alone" after service is terminated. Other families, with
more built-in vulnerability factors, can be expected—and
should be encouraged—to turn to the agency at periods in the
future when difficulties erupt again. The agency may have to
operate, for these families, as a kind of extended family, a programmatic aspect of settlement houses and community centers
serving impoverished communities. (See, for example, Dunu,
1979; Phillips, 1980; and Kaplan, 1986, pp. 75–78, concerning
the Lower East Side Family Union in New York City; and Kaplan, 1986, pp. 59–61, concerning the Center for Family Life in
Sunset Park, Brooklyn, NY.)

The practitioners need to know they will be backed by their
agency in their dealings with the community service system.

The agency must provide ongoing in-service training and time for collaboration with other staff. The role of the supervisor is a crucial one. He or she must be competent to teach and support practitioners working with multiproblem families; and that implies appreciable successful experience in this kind of practice. We suggest that the supervisor should herself be carrying at least one or two cases currently. Supervisors who perform the supervisory role only in the bureaucratic sense can, we suspect, be a major variable in the burnout and the poor quality of practice of their workers. Provence and Naylor emphasize that "a competent staff is essential. To put it simply, persons providing services should know what they are doing" (1983, p. 150). Supervisors, as well as practitioners, need to know what they are doing.

We suggest a proposition that would be interesting to test: That the practitioner will tend to relate to her clients the way she is related to by her agency. If the supervisor and the administration are insensitive to her emotional reactions to her work, and her professional needs for support and ongoing learning, she will be insensitive to her clients. If the agency is interested more in adherence to bureaucratic requirements than to the quality of the practitioner's practice, she will tend to relate to her clients in an equally stiff, by-the-book bureaucratic fashion. If the practitioner is angry with her agency, but feels her reaction is discounted, she will tend to "take it out" on her clients.

We suggest that burnout of staff working with multiproblem families is a function of the total agency-practitioner-client system, which indeed may be more multiproblem than are the client families who are only one subsystem in that total system. Because work with multiproblem families is emotionally and physically difficult, it would seem to be all the more important that an agency specializing in this service pay close attention to the above administrative matters.

High-risk families at whatever stage of the family life cycle need and deserve help. If choices have to be made and priorities set because of fiscal or other constraints, we would suggest preference being given to programs that concentrate on such families with very young children. Usually, in most communities, multiproblem families do not come dramatically to the attention of the service system until an urgent crisis erupts, often having to do with child abuse or neglect—although the family probably has been known to a number of agencies, in a fragmented way, for several years. Solid empirical evidence does not exist that programs serving young children and their families actually do an effective job of secondary prevention, and better outcome research is needed from these agencies. (See, for example, Halpern, 1984, who concludes that there is little quantitative evidence of the effectiveness of the early-childhood family-focused programs, because of deficiencies in the quality of their research.) In the meantime, however, it may be reasonable to hypothesize that if funds are insufficient to go around and necessitate difficult triage choices, they are better expended on programs that at least are attempting prevention, at the secondary level, by intervention at the point when early problems surface.

Solid data are not yet available about the cost-effectiveness of intensive services to multiproblem families. It is quite possible that these costs will be found to be, if probably not less expensive, no more expensive than the present pattern of uncoordinated, disorganized, and largely ineffectual services that duplicate service costs without the payoff of adequate service delivery. Innovative programs serving multiproblem families claim cost-effectiveness, usually by comparison with the costs of out-of-home placement. Until more solid research on more than short-term outcome is produced, however, it is difficult to assess these claims. Solnit, however, comments:

> The cost of *not* having such programs is unbearable economically, socially, and in terms of the wasted lives of children who without these services are likely to become the dependent, sick and unproductive adults of the future. Such children are also likely as parents to become the transmitters to the next generation of the deprivation, disorganization, and disruption that characterize those high-risk environments in which social deviation, educational deficits, and physical and mental ill health are evoked and elaborated. (From the foreword of Provence & Naylor, 1983, p. ix)

It is hard to imagine how anyone could disagree with this statement. But the issue of empirically demonstrated effectiveness of service still needs to be addressed. Competence as well as compassion is needed.

But—compassion and caring are indeed the bottom line. A practitioner writes about her families, who are

> parents who are truly living life on the edge. These are people whose lives are chaotic and whose histories are primarily a map of pain and adaptation to that pain. Their lives stun us with their bleakness, their boredom, their harshness and their hopeless- ness.... We struggle to find a way to make a relationship with them which will have in it some trust and some glimpse of hope.... We offer them our close attention, our concern and our understanding—but we are as helpless as they are to offer the social changes that might actually ease their days.... We are, I hope, patient and realistic. If we are not we will not see them again. And even if we are we may not, for though their lives are lived as on mired treadmills they do not quiet long enough for them initially even to remember us. It takes time for what we do together to matter to them. (Paul, 1987, p. 16)

Empirically demonstrated effectiveness of service, and bet- ter conceptual development and validation of theory, are indeed crucial elements for improved professional practice with multi- problem families. These necessary concerns with developing a scientifically based practice are not antithetical to, but are rather firmly grounded in a value base of compassion, concern, and commitment. The test of a truly civilized society is how it backs up by action its adherence to these values—how it imple- ments its compassion, concern, and commitment regarding the parents and children caught in "mired treadmills."

Bibliography and Selected Readings

Ackerman, N. (1954). The diagnosis of neurotic marital interaction. *Social Casework, 34*, 139–146.

Ackerman, N.W. (1958). *The psychodynamics of family life*. New York: Basic Books.

Ackerman, N.W., Beatman, F.L., & Sherman, S.N. (Eds.). (1961). *Exploring the base for family therapy*. New York: Family Service Association of America.

Addams, J. (1910). *Twenty years at Hull House*. New York: Macmillan.

Alexander, J.F., & Parsons, B. (1973). Short-term behavioral intervention with delinquent families. *Journal of Abnormal Psychology, 81*, 219–225.

American Psychiatric Association. (1987). *Diagnostic and statistical manual of mental disorders* (3rd ed., revised). Washington, D.C.: APA.

Aponte, H.J. (1976). Underorganization in the poor family. In P.J. Guerin (Ed.), *Family therapy: Theory and practice* (pp. 432–448). New York: Gardner Press.

Ascher, M.L., & Efran, J.S. (1978). Use of paradoxical intention in a behavioral program for sleep onset insomnia. *Journal of Consulting and Clinical Psychology, 46*, 547–550.

Auerswald, E.H. (1968). Interdisciplinary versus ecological approach. *Family Process, 7*, 202–215.

Auletta, K. (1982). *The underclass*. New York: Random House.

Ayres, B., & Lagey, J.C. (1961). *Checklist survey of multi-problem families in Vancouver City*. Vancouver, BC: Community Chest and Councils of the Greater Vancouver Area.

Bahr, S.J. (1979). Family determinants and effects of deviance. In W.R. Burr, R. Hill, F.I. Nye & I.L. Reiss (Eds.), *Contemporary theories about the family* Vol. I (pp. 615–643). New York: Free Press.

Bailey, D.B., Simeonsson, R.J., Winton, P.J., Huntington, G.S., Comfort, M., Isbell, P., O'Donnell, K.J., & Helm, J.M. (1986). Family focused intervention: A functional model for planning, implementing, and evaluating individualized family services in early intervention. *Journal of the Division for Early Childhood, 10*, 156–171.

Bateson, G., Jackson, D.D., Haley, J., & Weakland, J.H. (1956). Toward a theory of schizophrenia. *Behavioral Science, 1*, 251–264.

Bateson, G. (1972). *Steps to an ecology of mind.* New York: Ballantine.

Beatman, F.L. (1956). Family interaction: Its significance for diagnosis and treatment. Paper presented at Biennial Meeting of Family Association of America. (Published in *Social Casework, 38*, 111–118.)

Becker, D.F. (1963). Early adventures in social casework: The charity agent 1880–1910. *Social Casework, 44*, 255–261.

Becker, D.F. (1964). Exit Lady Bountiful: The volunteer and the professional social worker. *Social Service Review, 38*, 57–72.

Behrens, M.L., & Ackerman, N.W. (1956). The home visit as an aid in family diagnosis and therapy. *Social Casework, 37*, 11–19.

Beezley, P., Martin, H., & Alexander, H. (1976). Comprehensive family oriented therapy. In R. Helfer & C. Kempe (Eds.), *Child abuse and neglect.* Cambridge, MA: Ballinger.

Bell, N.W., & Vogel, E.F. (1960). Toward a framework for functional analysis of family behavior. In N.W. Bell & E.F. Vogel (Eds.), *A modern introduction to the family* (pp. 1–33). Glencoe, IL: Free Press.

Berleman, W.C. (1968). Mary Richmond's "Social diagnosis" in retrospect. *Social Casework, 49*, 395–402.

Bernstein, R. (1988). King's dream: America still haunted by problems of black poor. *New York Times: The Week in Review.* January 17, 1988, p. 1.

Birchler, G.R., & Spinks, S.H. (1981). Behavioral-systems marital and family therapy: Integration and clinical application. *American Journal of Family Therapy, 8*, 6–28.

Blechman, E.A., & Olson, D.H. (1976). Family contract game: Description and effectiveness. In D.H. Olson (Ed.), *Treating relationships* (pp. 133–149). Lake Hills, IA: Graphic Publishing.

Bordin, E.S. (1974). *Research strategies in psychotherapy.* New York: Wiley.

Boszormenyi-Nagy, I., & Ulrich, D.N. (1981). Contextual family therapy. In A.S. Gurman & D.P. Kniskern (Eds.), *Handbook of family therapy* (pp. 159–186). New York: Brunner/Mazel.

Bowen, M. (1960). A family concept of schizophrenia. In D.D. Jackson (Ed.), *The etiology of schizophrenia.* New York: Basic Books.

Bowen, M. (1978). *Family therapy in clinical practice.* New York: Aronson.

Brace, C.L. (1872). *The dangerous classes of New York.* New York: Wynkoop & Hallenbeck.

Braverman, L. (1986). Social casework and strategic therapy. *Social Casework, 67*, 234–239.

Breckenridge, S.B. (1934). *Family welfare work in a metropolitan community.* Chicago: University of Chicago Press.

Briar, S. (1968). The casework predicament. *Social Work, 13*, pp.5–11.

Brieland, D., Briggs, T., & Leuenberger, P. (1973). *The team model of social work practice.* Syracuse, NY: Syracuse University Press.

Bronfenbrenner, U. (1979). *The ecology of human development: Experiments by nature and design.* Boston: Harvard University Press.

Brown, G.B., Bhrolchain, M.N., & Harris, T. (1975). Social class and psychiatric disturbance among women in an urban population. *Sociology, 9,* 225–254.

Brown, G.E. (Ed.) (1968). *The multi-problem dilemma.* Metuchen, NJ: Scarecrow Press.

Bryce, M. & Lloyd, J. (Eds.) (1981). *Treating families in the home.* Springfield, IL: Charles C. Thomas.

Bullock, A., & Stallybrass, O. (1977). *The Harper dictionary of modern thought.* New York: Harper & Row.

Bureau of the Census. (1980). *Social indicators III.* Washington, DC: U.S. Government Printing Office.

Bureau of the Census. (1986). *Statistical abstract of the United States.* Washington, DC: U.S. Government Printing Office.

Bureau of the Census. (1987). *Statistical abstract of the United States.* Washington, DC: U.S. Government Printing Office.

Burt, M.R., & Balyeat, R. (1974). A new system for improving the care of neglected and abused children. *Child Welfare, 53,* 167–179.

Cabot, R.C. (1919). Discussion of paper by F.S. Chapin "The relations of sociology and social case work." *Proceedings of National Conference of Social Work, 1919* (p. 365). Chicago: Rogers & Hall.

Cahalan, D., Cisin, I.H., & Crossley, H.M. (1969). *American drinking practices.* New Brunswick, NJ: Rutgers University Center of Alcohol Studies.

Camasso, M.J., & Camasso, A.E. (1986). Social supports, undesirable life events, and psychological distress in a disadvantaged urban population. *Social Service Review, 60,* 378–394.

Cannon, W.B. (1932). *Wisdom of the body.* New York: Norton.

Cavan, R.S., & Ranck, K.H. (1938). *The family and the depression.* Chicago: University of Chicago Press.

Chafetz, J.S. (1978). *A primer on the construction and testing of theories in sociology.* Itasca, IL: Peacock.

Chafetz, M.E., & Task Force Staff associates (1971). *Alcohol and health: First special report to the U.S. Congress from the Secretary of Health, Education and Welfare,* (DHEW Publication No. HSM 72-9099). Washington, DC: U.S. Government Printing Office.

Chilman, C.S. (1966). Social work practice with very poor families: some implications suggested by the available research. *Welfare in Review, 4,* 13–22.

Cicchetti, D., & Rizley, R. (1981). Developmental perspectives on the etiology, intergenerational transmission, and sequelae of child maltreatment. *New Directions for Child Development, 11,* 31–55.

Cicchetti, D., & Toth, S.L. (1987). The application of a transactional risk model to intervention with multi-risk maltreating families. *Zero to Three: Bulletin of National Center for Clinical Infant Programs, 7,* 1–8.

Clark, T., Zalis, T., & Sacco, F. (1982). *Outreach family therapy.* New York: Aronson.

Cloward, R.A., & Epstein, I. (1965). Private social welfare's disengagement from the poor: the case of family adjustment agencies. In M.N. Zald (Ed.), *Social welfare institutions* (pp. 623–644). New York: Wiley.

Cohen, A.K. (1966). *Deviance and control.* Englewood Cliffs, NJ: Prentice-Hall.

Cohen, M.R. (1931). Reason in social science. In M.R. Cohen, *Reason and nature* (pp. 250–263). New York: Harcourt, Brace & Co. Reprinted in H. Fegel & M. Broderick (Eds.). (1953). *Readings in the philosophy of science* (pp. 663–673). New York: Appleton-Century Crofts.

Compton, B., & Galaway, B. (1984). The contract phase: Joint assessment, goal setting, and planning. In B. Compton & B. Galaway (Eds.), *Social work processes* (3rd ed.) (pp. 395–423). Chicago, IL: Dorsey.

Compton, B., & Galaway, B. (1984). Teamwork for social work practice. In B. Compton & B. Galaway (Eds.) *Social work processes* (3rd ed.) (pp. 515–550). Chicago, IL: Dorsey.

Constantine, L.L. (1978). Family sculpture and relationship mapping technique. *Journal of Marriage and Family Counseling, 40,* 13–23.

Cook, T. & Campbell, D. (1979). *Quasi-experimentation.* Boston: Houghton Mifflin

Coyle, G.L. (1962). Concepts relevant to helping the family as a group. *Social Casework, 43,* 347–354.

Dell, P.F. (1981). Some irreverent thoughts on paradox. *Family Process, 20,* 37–51.

Dell, P.F. (1982). Beyond homeostasis: Toward a concept of coherence. *Family Process, 21,* 21–41.

DeShazer, S. (1982). Some conceptual distinctions are more useful than others. *Family Process, 21,* 71–84.

DeWitt, K.N. (1978). The effectiveness of family therapy. *Archives of General Psychiatry, 35,* 549–561.

Dexter, E. (1926). The social case worker's attitude and problems as they affect her work. *The Family, 7,* 177–181.

Dizard, J. (1968). *Social change in the family.* Chicago: Community and Family Study Center, University of Chicago.

Dohrenwend, B.P. (1966). Social status and psychological disorder: An issue of substance and an issue of method. *American Sociological Review, 31,* 13–34.

Doyle, A.B., Gold, D., & Moskowitz, D.S. (Eds.). (1984). *Children in families under stress.* San Francisco: Jossey-Bass.

Drotar, D. (Ed.). (1983). *New directions in failure to thrive: Implications for research and practice.* New York: Plenum.

Dunu, M. (1979). The Lower East Side Family Union: Assuring community services for minority families. In S. Maybanks & M. Bryce (Eds.), *Home-based services for children and families: Policy, practice, and research* (pp. 211–224). Springfield, IL: Charles C. Thomas.

Duvall, E.M. (1957). *Family development.* Philadelphia: Lippincott.

Eiduson, B.T. (1964). Intellectual inbreeding in the clinic? *American Journal of Orthopsychiatry, 34,* 714–721.

Ellis, A. (1973a). *How to raise an emotionally healthy, happy child.* Hollywood, CA: Wilshire.

Ellis, A. (1973b). *Humanistic psychotherapy: The rational-emotive approach.* New York: McGraw-Hill.

Epstein, N., & Shainline, A. (1974). Paraprofessional parent aides and disadvantaged families. *Social Casework, 55*, 230–236.

Fantl, B. (1958). Integrating psychological, social, and cultural factors in assertive casework. *Social Casework, 3*, 30–37.

Fantl, B. (1961). Casework practice in lower-class districts. *Mental Hygiene, 45*, 425–438.

Feldman, L.B., & Pinsof, W.H. (1982). Problem maintenance in family systems: An integrative model. *Journal of Marital and Family Therapy, 7*, 295–308.

Fields, B. (1987). Toward tenacity of commitment: Understanding and modifying institutional practices and individual responses that impede work with multiproblem families. *Zero to Three: Bulletin of the National Center for Clinical Infant Programs, 7*, 9–12.

Fisher, L., Anderson, A., & Jones, J.E. (1981). Types of paradoxical intervention and indications/contraindications for use in clinical practice. *Family Process, 20*, 25–35.

Flexner, A. (1915). Is social work a profession? *Proceedings of the National Conference of Charities and Correction 1915*, 576–590. (Reprinted in R.E. Pumphrey & M.W. Pumphrey, 1961, pp. 301–307.)

Fontana, A. (1966). Familial etiology of schizophrenia: Is scientific method possible? *Psychological Bulletin, 66*, 214–227.

Framo, J.L. (1981). The integration of marital therapy with sessions with family of origin. In D.P. Kniskern & A.S. Gurman (Eds.), *Handbook of family therapy* (pp. 133–158). New York: Brunner/Mazel.

Frank, G.H. (1965). The role of the family in the development of psychopathology. *Psychological Bulletin, 64*, 191–205.

Frankel, H. (1968). Family-centered, home-based services in child protection: A review of the research. *Social Service Review, 62*, 137–157.

Freed, A.O. (1982). Building theory for family practice. *Social Casework, 63*, 472–481.

Fried, M. (1976). Social differences in mental health. In J. Kosa & I.K. Zola (Eds.), *Poverty and health: A sociological analysis* (pp. 135–192). Cambridge, MA: Harvard University Press.

Fromm-Reichmann, F. (1948). Notes on the development of treatment of schizophrenics by psychoanalytical psychotherapy. *Psychiatry, 11*, 263–273.

Gambrill, E.D. (1977). *Behavior modification: Handbook of assessment, intervention, and evaluation.* San Francisco: Jossey-Bass.

Gambrill, E.D. (1981). A behavioral perspective of families. In E.R. Tolson & W.J. Reid (Eds.), *Models of family treatment* (pp. 64–104). New York: Columbia University Press.

Garbarino, J. (1983). Social support networks: Rx for the helping professions. In J.K. Whittaker & J. Garbarino (Eds.) *Social support networks: Informal helping in the human services* (pp. 3–28). New York: Aldine.

Garbarino, J.,& Gilliam, G. (1980). *Understanding abusive families.* Lexington, MA: Lexington.

Gecas, V. (1979). The influence of social class on socialization. In W.R. Burr, R. Hill, F.I. Nye, & I.L Reiss (Eds.), *Contemporary theories about the family*, Volume I (pp. 365–404). New York: Free Press.

Geismar, L.L. (1957). *Report on checklist survey.* St. Paul, MN: Family Centered Project of Greater St. Paul Community Chest and Councils.

Geismar, L.L. (1963). The social functioning of the ADC family. *The Welfare Reporter, 14*, 43–54.

Geismar, L.L. (1964). Family functioning as an index of welfare services. *Family Process, 3*, 99–113.

Geismar, L.L. (1969). *Preventive intervention in social work.* Metuchen, NJ: Scarecrow Press.

Geismar, L.L. (1971). Implications of a family life improvement project. *Social Casework, 52*, 455–465.

Geismar, L.L. (1973). *555 families: A social psychological study of young families in transition.* New Brunswick, NJ: Transaction Books.

Geismar, L.L. (1980). *Family and community functioning.* Metuchen, NJ: Scarecrow Press.

Geismar, L.L. & Ayres, B. (1958). *Families in trouble: An analysis of basic social characteristics of one hundred families served by the Family Centered Project of St. Paul.* St. Paul, MN: Family Centered Project of Greater St. Paul Community Chest and Councils.

Geismar, L.L. & Ayres, B. (1959a). A method of evaluating the social functioning of families under treatment. *Social Work, 4*, 102–108.

Geismar, L.L. & Ayres, B. (1959b). *Patterns of change in problem families.* St. Paul, MN: Family Centered Project of Greater St. Paul Community Chest and Councils.

Geismar, L.L. & Ayres, B. (1960). *Measuring family functioning.* St. Paul, MN: Family Centered Project of Greater St. Paul Community Chest and Councils.

Geismar, L.L., & Krisberg, J. (1967). *The forgotten neighborhood: Site of an early skirmish in the war on poverty.* Metuchen, NJ: Scarecrow Press.

Geismar, L.L. & Lagay, B. (1985). Prevention in social work: A postmortem of an experiment on preventive intervention. *The Journal of Applied Behavioral Science, 21*, 329–338.

Geismar, L.L., Lagay, B., Wolock, I., Gerhart, U.C., & Fink, H. (1972). *Early supports for family life.* Metuchen, NJ: Scarecrow Press.

Geismar, L.L., LaSorte, M.A., & Ayres, B. (1962). Measuring family disorganization. *Marriage and Family Living, 24*, 51–56.

Geismar, L.L., & LaSorte, M. (1964). *Understanding the multiproblem family.* New York: Association Press.

Geismar, L.L., & Wood, K.M. (1986). *Family and delinquency: Resocializing the young offender.* New York: Human Sciences Press.

Gelles, R.J. (1980). A profile of violence toward children in the United States. In G. Gerbner, C.J. Ross, & E. Zigler, (Eds.), *Child abuse: An agenda for action* (pp. 82–105), New York: Oxford University Press.

Gelles, R.J. (1987). The family and its role in the abuse of children. *Psychiatric Annals, 17*, 229–232.

Germain, C.B. (Ed.). (1979). *Social work practice: People and environments.* New York: Columbia University Press.

Germain, C.B. (1981). The ecological approach to people-environment transactions. *Social Casework, 62*, 323–331.

Germain, C.B., & Gitterman, A. (1980). *The life model of social work practice.* New York: Columbia University Press.

Germain, C.B., & Hartman, A. (1980). People and ideas in the history of social work practice. *Social Casework, 61*, 323–331.

Gil, D. (1970). *Violence against children: Physical child abuse in the United States.* Cambridge, MA: Harvard University Press.

Gilbert, M. (1976). Behavioral approach to the treatment of child abuse. *Nursing Times, 72*, 140–143.

Glaser, B.G., & Strauss, A.L. (1967). *The discovery of grounded theory: Strategies for qualitative research.* New York: Aldine.

Glick, P. (1947). The family life cycle. *American Sociological Review, 12*, 164–174.

Goldmeier, B.J. (1973). The legacy of Mary Richmond in education and practice. *Social Casework, 54*, 276–283.

Goldstein, H. (1970). *Social work practice: A unitary approach.* Columbia, SC: University of South Carolina Press.

Gomberg, M.R. (1944). The specific nature of family case work. In J. Taft (Ed.), *A functional approach to family case work* (pp. 111–147). Philadelphia: University of Pennsylvania Press.

Gomberg, M.R. (1948). Counseling as a service of the family agency. In J. Taft (Ed.), *Family casework and counseling* (pp. 191–261). Philadelphia: University of Pennsylvania Press.

Gomberg, M.R. (1958). Family diagnosis: Trends in theory and practice. *Social Casework, 39*, 3–10.

Gomberg, M.R. and Levinson, F.T. (1951). *Diagnosis and process in family counseling.* New York: Family Service Association of America.

Gordon, T. (1970). *Parent effectiveness training.* New York: Wyden.

Gove, W., & Crutchfield, R. (1982). The family and juvenile delinquency. *The Sociological Quarterly, 23*, 301–319.

Grinnell, R.M. (1973). Environmental modification: Casework's concern or casework's neglect? *Social Service Review, 47*, 208–220.

Grinnell, R.M., Kyte, N.S., & Bostwick, G.J. (1981). Environmental modification. In A.N. Maluccio (Ed.), *Promoting competence in clients: A new/old approach to social work practice* (pp. 152–184). New York: Free Press.

Guerin, P.J. (1976). Family therapy: The first twenty-five years. In P.J. Guerin (Ed.), *Family therapy: Theory and practice* (pp. 2–22). New York: Gardner.

Gurman, A.S., & Kniskern, D.P. (1978). Research on marital and family therapy: progress, perspective, and prospect. In S.L. Garfield & A.E. Bergin (Eds.), *Handbook of psychotherapy and behavior change* (2nd ed.) (pp. 817–901). New York: Wiley.

Gurman, A.S., & Kniskern, D.P. (Eds.) (1981). *Handbook of family therapy.* New York: Brunner/Mazel.

Gurman, A.S., & Razin, A.M. (1977). *Effective psychotherapy: A handbook of research.* New York: Pergamon.

Haapala, D., & Kinney, J. (1979). Homebuilders' approach to the training of in-home therapists. In S. Maybanks & M. Bryce (Eds.), *Home-based services for children and families: policy, practice and research* (pp. 248–259). Springfield, IL: Charles C. Thomas.

Haley, J. (1963). *Strategies of psychotherapy*. New York: Grune & Stratton.

Haley, J. (1976). *Problem solving therapy*. San Francisco: Jossey-Bass.

Haley, J. (1980). *Leaving home: The therapy of disturbed young people*. New York: McGraw-Hill.

Haley, J. (1984). *Ordeal therapy*. San Francisco: Jossey-Bass.

Hallowitz, D., Clement, R.G., & Cutter, A.V. (1957). The treatment process with both parents together. *American Journal of Orthopsychiatry, 27*, 587–601.

Halper, G., & Jones, M.A. (1981). *Serving families at risk of dissolution: public preventive services in New York City*. New York: Human Resources Administration.

Halpern, R. (1984). Lack of effects for home-based early intervention? Some possible explanations. *American Journal of Orthopsychiatry, 54*, 33–42.

Hamilton, G. (1940; Rev. ed., 1951). *Theory and practice of social casework*. New York: Columbia University Press.

Hamilton, G. (1958). A theory of personality: Freud's contribution to social work. In H.J. Parad (Ed.), *Ego psychology and dynamic casework* (pp. 11–37). New York: Family Service Association of America.

Hansen, C.C. (1968). An extended home visit with conjoint family therapy. *Family Process, 1*, 67–87.

Hartman, A. (1971). But what is social casework? *Social Casework, 52*, 411–419.

Hartman, A. & Laird, J. (1983). *Family-centered social work practice*. New York: Free Press.

Hartmann, H. (1958). *Ego psychology and the problem of adaptation*. New York: International Universities Press.

Havens, L. (1973). *Approaches to the mind*. Boston: Little, Brown.

Hearn, G.A. (Ed.). (1969). *The general system approach: Contributions toward an holistic conception of social work*. New York: Council on Social Work Education.

Heineman, M.B. (1981). The obsolete scientific imperative in social work research. *Social Service Review, 55*, 371–397.

Helfer, R., & Kempe, C. (Eds.) (1976). *Child abuse and neglect*. Cambridge, MA: Ballinger.

Helfer, R. (1982). A review of the literature on the prevention of child abuse and neglect. *Child Abuse and Neglect, 6*, 251–261.

Henry, C.S. (1958). Motivation in non-voluntary clients. *Social Casework, 39*, 130–135.

Hersen, M., & Barlow, D.H. (1976). *Single-case experimental designs*. New York: Pergamon.

Hersen, M., Eisler, R.M., & Miller, P.M. (Eds.). (1978). *Progress in behavior modification*. New York: Academic Press.

Hicks, M.W., & Platt, M. (1970). Marital happiness and stability: A Review of the research in the sixties. *Journal of Marriage and the Family, 32*, 553–574.

Hill, R. (1958). Social stresses on the family: Generic features of families under stress. *Social Casework, 39*, 139–149.

Hill, R. (1971). *The strengths of black families*. New York: Emerson Hall.

Hill, R., & Rodgers, R.H. (1964). The developmental approach. In H.T. Christenson (Ed.), *Handbook of marriage and the family* (pp. 171–211). Chicago: Rand-McNally.

Hobbs, N. (1962). Sources of gain in psychotherapy. *American Psychologist, 17,* 741–747. Reprinted in B.R. Compton & B. Galaway (Eds.). (1975). *Social work processes* (pp. 360–370). Homewood, IL: Dorsey Press.

Hoffman, L., & Long, L. (1969). A systems dilemma. *Family Process, 8,* 211–234.

Hollis, F. (1949). *Women in marital conflict.* New York: Family Service Association of America.

Hollis, F. (1965). *Casework: a psychosocial therapy.* New York: Random House.

Hollis, F. (1971). Social casework: the psychosocial approach. In *Encyclopedia of Social Work* (pp. 1217–1226). New York: National Association of Social Workers.

Hollis, F. (1980). On revisiting social work. *Social Casework, 61,* 3–10.

Horejsi, C.R. (1981). The St. Paul family-centered project revisited: Exploring an old gold mine. In M. Bryce & J.C. Lloyd (Eds.), *Treating families in the home.* Springfield, IL: Charles C. Thomas.

Howells, J.G., & Guirguis, W.R. (1985). *The family and schizophrenia.* New York: International Universities Press.

Ilfeld, F.W., Jr. (1978). Psychological status of community residents along major demographic dimensions. *Archives of General Psychiatry, 35,* 716–724.

Information please almanac. (1986). Boston: Houghton Mifflin.

Jackson, D.D. (Ed.). (1960). *The etiology of schizophrenia.* New York: Basic Books.

Jacobson, N.S. (1977). Problem-solving contingency contracting in the treatment of marital discord. *Journal of Consulting and Clinical Psychology, 48,* 92–100.

Jacobson, N.S., & Margolin, G. (1979). *Marital therapy: Strategies based on social learning and behavior exchange principles.* New York: Brunner/Mazel.

Jaffe, L. (1969). Family anomie and delinquency: Development of the concept and some empirical findings. *British Journal of Criminology, 9,* 376–388.

James, D.B. (1972). *Poverty, politics and change.* Englewood Cliffs, NJ: Prentice-Hall.

Janzen, C., & Harris, O. (1986). *Family treatment in social work practice.* Itasca, IL: Peacock.

Jarrett, M.C. (1919). The psychiatric thread running through all social case work. In *Proceedings of National Conference of Social Work, 1919* (pp. 587–593). Chicago: Rogers & Hall.

Jefferson, C. (1978). Some notes on the use of family sculpture in therapy. *Family Process, 17,* 69–76.

Jeffrey, M. (1976). Practical ways to change parent-child interaction in families of children at risk. In R. Helfer & C. Kempe (Eds.), *Child abuse and neglect.* Cambridge, MA: Ballinger.

Johnson, H.C. (1986). Emerging concerns in family therapy. *Social Work, 31,* 299–306.

Johnstone, J. (1978). Juvenile delinquency and the family: A contextual interpretation. *Youth and Society, 9,* 299–314.

Jones, M.A. (1983). *A second chance for families—five years later: Follow-up of a program to prevent foster care.* New York: Child Welfare League of America.

Jones, M.A., Magura, S., & Shyne, A.W. (1981). Effective practice with families in protective and preventive services: what works? *Child Welfare, 60,* 67–80.

Josselyn, I.M. (1953). The family as a psychological unit. *Social Casework, 34,* 336–343.

Kane, R. (1975). The interprofessional team as a small group. *Social Work in Health Care, 1,* 19–32.

Kaplan, L. (1986). *Working with multiproblem families.* Lexington, MA: Lexington Books.

Keeney, B.F. (1982). What is an epistemology of family therapy? *Family Process, 21,* 153–168.

Kinney, J.M., Godfrey, C., Haapala, D.A., & Madsen, B. (1979). Homebuilders; keeping families together. In G. Landsbert, W. Neigher, R. Hammer, C. Windle & J.K. Woy (Eds.). *Evaluation in practice: A sourcebook of program evaluation studies from mental health care systems in the United States.* Washington, DC: U.S. Government Printing Office.

Kinney, J.M., Haapala, D., & Gast, J.E. (1981). Assessment of families in crisis. In M. Bryce & J. Lloyd (Eds.), *Treating families in the home* (pp. 50–67). Springfield, IL: Charles C. Thomas.

Kinney, J.M., Madsen, B., Fleming, T., & Haapala, D. (1977). Homebuilders: Keeping families together. *Journal of Clinical and Consulting Psychology, 45,* 667–673.

Kniskern, D.P., & Gurman, A.S. (1979). Research on training in marriage and family therapy: Status, issues and directions. *Journal of Consulting and Clinical Psychology, 5,* 83–94.

Kohler, W. (1959). *Gestalt psychology.* New York: Mentor.

Kohn, M.L. (1973). Social class and schizophrenia: A critical review and a reformulation. *Schizophrenia Bulletin, 7,* 60–79.

Kolevzon, M.S., & Green, R.G. (1985). *Family therapy models.* New York: Springer.

Kreisman, D.E., & Joy, V.D. (1981). Family response to the mental illness of a relative: A review of the literature. *Schizophrenia Bulletin, 10,* 34–57.

Kris, E. (1947). The nature of psychoanalytic propositions and their validation. In S.K. Hook & M.R. Konwitz (Eds.), *Freedom and experience.* Ithaca, NY: Cornell University Press.

Kuhn, T.S. (1957). *The Copernican revolution.* Cambridge, MA: Harvard University Press.

Kuhn, T.S. (1970). *The structure of scientific revolutions* (2nd ed.). Chicago: University of Chicago Press.

Lagey, J.C., & Ayres, B. (1962). *Community treatment programs for multi-problem families,* Vancouver, BC: Community Chests and Councils of the Greater Vancouver Area.

Lansky, M.R. (1981). *Family therapy and major psychopathology.* New York: Grune & Stratton.

Lee, P.R. (1919). The fabric of the family. *Proceedings of National Conference of Social Work, 1919* (pp. 319–326). Chicago: Rogers & Hall.

Leiby, J. (1978). *A history of social welfare and social work in the United States.* New York: Columbia University Press.

Leighton, D.C., Harding, J.S., Macklin, D.B., Macmillan, A.M. & Leighton, A.H. (1963). *The character of danger*. New York: Basic Books.

Lewin, K. (1935). *A dynamic theory of personality: Selected papers*. New York: McGraw-Hill.

Lewin, K. (1936). *Principles of topological psychology*. New York: McGraw-Hill.

Lewin, K. (1951). *Field theory in social science*. New York: Harper.

Lewis, O. (1959). *Five families*. New York: Basic Books.

Lewis, J.M., Beavers, W.R., Gossett, J.T., & Phillips, V.A. (1976). *No single thread: Psychological health in family systems*. New York: Brunner/Mazel.

Lidz, T., Cornelison, A., Terry, D., & Fleck, S. (1958). Intrafamilial environment of the schizophrenic patient: VI. The transmission of irrationality. *Archives of Neurological Psychiatry, 79*, 305–316.

Lidz, T., Fleck, S., & Cornelison, A. (1965). *Schizophrenia and the family*. New York: International Universities Press.

Lidz T., Parker, B., & Cornelison, A. (1956). The role of the father in the family environment of the schizophrenic patient. *American Journal of Psychiatry, 113*, 126–132.

Liem, J.H. (1980). Family studies of schizophrenia: An update and commentary. *Schizophrenia Bulletin, 6*, 429–455.

Lindenberg, R.E. (1958). Hard to reach: Client or casework agency? *Social Work, 3*, 23–29.

Linder-Pelz, S., Levy, S., Tamir, A., Spenser, T., & Epstein, L.M. (1984). A measure of family functioning for health care practice and research in Israel. *Journal of Comparative Family Studies, 15*, 211–230.

Loomis, C.P., & Hamilton, C.H. (1936). Family life cycle analysis. *Social Forces, 15*, 225–231.

Lowe, R.N. (1982). Adlerian/Dreikursian family counseling. In A.M. Horne & M.M. Ohlsen (Eds.), *Family counseling and therapy* (pp. 329–359). Itasca, IL: Peacock.

Lowry, F. (1936). Problems of therapy in family case work. *Social Service Review, 10*, 195–205.

Lowry, F. (1948). Case-work principles guiding the worker in contacts of short duration. *Social Service Review, 22*, 234–239.

Lowry, F. (1957). The caseworker in short contact services. *Social Work, 2*, 52–56.

Lubove, R. (1965). *The professional altruist: The emergence of social work as a career, 1880–1930*. Cambridge, MA: Harvard University Press.

Magura, S. (1981). Are services to prevent foster care effective? *Children and Youth Services Review, 3*, 193–212.

Mailick, M. (1977). A situational perspective in casework theory. *Social Casework, 58*, 401–411.

Maluccio, A.N., & Marlow, W.D. (1974). The case for the contract. *Social Work, 19*, 28–37.

Manis, J.G., Brower, M.J., Hunt, C.L., & Kercher, L.C. (1964). Estimating the prevalence of mental illness. *American Sociological Review, 29*, 84–89.

Martindale, D., & Martindale, E. (1971). *The social dimensions of mental illness, alcoholism and drug dependence*. Westport, CT: Greenwood.

Mash, E.J., Handy, L.C., & Hamerlynck, L.A. (1974). *Behavior modification approaches to parenting.* New York: Brunner/Mazel.

Mash, E.J., Hamerlynck, L.A., & Handy, L.C. (Eds.). (1976). *Behavior modification and families.* New York: Brunner/Mazel.

Masten, A.S. (1979). Family therapy as a treatment for children: a critical review of outcome research. *Family Process, 18,* 323–335.

Maybanks, S., & Bryce, M. (Eds.). (1979). *Home-based services for children and families: Policy, practice and research.* Springfield, IL: Charles C. Thomas.

McAdoo, H. (1977). Family therapy in the black community. *American Journal of Orthopsychiatry, 47,* 75–79.

McKinney, G.E. (1970). Adapting family therapy to multideficit families. *Social Casework, 51,* 327–333.

Merton, R.K. (1957). *Social theory and social structure* (2nd ed.). New York: Glencoe.

Meyer, C.H. (1976). *Social work practice: The changing landscape* (2nd ed.). New York: Free Press.

Meyer, C.H. (1982). *Clinical social work in the eco-systems perspective.* New York: Columbia University Press.

Middleman, R.R., & Goldberg, G. (1974). *Social service delivery: a structural approach to social work practice.* New York: Columbia University Press.

Miller, J.G. (1978). *Living systems.* New York: McGraw-Hill.

Minuchin, S., & Montalvo, B. (1967). Techniques for working with disorganized low socio-economic families. *American Journal of Orthopsychiatry, 37,* 880–887.

Minuchin, S., Montalvo, B., Guerney, B., Rosman, B., & Schumer, F. (1967). *Families of the slums.* New York: Basic Books.

Mosher, L.R., & Gunderson, J.G. (1973). Special report: schizophrenia. *Schizophrenia Bulletin, 7,* 10–52.

Mullen, E.G., Dumpson, J.R., & Associates. (1972). *Evaluation of social intervention.* San Francisco: Jossey-Bass.

Nathan, P.E., & Harris, S.L. (1980). *Psychopathology and society.* New York: McGraw-Hill.

Nelsen, J.C. (1983). *Family treatment: An integrative approach.* Englewood Cliffs, NJ: Prentice-Hall.

New York Times (1988). AIDS antibodies in New York infants. January 15, 1988, p. 6.

Nock, S.L. (1979). The family life cycle: Empirical or conceptual tool? *Journal of Marriage and the Family, 41,* 15–26.

Norton, A.J. (1983). Family life cycle: 1980. *Journal of Marriage and the Family, 45,* 267–275.

Nugent, W.R. (1987). Use and evaluation of theories. *Social Work Research and Abstracts, 23,* 14–19.

Nye, F.I. (1976). *Role structure and analysis of the family.* Beverly Hills, CA: Sage Publications.

Nye, F.I., & McLaughlin, S. (1976). Role competence and marital satisfaction. In F.I. Nye (Ed.), *Role structure and analysis of the family* (pp. 191–205). Beverly Hills, CA: Sage Publications.

Ogburn, W.F. (1938). The changing family. *The Family, 19,* 139–143.

Olson, D.H. (1970). Marital and family therapy: Integrative review and critique. *Journal of Marriage and the Family, 32,* 501–538.

Olson, D.H., Sprenkle, D.H., & Russell, C.S. (1979). A circumplex model of marital and family systems: 1. Cohesion and adaptability dimensions, family types and clinical adaptations. *Family Process, 18,* 3–28.

Olson, D.H., McCubbin, H.I., & associates (1983). *Families: What makes them work.* Beverly Hills, CA: Sage Publications.

Orcutt, B.A. (1977). Family treatment of poverty level families. *Social Casework, 58,* 92–100.

O'Reilly, J.B. (1886) *In bohemia.* Quoted in Leiby, 1978, p. 116.

Overton, A. (1953). Serving families who don't want help. *Social Casework, 34,* 304–309.

Overton, A. (1956). Casework as a partnership. *Children, 3,* 181–186.

Overton, A. (1960). Taking help from our clients. *Social Work, 5,* 42–50.

Overton, A., Tinker, K.H., & associates (1957). *Casework notebook.* St. Paul, MN: Family Centered Project of Greater St. Paul. (Reprinted, 1978, by United Way of The St. Paul Area, 333 Sibley St., St. Paul, MN 55101; cost $4.50 plus $.94 postage.)

Papp, P. (1976). Family choreography. In P.J. Guerin (Ed.), *Family therapy: Theory and practice* (pp. 465–479). New York: Gardner.

Park, R.E., Burgess, E.W., & McKenzie, R.D. (1925). *The city: The ecological approach to the study of human community.* Chicago: University of Chicago Press.

Parloff, M.B., Waskow, I.E., & Wolfe, B.E. (1978). Research on therapist variables in relation to process and outcome. In S.L Garfield & A.E. Bergin (Eds.), *Handbook of psychotherapy and behavior change* (2nd ed.) (pp. 233–282). New York: Wiley.

Parsons, T., & Bales, R.F. (1958). *Family, socialization and interaction process.* Glencoe, IL: Free Press.

Patterson, G.R., Reid, J.B., Jones, R.R., & Conger, R.E. (1975). *A social learning approach to family intervention: I. Families with aggressive children.* Eugene, OR: Castalia.

Patterson, G.R., Weiss, R.L., & Hops, H. (1976). Training of marital skills: some problems and concepts. In H. Leitenberg (Ed.), *Handbook of behavior modification and behavior therapy* (pp. 242–254). Englewood Cliffs, NJ: Prentice-Hall.

Paul, J. (1987) Working with infants, toddlers and their families: What we do and how we keep going. *Zero to Three: Bulletin of National Center for Clinical Infant Programs, 5,* 15–17.

Peck, H.B., Kaplan, S.R., & Roman, M. (1966). Prevention, treatment and social action: A strategy of intervention in a disadvantaged urban area. *American Journal of Orthopsychiatry, 36,* 60. (Quoted in Berleman, 1968, p. 401.)

Pelton, L.H. (1987a). Child abuse and neglect: The myth of classlessness. In L.H. Pelton (Ed.), *The social context of child abuse and neglect* (pp. 23–38). New York: Human Sciences Press.

Pelton, L.H. (1987b) *The social context of child abuse and neglect.* New York: Human Sciences Press.

Perlman, H.H. (1957). *Social casework: a problem solving process.* Chicago: University of Chicago Press.

Peterson, K.J. (1979). Assessment in the life model: A historical perspective. *Social Casework, 60,* 586–596.

Phillips, M. et al. (1980). *The forgotten ones.* New York: Henry Street Settlement Urban Life Center.

Philp, A.F. (1963). *Family failure.* London: Farber & Farber.

Piaget, J. (1963). *The origin of intelligence in children.* New York: Norton.

Piaget, J., & Inhelder, B. (1958). *The growth of logical thinking from childhood to adolescence.* New York: Basic Books.

Pincus, A., & Minahan, A. (1973). *Social work practice: Model and method.* Itasca, IL: Peacock.

Pinsof, W. (1983). Integrative problem-centered therapy: Toward the synthesis of family and individual psychotherapies. *Journal of Marital and Family Therapy, 9,* 19–35.

Pless, I.B., & Satterwhite, B.B. (1973). A measure of family functioning and its application. *Social Science and Medicine, 7,* 613–621.

Popper, K.R. (1965). *Conjectures and refutations: The growth of scientific knowledge.* New York: Harper & Row.

Provence, S., & Naylor, A. (1983). *Working with disadvantaged children and their families.* New Haven, CT: Yale University Press.

Pumphrey, M.W. (1973). Lasting and outmoded concepts in the caseworker's heritage. *Social Casework, 54,* 259–267.

Pumphrey, R.E., & Pumphrey, M.W. (1961). *The heritage of American social work.* New York: Columbia University Press.

Random House Dictionary of the English Language, College Edition (1968). New York: Random House.

Rapaport, D. (Ed.). (1951). *Organization and pathology of thought.* New York: Columbia University Press.

Rapaport, D. (1959). A historical survey of psychoanalytic ego psychology. In E.H. Erikson (Ed.), *Identity and the life cycle* (pp. 5–17). New York: International Universities Press.

Rapaport, L. (1968) Social casework: An appraisal and an affirmation. *Smith College Studies in Social Work, 39,* p. 225 (Quoted by Hartman, A., 1971.)

Regensburg, J. (1954). Reaching children before the crisis comes. *Social Casework, 35,* 104–111.

Reid, W.J. (1985). *Family problem solving.* New York: Columbia University Press.

Reynolds, B.C. (1963). *An uncharted journey.* New York: Citadel Press.

Rich, M.E. (1956). *A belief in people: A history of family social work.* New York: Family Service Association of America.

Richmond, M.E. (1899). *Friendly visiting among the poor: A handbook for charity workers.* New York: Macmillan.

Richmond, M.E. (1907). *The good neighbor in the modern city.* Philadelphia: Lippincott.

Richmond, M.E. (1917). *Social diagnosis.* New York: Russell Sage Foundation.

Richmond, M.E. (1922). *What is social case work?*. New York: Russell Sage Foundation.

Richmond, M.E. (1930). *The long view: papers and addresses by Mary E. Richmond.* J.D. Colcord & R.Z. Mann (Eds.). New York: Russell Sage Foundation.

Richmond, M.E., & Hall, F. (1913). *A study of nine hundred eighty-five widows known to certain Charity Organization Societies in 1910.* New York: Russell Sage Foundation.

Robin, A. (1981). Parent-adolescent conflict: A skill training approach to the treatment of parent-adolescent conflict. *Behavior Therapy, 12*, 593–609.

Robinson, V. (1930). *A changing psychology in social case work.* Chapel Hill, NC: University of North Carolina Press.

Rodgers, R.H. (1973). *Family interaction and transaction: the developmental approach.* Englewood Cliffs, NJ: Prentice-Hall.

Roffman, R.A. (1987). Drug use and abuse. In *Encyclopedia of Social Work* (pp. 477–487). Silver Spring, MD: National Association of Social Workers.

Roghman, K.J., Hecht, P.D., & Haggerty, R.J. (1973). Family coping with everyday illness: Self report from a household survey. *Journal of Comparative Family Studies, 4*, 49–62.

Roosa, M.W., Fitzgerald, H.E., & Carlson, N.A. (1982). Teenage parenting and child development: A literature review. *Infant Mental Health Journal, 3*, 4–18.

Rosen, S.M., Fanshel, D., & Lutz, M.E. (Eds.). (1987). *Face of the nation 1987.* Silver Spring, MD: National Association of Social Workers.

Rowe, G.P. (1981). The developmental conceptual framework to the study of the family. In F.I. Nye & F.M. Berardo (Eds.), *Emerging conceptual frameworks in family analysis* (pp. 198–222). New York: Praeger.

Rowntree, B.S. (1901). *Poverty: a study of town life.* New York: Macmillan.

Ryan, W. (1976). *Blaming the victim.* New York: Vintage.

Sanborn, F.B. (1890). Indoor and outdoor relief. *Proceedings of the National Conference on Charities and Correction.* In R.E. Pumphrey & M.W. Pumphrey (Eds.), *The heritage of American social work* (pp. 219–221). New York: Columbia University Press, 1961.

Satir, V. (1967). *Conjoint family therapy.* Palo Alto, CA: Science and Behavior Books.

Scherz, F. (1953). What is family centered casework? *Social Casework, 34*, 343–349.

Scherz, F. (1970). Theory and practice of family therapy. In R.R. Roberts & R.H. Nee (Eds.), *Theories of social casework.* Chicago: University of Chicago Press.

Schmidt, W., Smart, R.G., & Moss, M.K. (1970). *Social class and the treatment of alcoholism.* Toronto: University of Toronto Press.

Schon, D.A. (1983). *The reflective practitioner: How professionals think in action.* New York: Basic Books.

Schram, R.W. (1979). Marital satisfaction over the family life cycle: a critique and proposal. *Journal of Marriage and the Family, 41*, 7–12.

Schwartz, A.C. (1962). Problems of integrating new treatment approaches into agency programs. *Social Casework, 43*, 292–297.

Schwartz, W. (1971). On the use of groups in social work practice. In W. Schwartz

& S.R. Zalba (Eds.) *The practice of group work.* New York: Columbia University Press.

Schwartz, W. (1977). Social group work: The interactionist approach. In *Encyclopedia of Social Work* (pp. 1328–1338). Washington, DC: National Association of Social Workers.

Seabury, B. (1976). The contract: uses, abuses, and limitations. *Social Work, 21,* 16–21.

Selvini-Palazzoli, M.S., Boscolo, L., Ceccin, G., & Prata, G. (1978). *Paradox and counterparadox.* New York: Aronson.

Shaw, M.E. (1980). *Role playing.* San Diego: University Associates.

Sheffield, A.E. (1922). *Case-study possibilities.* Boston: Research Bureau on Social Casework.

Sheffield, A.E. (1923). What is the case worker really doing? *Journal of Social Forces, 1,* 362–366.

Sheffield, A.E. (1924). Three interviews and the changing situation. *Journal of Social Forces, 2,* 692–697.

Sheffield, A.E. (1931). The situation as the unit of family case study. Paper delivered to the Section on Sociology and Social Work of the American Sociological Society, December 1930. (Published in *Journal of Social Forces, 9,* 465–474.)

Sheffield, A.E. (1937). *Social insight in case situations.* New York: Appleton-Century.

Sherman, S.N. (1961). The concept of the family in casework theory. In N.W. Ackerman, F.S. Beatman, & S.N. Sherman (Eds.), *Exploring the base for family therapy* (pp. 14–28). New York: Family Service Association of America.

Sherwood, J.J., & Hoylman, F.M. (1977). *Utilizing human resources: individual versus group approaches to problem-solving and decision-making.* Lafayette, IN: Purdue University Press.

Singer, M.T., & Wynne, L.C. (1965). Thought disorder and family relations of schizophrenics: III. Methodology using projective techniques. *Archives of General Psychiatry, 12,* 187–200.

Singer, M.T., & Wynne, L.C. (1965). Thought disorder and family relations of schizophrenics: IV. Results and implications. *Archives of General Psychiatry, 12,* 201–212.

Siporin, M. (1970). Social treatment: A new-old helping method. *Social Work, 15,* 13–25.

Siporin, M. (1972). Situational assessment and intervention. *Social Casework, 53,* 91–109.

Siporin, M. (1975). *Introduction to social work practice.* New York: Macmillan.

Siporin, M. (1980). Marriage and family therapy in social work. *Social Casework, 61,* 11–21.

Slater, E.P., & Harris, W.R. (1978). Therapy at home. *Practice Digest, 1,* 20–21.

Smilkstein, G. (1978). The family APGAR: A proposal for a family function test and its use by physicians. *Journal of Family Practice, 6,* 1231–1239.

Smith, S.L. (1984). Significant research findings in the etiology of child abuse. *Social Casework, 65,* 337–346.

Smith, Z. (1890). *A belief in people: A history of family social work* (p. 14). (Quoted in Rich, M.E., 1956.) New York: Family Service Association of America.

Sorokin, P., Zimmerman, C.C., & Galpin, C.J. (1931). *A systematic sourcebook in rural sociology, Vol. 2*. Minneapolis: University of Minnesota Press.

Southard, E.E. (1919). The individual versus the family as unit of interest in social work. *Proceedings of National Conference of Social Work, 1919* (pp. 582–587). Chicago: Rogers & Hall.

Spanier, G.B. & Glick, P.C. (1980). The life cycle of American families: an expanded analysis. *Journal of Family History 5*, 97–111.

Spanier, G.B., Lewis, R.A., & Cole, C.L. (1975). Marital adjustment over the family life cycle: The issue of curvilinearity. *Journal of Marriage and the Family, 37*, 263–275.

Spanier, G.B., Sauer, W., & Larzelere, R. (1979). An empirical evaluation of the life cycle. *Journal of Marriage and the Family, 41*, 27–38.

Spaulding, E.R. (1919) The training school of psychiatric social work at Smith College. *Proceedings of National Conference of Social Work, 1919* (pp. 606–611). Chicago: Rogers & Hall.

Spencer, J.C. (1963). The multi-problem family. In B. Schlesinger, (Ed.), *The multi-problem family*. Toronto: University of Toronto Press.

Srole, L. Langner, T.S., Michael, S.T., Kirkpatrick, P., Opler, M.K., & Rennie, T.A. (1978). *Mental health in the metropolis* (rev. ed.). New York: New York University Press.

Stein, H. (1960). The concept of the social environment in social work practice. *Smith College Studies in Social Work, 30*, 187–210.

Steinmetz, S.K., & Straus, M.A. (1974). Intra-family violence. In S.K. Steinmetz & M.A. Straus (Eds.), *Violence in the family*. (pp. 3–25). New York: Harper & Row.

Sterling, A. (1980). Critical analysis of a systems dilemma. Paper delivered at New York University School of Social Work. Quoted by Mishne, J.M. (1982). The missing system in social work's application of systems theory. *Social Casework, 63*, p. 548.

Stuart, R.B. (1980). *Helping couples change: A social learning approach to marital therapy*. New York: Guilford.

Studt, E. (1954). An outline for study of social authority factors in casework. *Social Casework, 35*, 231–238.

Sullivan, H.S. (1953). *The interpersonal theory of psychiatry*. New York: Norton.

Sullivan, H.S. (1962). *Schizophrenia as a human process*. New York: Norton.

Sunley, R. (1970). Family advocacy: From case to cause. *Social Casework, 51*, 347–357.

Taft, J. (1919). Qualifications of the psychiatric social worker. *Proceedings of National Conference of Social Work, 1919* (pp. 593–599). Chicago: Rogers & Hall.

Taft, J. (Ed.). (1944). *Family case work: A functional approach*. Philadelphia: University of Pennsylvania Press.

Taft, J. (Ed.). (1948). *Family casework and counseling*. Philadelphia: University of Pennsylvania Press.

Terkelson, K.G. (1983). Schizophrenia and the family: II. Adverse effects of family therapy. *Family Process, 22*, 191–200.

Thomas, E.J., & Carter, R.D. (1971). Instigative modification with a multiproblem family. *Social Casework, 52*, 444–454.

Tinker, K.H. (1957). *Let's look at our failures.* St. Paul, MN: Family Centered Project (mimeograph).

Torrey, E.F. (1983). *Surviving schizophrenia: A family manual.* New York: Harper & Row.

Truax, C.B., & Mitchell, K.M. (1971). Research on certain therapist interpersonal skills in relation to process and outcome. In A.E. Bergin & S.L. Garfield (Eds.), *Handbook of psychotherapy and behavior change: an empirical analysis* (pp. 299–344). New York: Wiley.

Umbarger, C. (1972). The paraprofessional and family therapy. *Family Process, 11*, 147–162.

von Bertalanffy, L. (1950). The theory of open systems in physics and biology. *Science, 3*, 23–29.

von Bertalanffy, L. (1968). *General systems theory: Foundations, development, applications.* New York: George Braziller

von Bertalanffy, L. (1969). *General systems theory: Essays on its foundations and development,* (rev. ed.). New York: George Braziller.

Waite, F.T. (1941). Case work—today and fifty years ago. *The Family, 21*, 315–322. (Quoted by Sherman, 1961, p. 19).

Wallace, D. (1967). The Chemung County evaluation of casework service to dependent multiproblem families: Another problem outcome. *Social Service Review, 41*, 379–389.

Walsh, F. (Ed.). (1982). *Normal family processes.* New York: Guilford.

Walsh, F. (1983). Family therapy: A systemic orientation to treatment. In A. Rosenblatt & D. Waldfogel (Eds.), *Handbook of clinical social work* (pp. 466–489). San Francisco: Jossey-Bass.

Wattenberg, E. (1987). Family: One parent. In *Encyclopedia of Social Work* (pp. 548–555). Silver Spring, MD: National Association of Social Workers.

Watzlawick, P., Weakland, J. & Fisch, R. (1974). *Change: Principles of problem formation and problem resolution.* New York: Norton.

Weider, S., Jasnow, M., Greenspan, S.I., & Strauss, M. (1983). Identifying the multi-risk family prenatally: Antecedent psychosocial factors and infant development trends. *Infant Mental Health Journal, 4*, 165–201.

Wells, R.A. (1981). The empirical base of family therapy: Practice implications. In E.R. Tolson & W.J. Reid (Eds.), *Models of family treatment* (pp. 248–305). New York: Columbia University Press.

Wells, R.A., & Dezen, A.E. (1978). The results of family therapy revisited: The nonbehavioral methods. *Family Process, 17*, 251–274.

Wells, R.A., Dilkes, T.C., & Trivelli, N. (1972). The results of family therapy: A critical review of the literature. *Family Process, 7*, 189–207.

Weltner, J.S. (1982). A structural approach to the single parent family. *Family Process, 21*, 203–210.

Weltner, J.S. (1985). Matchmaking: Choosing the appropriate therapy for families at various levels of pathology. In M.P. Mirkin & S.L.Koman (Eds.), *Handbook of adolescents and family therapy* (pp. 39–50). New York: Gardner.

Whitaker, C. (1976). The hindrance of theory in clinical work. In P.J. Guerin (Ed.), *Family therapy: Theory and practice* (pp. 154–164). New York: Gardner.

White, R.W. (1959). Motivation reconsidered: the concept of competence. *Psychological Review, 66,* 297–333.

White, R.W. (1963). *Ego and reality in psychoanalytic theory.* New York: International Universities Press.

Wiener, N. (1948). *Cybernetics,* New York: Wiley.

Wiener, N. (1954). *The human use of human beings.* Boston: Houghton-Mifflin.

Wilkerson, I. (1987). New studies zeroing in on poorest of the poor. *The New York Times National News.* Sunday, December 20, 1987, p. 26.

Wilkinson, K. (1974). The broken home and juvenile delinquency: Scientific explanation or ideology? *Social Problems, 21,* 727–737.

Wilson, W.J. (1985). Cycles of deprivation and the underclass debate. *Social Service Review, 59,* 541–559.

Wiltse, K.T. (1954). Social casework services in the Aid to Dependent Children program. *Social Service Review, 28,* 173–185.

Wiltse, K.T. (1958). The hopeless family. *Social Work, 3,* 12–22.

Wolock, I., & Horowitz, B. (1979). Child maltreatment and material deprivation among AFDC recipient families. *Social Service Review, 53,* 175–194.

Wood, K.M. (1971). The contribution of psychoanalysis and ego psychology to social casework. In H. Strean (Ed.), *Social casework: Theories in action* (pp. 45–122). Metuchen, NJ: Scarecrow Press

Wood, K.M. (1978). Casework effectiveness: A new look at the research evidence. *Social Work, 23,* 437–458. Reprinted in N. Gilbert & H. Specht (Eds.), (1981). *The emergence of social welfare and social work* (pp. 365–408). Itasca, IL: Peacock.

Wood, K.M. (1980). Experiences in teaching the practitioner-researcher model. In R. Weinback & A. Rubin (Eds.), *Teaching social work research: Alternative programs and strategies* (pp. 13–22). New York: Council on Social Work Education.

Woodward, C. A., Santa-Barbara, J., Streiner, D.L., Goodman, J.T., Levin, S., & Epstein, N.B. (1981). Client, treatment and therapist variables related to outcome in brief systems oriented family therapy. *Family Process, 209,* 189–197.

Wright, H.R. (1954). Three against time: Edith and Grace Abbott and Sophonisba P. Breckenridge. *Social Service Review, 38,* 41–53.

Wright, L. (1924). The worker's attitude as an element in social casework. *The Family, 5,* 103–109.

Wynne, L.C., Ryckoff, I.M., Day, J., & Hirsch, S.I. (1958). Pseudomutuality in the family relations of schizophrenics. *Psychiatry, 21,* 205–220.

Younker, I.M. (1948). Family counseling in action today. *Social Casework, 29,* 106–111.

Zimbalist, S.E. (1952). Organismic social work versus partialistic research. *Social Casework, 33,* 3–10.

Author Index

Subject Index